**James M. Russell** has ~~a post-graduate~~ University of Cambridge, a post-graduate qualification in critical theory, and has taught at the Open University in the UK. He lives in north London.

Recent titles in the series

# A Brief Guide to Philosophical Classics

James M. Russell

ROBINSON

ROBINSON

First published in Great Britain in 2007 by Magpie Books,
an imprint of Constable & Robinson Ltd.
This paperback edition published in 2015 by Robinson

A CIP catalogue record for this book
is available from the British Library.

ISBN 978-1-84901-001-6

Typeset in Great Britain by SX Composing DTP, Rayleigh, Essex
Printed and bound in Great Britain by Clays Ltd., Elcograf S.p.A.

Papers used by Robinson are from well-managed forests
and other responsible sources

Robinson
An imprint of
Little, Brown Book Group
Carmelite House
50 Victoria Embankment
London EC4Y 0DY

An Hachette UK Company
www.hachette.co.uk

www.littlebrown.co.uk

# Contents

## Meditations: Contemplation as Philosophy 105

## Psychodrama: How to Live your Life 143

## Twentieth-Century "Isms": 172
##   Political and Personal Issues

# Introduction

The aim of this book is to provide brief introductions to philosophical classics. We have selected sixty-seven books and given a brief description of each. There were two main challenges in doing this. Firstly, it is rather difficult to give an accurate impression of a complex work of philosophy in a thousand words or so. And secondly: what books should we describe as "philosophical classics" in the first place?

In choosing the books, we have intentionally cast our net beyond the realm of traditional philosophy. Our selection includes novels, children's books, works of science fiction and political tracts as well as more academic works. We wanted to reflect the fact that many books that provide philosophical inspiration are not strictly speaking philosophy books. Many would argue with some of the eclectic list of titles that have been included. And inevitably a lot of important and interesting books have had to be omitted. However we hope that the final list contains books that are thought-provoking and philosophically useful, as well as giving an overview of the sheer range of books in which philosophical ideas can be discovered.

The difficulty of explaining a writer's thinking in a short

piece has sometimes influenced the choice of which books to include. Where possible we have preferred titles that can be succinctly summarized. There are of course indispensable titles (such as Kant's *Critique of Pure Reason*) which are almost impossible to boil down to a compressed version. In this case we have tried to home in on a few key ideas which can be explained in the space available, in order to give a brief taste of what the book is like.

We have aimed to make the book as accessible as possible. Our guiding principle was to explain why each book is important or regarded as being so. But we also wanted to answer the question "Would I enjoy reading this book?" The "Speed Reads" included at the end of each entry are intended to convey a quick sense of what the writer is like to read. They also provide a compressed (and occasionally humorous) summary of the main points of the book in question.

Overall we have aimed for a chatty and comprehensible style, even if this occasionally risks criticism for not being sufficiently serious. We have explained the books as we would to an interested friend, rather than as a philosophy tutor would explain them to a student, and we hope that this makes for a readable and interesting tour.

Each piece here is self-contained and there is no reason why you shouldn't use the book as a reference, or for "dipping into." However the book does have a structure that would give it some narrative continuity if you choose to read it straight through. It is divided into seven sections, each of which takes a look at different aspects of the philosophical tradition.

First we take a whirlwind tour through Western philosophy, from Plato through to Wittgenstein. Then we consider a few of the "outsiders" of the philosophical tradition, such as Kierkegaard and Dostoevsky. The sections on *Meditations* and *Psychodrama* widen the net further to take in a variety of books that have contemplated the meaning of life, or added to our understanding of how the mind works, or considered the question of "how you should live your life." Then, following a look at a few of the last century's most prominent kinds of political and philosophical idealism, we include a section that provides a sampler of more recent western philosophy. Finally we take a closer look at the continental tradition and at the critical theory.

There are a couple of general points that need to be made. Firstly, the quotes given at the start of each section are not always from the work being summarized. In a number of cases we found quotes from elsewhere in an author's body of work that seemed better mottoes, because they were more apposite, pithy, or amusing. Secondly, there are books where the title or publication date could have been given with provisos. Some (such as *On Sexuality* by Freud) were originally published under different titles. Other books have complicated bibliographic histories with regard to the publication date – for instance, books that were published privately, or books like *Fictions* by Jorge Luis Borges, which was originally published as two separate titles, and only translated into English twenty years later.

Rather than complicate our presentation, we have made an editorial choice as to which title and date to give. In terms of the titles we have preferred the title that is generally used on modern editions and which would enable a browser to find the book in a bookstore or on the internet. In a few cases such as Primo Levi's *If This Is a Man,* which was published under a different title in the United States, we have explained our choice in the text. However as a general rule we felt that giving too many detailed explanations of the publication history or titling would be rather pedantic, and would distract from our main purpose, which is to explain and describe the books.

This book has been enormously enjoyable to compile and I'd like to thank the contributors, who wrote entries for titles which fall into their special field, as well as Duncan Proudfoot at Constable & Robinson and Stuart Miller at Barnes & Noble for their feedback and input. The question of which books are philosophical classics is a fascinating one to grapple with, and I hope that *Philosophical Classics* will be as interesting and entertaining for readers as it was for me to produce.

James M. Russell

# A Whirlwind Tour:
# The Tradition of Philosophy

## *Introduction*

In this section we have attempted to compile a brief but coherent account of the main Western philosophical tradition. We have chosen books and writers that can be regarded as highlights or turning points of philosophy, or that are representative of a certain way of thinking.

Inevitably there are many omissions, and there are books and writers included here that others might exclude. Any whirlwind tour of this nature will be highly subjective – all that we can attempt is to give a brief taste of the ways in which philosophers have developed ideas and theories, often in response to those who have gone before.

One important bias that we should acknowledge is that the story told in this section is largely the story of the Anglo-American school of philosophy. The European philosophers who are included in this section, such as Kant, Hegel and Descartes, are generally seen as part of the classic tradition of philosophy which is shared by both Anglo-American and continental traditions. The reason for focusing on the Anglo-American tradition here is to keep the story relatively simple. As one reaches the nineteenth and twentieth centuries, Western philosophy becomes more fragmented, and to follow all the different strands of thought that followed on from the era of Kant and Hegel would be extremely complex and confusing. Instead we have tried to give a taste of the later continental tradition in the final section of this book.

The story of philosophy from the Greeks through to the modern tradition covers many different philosophical questions, but one key question that crops up repeatedly is the problem of knowledge. What certain knowledge can we have? And can we know that the world we perceive is the real one? From Plato's cave dwellers through to Descartes' demon, this is a question that has haunted many great thinkers. One recurring theme of this section is the many ways in which philosophers have tried to solve this problem.

The titles are listed chronologically, with the one exception of Bertrand Russell's *The Problems of Philosophy*, which seems an appropriate starting point for an exploration of the history of philosophical thought, as it gives a brief overview of the most well-known philosophical questions. Then we go back to Plato, the father of modern philosophy, rather than going back to the pre-Socratic philosophers who, fascinating though they are, fall beyond the scope of this book. Then we pass from Aristotle and Augustine through to the point where medieval thought started to be transformed into renaissance philosophy in the work of thinkers such as Hobbes and Descartes. We contrast the attempts of rationalists to build a perfect system of pure reason with the empiricist project of gaining an understanding of the world purely from our experience of that world.

We then consider Berkeley's idealism (including his rather surprising assertion that matter doesn't exist) and Hume's scepticism before taking a brief look at the grand system-building of Kant and Hegel. Moving towards the relativism and psychological insights of modern philosophy via Schopenhauer and John Stuart Mill, we finally reach the twentieth century. Here we briefly consider whether or not Wittgenstein and Gödel represent the end of Western philosophy in its traditional form.

On this very compressed journey, we don't have space for many great philosophers, including the likes of Bacon, Spinoza and Rousseau. Nietzsche and Kierkegaard could have been included in this section, but are elsewhere in the book instead. We have had to exclude mention of whole traditions of thought such as the great Arab and Persian philosophers of the Middle Ages, or the Jewish tradition exemplified by Maimonides. And our account of twentieth century thought is by necessity more of a sampler than a coherent narrative.

Nonetheless this section gives an overview of the ways in which the philosophical tradition has progressed – through breakthrough ideas, debate, and subsequent opposition and refinement of existing theories. The story of philosophy often feels like an ongoing conversation between the world's great thinkers. By tracing the development of a few key ideas throughout this section, we hope that we can give a flavour of that big conversation.

## *The Problems of Philosophy,* 1912

### Bertrand Russell

*"Is there any knowledge in the world which is so certain that no reasonable man could doubt it?"*

If you go to the philosophy section in a bookshop or library, you will find many books which are hard to read without understanding a lot of jargon and a great deal of previous theory. It is harder to find a general introduction to philosophy for the layman. There are not many books that set out the basic problems of philosophy for the general reader without assuming a great deal of previous knowledge or oversimplifying the subject.

Almost a century after it was first published, *The Problems of Philosophy* remains one of the best basic introductions to the whole subject of philosophy. It is a short book (120 pages or so) in which Bertrand Russell attempts to explain standard philosophical problems to a general reader.

Russell's greatest achievements were actually within the rather abstract and difficult field of mathematical logic. *Principia Mathematica*, which he wrote with Alfred Whitehead, is still recognized as an extraordinary achievement within this specialist area. It was an attempt to reduce mathematics to a rigorous, logical basis. He did not solve every problem he attempted. Indeed, as we will see, a few of the problems he identified led directly on to later work which undermined the whole project he had undertaken – Kurt Gödel eventually proved that a logical mathematical system could not be fully consistent and complete as Russell had hoped. But nonetheless, Russell's work in this field was extraordinary.

Beyond this, Russell's influence as a philosopher was broad. He was a prolific writer, and so prominent that many philosophers of the period responded directly to his ideas in their writing. He is seen as the founder of analytic philosophy, a strand of thought that tried to make general philosophy as close to common sense as possible. He objected to excessive use of complex ideas, and needless jargon, and felt that a close analysis of language and careful use of words would solve most problems. Russell often recommended the use of Occam's Razor (a historical theory which suggests that where there is a simple or complex explanation for the same thing, the simple explanation is to be preferred). In this respect he influenced his student Ludwig Wittgenstein's early work, although he came to disagree with Wittgenstein's later, more complex writing. In retrospect, his enduring influence beyond the sphere of mathematical logic is slight, except in the ways that other philosophers of his period reacted against his ideas. But at the time he was a highly respected figure.

His writing is a mixed bag. He was somewhat compulsive about expressing his opinions and wrote on an extraordinary range of topics. His book in praise of idleness is a charming meditation, his polemics about pacifism and disarmament reveal a committed radical (sometimes right, sometimes wrong, but always passionate), and his other work ranges over topics as varied as ethics and the theory of relativity.

*The Problems of Philosophy* was published in 1912, and is still a highly readable guide. At times Russell's writing is infuriatingly patrician and condescending, but for the most part he merely takes it on himself to lay out the foundations of philosophy in the most accessible form possible. He deliberately restricts himself in the book to problems where he feels that he can make a sensible and brief analysis. Rather than merely describe each problem, he works his way through a simple attempt at answering it, and it is partly this that makes the book such a model introduction to philosophy. In each section he sets out a problem and then wrestles with an attempt to answer it in a way that invites us to join him in thinking about why this problem is so important. Often we might disagree with parts of his answer, and this is an essential part of starting to read philosophy. This is because philosophy is about the debate between opposing viewpoints and the conversation that ensues, not just about learning a set of problems and answers.

The problem of knowledge is a central part of this book, as it is throughout the history of philosophy. Russell starts the book by asking what certain knowledge we can have. This is a thorny question that was addressed directly by philosophers from Plato to Descartes, to Locke, Hume and beyond. Russell gives a beginners' guide to some of the historical answers, as well as giving his own views on the distinction between appearance and reality.

Russell goes on to examine subjects such as idealism, the existence of matter, the problem of induction (which can be summarized as whether or not we truly know that the sun will rise tomorrow) and the limits of what we can possibly discover through philosophical enquiry.

*The Problems of Philosophy* is by turns irritatingly patronizing, endearingly useful, and remarkably insightful. In places it is dated, as twentieth century philosophy has moved a long way since Russell's time. Nonetheless if we had to choose a single book as a basic primer on the question of "what is philosophy about?," it would still be this one.

---

### *The Problems of Philosophy*
## The Speed Read

I am very clever. You are probably not as clever as me, but don't be alarmed, I will speak very slowly. Philosophy is extremely interesting, and in this little book I will explain why. What can we possibly know? How do we know it? What is reality, and how can we tell it apart from mere appearance? What is matter? Will the future be similar to the past? Many philosophical problems can be explained by the application of simple common sense. (But only if you are as clever as me.)

---

## *The Republic*, 5th Century BC

### Plato

*"Necessity, who is the mother of invention."*

The real story of Western Philosophy starts with Plato, and his mentor Socrates, whose teachings he immortalized. Many of the pre-Socratic philosophers are known to us only through fragments, and summaries of their main ideas. But with Socrates, Plato gave us a vivid depiction of philosophizing – which he shows as a process of doubting and questioning everything that we believe, in order to try to uncover the truth.

The pre-Socratics had principally been concerned with the nature of reality – for instance whether or not the world is composed of atoms or elements, whether the world is unified and stable as Parmenides believed, or in a state of permanent flux as Heraclitus taught. (Zeno's famous paradoxes were formulated as an attempt to prove Heraclitus wrong in this respect.)

In the fifth century BC, Athens was a flourishing city state, and a democracy (for those lucky enough to be citizens rather than slaves). A school of philosophers known as the Sophists flourished by teaching citizens how to win arguments – the word "sophistry," which derives from their name, is testament to the fact that (like many modern lawyers) they were more concerned with winning the argument than with ideals of truth or justice.

Socrates frequently clashed with Sophists, largely because he believed it was important to use philosophy to discover the truth. The series of dialogues which his student Plato wrote show him debating such matters as "What is the highest form of love?" and "What is virtue?" with his contemporaries. He is also (in *The Apology*) depicted bravely awaiting his execution, having chosen truth over the alternative of exile or renouncing his philosophy (which was upsetting his fellow Athenians to the degree that they had passed sentence of death on him).

Plato's dialogues can often feel like a fixed boxing match. Socrates will interrogate his acquaintances on their beliefs, gradually demonstrating to them the falsity of what they have proposed. At this point they generally roll over and concede defeat with the immortal words "I see now that you are right, Socrates." Socrates then proceeds to tell them his version of the truth. Twenty-five centuries later, his views can often seem bizarre and self-justifying. For instance at the end of *The Symposium* Socrates "proves" that the highest form of love is that between an older teacher and an attractive young man (like most of his fellow Athenians, Socrates saw homosexuality as perfectly normal).

So why do we still see Plato as such a central part of the philosophical tradition? Firstly because Socrates presents us with such an engaging (and roguish) example of the philosopher, a restless and inquisitive seeker of truth, who will question even the simplest matters of experience and reality with the aim of learning more about the world. And secondly because the Socratic method of dialectic, a process of testing out possible answers to a question, teasing out logical inconsistencies and errors until we gradually approach the truth, lies at the heart of over two thousand years of philosophy.

*The Republic* is the most complete statement of Socrates' beliefs (or at least of Plato's version of those beliefs). The main question addressed is that of the meaning of justice. But in the process, Plato sets out a complete system of beliefs about reality and human society.

In the "Allegory of the Cave," he gives us one of the most enduring images of philosophy. A group of people who live in a cave experience the outside world only through reflections and shadows that are cast by a fire on to the wall of their cave. If one member of this group were to travel to the outside and then come back to tell his colleagues about what he had seen, they might well be disbelieving and dismissive of his tales of the real world. This allegory vividly expresses the primal fear that the world we experience might not be the "real world." What if, like the character of Neo in *The Matrix,* we are experiencing a false reality? (This won't be the last time we mention *The Matrix* – later in the book we will see how Descartes pictured himself in a very similar plight at the start of his attempt to understand the problem of knowledge.)

Plato argued that the "real world" was made of eternal "forms," essential, unchanging aspects of reality. Our task as thinkers is to try to see past the misleading phantoms and shadows of everyday perception, to understand the true forms of existence. And like the enlightened traveller, we must then return to tell the ordinary people what we have discovered.

In trying to answer the question of what justice is, Plato goes on to suggest that if we think clearly and perceive the true forms of reality, we will naturally want to do the just thing in any given situation. This is a questionable theory, but accepting that it is true he goes on to try to describe a society in which people would be better able to perceive truth and justice. This is where his argument gets a bit wobbly. Rejecting the democracy of his time, Plato suggests a society where men and women are equally educated (an outrageous idea for his contemporaries), and where children are removed from their natural parents and brought up for the collective good of the society. In spite of having been a poet himself, Plato also suggests that art and fiction in particular should be banned from the republic, because they interfere with the quest for truth and beauty. Finally, the laws in this ideal society are to be made by those citizens with the highest state of knowledge. These citizens would, of course, be the philosophers.

So from a basic enquiry into the nature of justice, Plato ends up suggesting a rather repressive society ruled by philosopher-kings, among whose number he would presumably expect himself to be included. This self-aggrandizing and hubristic conclusion demonstrates one of the dangers of the Socratic method, which is that ridiculous and dubious arguments can be made to appear wise by a persuasive and skilled exponent. Plato regarded the Sophists with contempt, but could nonetheless use his dialectical skill to reach conclusions every bit as bizarre as anything they ever taught.

However, in spite of this, there are a wealth of fascinating ideas scattered throughout *The Republic* and other Socratic dialogues, and Socrates is always an intriguing and inspiring character. Plato's work is critical for an understanding of western philosophy. He reports Socrates at his trial as saying that the unexamined life is not worth living. If Plato teaches us one thing, it is that the first steps on the road to knowledge are doubt, intelligent debate, and a burning desire for the truth.

---

### *The Republic*

## The Speed Read

What is justice? We will naturally recognize the virtuous and correct path of action when we are properly educated to seek after the truth. The world we perceive is just a shadow of the real world of forms. Philosophers can learn to perceive the true forms of reality. Therefore an ideal society is one where all are educated on enlightened principles, and where the philosopher-kings tell everyone what to do.

---

## *The Nicomachean Ethics*, 4th Century BC

### Aristotle

*"For the things we have to learn before we can do them, we learn by doing them."*

Aristotle was a student of Plato, but he went on to have a lasting impact on philosophy in his own right. It is often said that Western philosophers could be broadly divided into Platonists and Aristotelians. One way of explaining this distinction is to use modern terms that neither would have been familiar with.

We can call Plato a rationalist – he believed that to achieve true understanding we need to understand the "form" or "thing-in-itself" that lies behind the reality that we perceive. So he used pure rational thought to try to comprehend the nature of the universe. By contrast we might call Aristotle an empiricist, meaning that he preferred to proceed from observation of the world (rather than pure reason) to his conclusions.

Aristotle rejected the Platonic idea of forms, believing that we can't separate the pure form of an object from the manifestations of that object in the world. Given that our category "tree" is based on observations of many trees, Plato would say that each tree we perceive is an example of the pure universal form "tree." Whereas Aristotle would say that universals are not real, and that "tree" is simply a category we have developed to describe trees, rather than being a pure metaphysical object.

The "rationalist versus empiricist" division doesn't fully capture the range of Aristotle's thinking. He wrote on a wide variety of subjects, including biology, politics, and physics, and deductive reasoning. Above all Aristotle was the great categorizer – in his writing he frequently starts by splitting his subject into various groups and categories, which he then analyses in forensic detail. For instance when looking at the concept of causation, he starts by subdividing causes into *material causes, formal causes, final causes,* and *efficient causes*. In truth, this method makes Aristotle's writing heavy going. He broke new ground in many subjects, but to a modern reader he can seem pedantic. But one can nonetheless admire the subtlety and detail of his thinking.

*The Nicomachean Ethics* was, as the title suggests, his greatest work on ethics. In particular he looks at the question of what it is that makes someone a "good person." He starts by considering what is the "good" that is the aim of human life. He considers the idea that happiness is the goal of life, but qualifies this initial idea to the degree that he concludes that human life must aim towards virtue in order to be truly good.

Next he considers what virtuous behaviour must consist of. He suggests that each virtue is a mean, or midway point, between two extremes. So for instance courage is the mean which lies between the extremes of cowardice and rashness, while generosity lies between the extremes of wastefulness and meanness. This is the notion which has been immortalized as the "virtuous mean." We could also describe it as a kind of "Goldilocks" morality, where we should be "not too hot, not too cold, but just right."

The interesting thing about the idea that virtues are a mean is that it makes Aristotle's ethics much more of a practical exercise than Plato's. For Plato all we needed to do to behave virtuously was to be educated to understand virtue. In this view, knowing what is a good thing leads us naturally to want to do that good thing.

Aristotle is putting forward a very different theory. He believes that we have to walk an ethical tightrope, working out from experience when we have deviated from virtuous behaviour towards one or the other extreme. This is a much more flexible and realistic approach to ethics and was a key part of much Christian philosophy in later centuries.

To act virtuously in Aristotle's ethics, one needs to practise constantly, to learn from one's mistakes, to continuously monitor one's own behaviour. This makes ethics an everyday discipline – we develop virtuous behaviour by understanding our own actions in many different situations in everyday life.

Aristotle also considers the notion of responsibility, noting that a person cannot be held to be behaving badly if they are acting under duress or if they are ignorant of the consequences of their actions. However if they are acting freely and in full knowledge of the consequences then he concludes that they are responsible for those consequences.

He then develops more fully the idea that people do not always act virtuously, even when they know what would be virtuous. He notes that there are two different ways in which people fail to do the right thing. Firstly there is the person with an "incontinent" will – this person knows the right thing to do, but is momentarily overcome by a desire for pleasure or self-indulgence that derails their best intentions. Secondly there are people who are intemperate, who don't wish to do the right thing and whose only goal is pleasure.

Aristotle considered that an incontinent will could be overcome, because the person who fails to do the right thing through weakness of will can still apprehend virtue as the ideal goal. Whereas he regarded an intemperate person as being beyond help as they do not even aim for virtue in the first place.

Finally Aristotle considers happiness at greater length. While he thinks that pleasure in itself is not the goal of virtue, he concedes that many virtuous activities have their own pleasures. So it is acceptable to be guided in life by a general preference for pleasurable activities, but in the end true happiness lies in actions that lead us to virtue.

*The Nicomachean Ethics* is typical of Aristotle's work in that it can seem very dry and analytical, but contains great insights that would go on to form the foundations of later philosophy. His views feel far more human and flexible than Plato's rather cold and rationalized ideas on the subject of "how to be a good person" – and this is what makes this book a key part of the history of ethics.

### The Nicomachean Ethics

## The Speed Read

We understand the world by analyzing our experience rather than through pure reason. So what does it take to be a good person? Plato was wrong to say that we will always do the right thing so long as we know what it is. Ethics is more of a balancing act, where each virtue is a mean between two vicious extremes. We may fail to do the right thing because we don't want to achieve virtue, or because we suffer from momentary weakness. But if we contemplate virtue and repeatedly practise doing the right thing in our everyday lives, we can learn to live a good life.

## *The Confessions*, 5th Century AD

### Augustine of Hippo

*"I believe in order that I may understand."*

Medieval philosophy was mostly fairly dull, from a modern point of view. In the Christian, Jewish and Muslim religions, the main aim of philosophers in this period was to synthesize philosophy with religious orthodoxy. Philosophical arguments were mostly wielded to back up and justify theological points. One consequence of this was that large elements of the philosophy of Plato (at least as he was interpreted by the Egyptian philosopher Plotinus) and Aristotle were adapted as the basis of a religious metaphysics. As a result a large part of modern Christian thought was heavily influenced by the ancient Greeks as well as by the Bible, and philosophy made little genuine progress.

Augustine of Hippo, a North African thinker who converted to Christianity, stands out from the medieval philosophers as worthy of mention for a number of reasons. The first is the fact that in *The Confessions*, Augustine brought autobiography into philosophy. *The Confessions* is often regarded as the first autobiographical book in the modern sense. In the first part of the book, Augustine gives a detailed psychological account of his early life, as an explanation of how he came to Christianity. He especially struggled with the idea of chastity and his carnal nature preventing him from becoming a Christian for many years, before a chance hearing of a child who seemed to be singing "Take it, read it" led him to pick up the Bible. He opened it and read a passage from St Paul condemning licentiousness, and this was the trigger for his own conversion.

This book is a fascinating read, and a remarkable portrait of a life from a completely different era to our own. Augustine had been a believer in Manichaenism, a belief system that emphasized the dualism between good and evil. In his *Confessions* he emphasizes the evil and weakness that he feels marked his early life. In doing this, he is also laying down the basis of his theological beliefs. He saw mankind as essentially weak, and believed that the only redemption we can achieve is through the grace of God. Rather than seeing evil as a force in its own right, as the Manicheans did, he chose to describe evil as the absence of good.

As a result, Augustine saw human rationality and philosophy as subservient to faith in God. He believed that philosophy was only truly useful to a believer. However he accepted that philosophy was important as part of a Christian faith, and much of his writing was important for philosophical as well as theological reasons. Like Descartes, ten centuries later, Augustine rejected the sceptics' idea that we can't truly know anything. He asserted that "Si fallor, sum" ("If I am mistaken, I exist") a prefiguring of the Cartesian line "I think therefore I am." And like Descartes (although with a less detailed exposition), he also went on from this foundation to conclude that we can trust our perceptions because of God.

Augustine's proof for the existence of God followed Plato, in that he saw mathematical truths as proof that we can perceive immaterial, immortal truths. He concluded from this that we have immaterial souls, and that the truths we believe must emanate from a greater power, God. He did, however, believe that even the necessary truths of mathematics must be dependent on God's will – meaning that God could make it true that $2 + 2 = 5$ if he chose to.

The infinite will of God raises the important question of human freedom. *The Confessions* is split into two parts – in the first, Augustine writes about his own life. In the second he offers some interpretations of *Genesis*. (He originally hoped to comment on the whole Bible, but realized that this was an impossible task.) When he considers what is meant by the statement that God created man in his own image, he decides that this doesn't mean a physical resemblance. Instead he suggests that man is like God because he knows the difference between good and evil. Man is born with original sin, but can, through the grace of God, find his way to goodness.

However, if God wills everything that happens in the universe, does this not mean that when we do an evil deed, it is because of God's will? In which case how can we be held responsible for our actions?

Augustine's answer to this is to consider the nature of time. Since God stands outside of time, he knows everything that has happened and will happen. However as humans we do not have this knowledge. Time only flows forward for us, and at any given stage of the progress of time, we are faced with choices for which we cannot know the outcome.

It is an essential feature of the divine plan that we have free will, and while God may know in advance what choices we will make, we still have to make those choices for ourselves, within the limitations of our perception of time.

Whether or not we accept Augustine's solution to the thorny problem of how to reconcile human free will with an all-powerful deity, his account of his personal path from sin to religion is a compelling one, which gives his idea of redemption through the grace of God real power.

Augustine's other great work *City of God*, takes a slightly different tack. Inspired by Alaric's sacking of Rome in AD 410, he contrasts Roman paganism with Christianity. He portrays the whole of human history as part of God's endeavour to build his kingdom, and he looks forward to the eventual victory of the faithful. As part of this endeavour, he considers an astonishing range of theological and philosophical puzzles, such as the nature of angels, the meaning of original sin, the constitution of souls, and, once again, the non-existence of actual evil. This is a harder book to read, but one that also had a profound influence on the development of Christian thought. (Some argue that *City of God* has had a problematic heritage in that it was a strong influence in creating the idea of Christianity as an ongoing battle against the pagan or infidel horde, an idea which influenced the Crusaders, and can still be perceived in the more extreme elements of modern evangelism.)

Augustine is theologically interesting, and his personal take on Christianity still reverberates today. But his philosophy is also fascinating, and is one of the more subtle examples of how medieval philosophers struggled to apply ideas from the Greeks and Romans to the religious world in which they lived.

## The Confessions

# The Speed Read

I lived a bad life, a life of weakness and original sin. I was disappointed by my Manichean teachers, but then I heard a child singing "Take it, read it" and picked up the Bible. I became a Christian and realized that knowledge is nothing without faith. No matter what else I may doubt, I know that I exist. God wills everything that happens in the world, even the necessary truths of mathematics. But it is his plan to give me free will, as we must choose between good and evil, which is merely the absence of good.

## *Meditations on First Philosophy,* 1641

### René Descartes

*"It is only prudent never to place complete confidence in that by which we have even once been deceived."*

As a devout Catholic, Descartes was troubled by the scepticism of contemporaries such as Montaigne. To counter these ideas he aimed to build a system for attaining certain knowledge about the world. Descartes was also a mathematician and like previous philosophers (including St Augustine), he saw the perfect, necessary truths of mathematics as a possible starting point for building a system of knowledge about the world.

In the *Meditations*, Descartes started out by trying to strip away all knowledge that was not certain, in order to find the most basic building blocks of logic. Using his "Method Of Doubt," he reasoned that it was possible to doubt our perceptions, as it might be that everything we perceive is a dream. This would not however render the truths of mathematics unreliable as they are necessary truths (in other words, it is impossible for 2 + 2 = 4 to be wrong).

However, taking his doubts even further, in order to start from a position more sceptical than the most extreme sceptic, he further imagined that he might be the prisoner of a deceiving god, a demon who held him captive and who placed all the thoughts he had into his mind. In this circumstance, even the necessary truths he believed might be false, as the deceiving god could simply change the world to render those truths false.

With this most extreme moment of doubt, Descartes was expanding on Plato's original allegory of the cave, and at the same time prefiguring the plot of *The Matrix* (where most humans are kept in vats, and fed false perceptions by the machines) by 350 years or so. He had also painted himself into something of a corner, as this level of scepticism seems inescapable. If it is indeed possible that a demon is deceiving us, how can we be certain of anything at all. If we are in a vat, being fed our every sensation and idea, how could we possibly know that to be the case?

Undeterred, Descartes proceeded to pull his first rabbit out of the hat, by concluding that there was indeed one thing he could be certain of – "Cogito ergo sum" ("I think therefore I am"). Even if every thought in his head was false, he could at least be certain that he was thinking.

(Various later philosophers have pointed out that even this step can be doubted as it makes a leap from "There is a thought" to "There is an 'I' that is thinking," thereby assuming the identity and coherence of the thinking subject. But for now, let's ignore that.)

Descartes now needs some more fancy footwork to build towards a system of certain knowledge. He first observes that the ideas in his head are "clear and distinct," and that

such clear and distinct ideas can be conceived to represent aspects of reality. These ideas might be adventitious
(from the outside world), factitious (self-created) or innate
(inscribed on the mind by God).

Now Descartes considers the idea of God. Since it is
possible to conceive of a perfect being, he argues that this
idea could only be an innate idea, as it couldn't be from the
outside (one can't directly experience God) or self-created
(as one can't perceive perfection in oneself). Therefore he
concludes that God exists.

Finally in order to complete his basis for knowledge he
reasons that since our conception of God is one of perfection, and since all aspects of this being must be perfect, there
would be no reason for God to deceive us. So on this basis
we can accept the basic necessary truths of mathematics and
logic as the first building blocks of knowledge.

These last two steps are of course riddled with problems,
as many critics of Descartes' time and since have pointed
out. It is far from obvious what a "clear and distinct idea"
is. And there is a circularity in the argument as Descartes
makes assumptions about these ideas before proving the
existence and truthfulness of God, thereby proving the reli-
ability of clear and distinct ideas. In fact a close study of
Descartes' *Meditations* leaves many modern readers feeling
that it is actually impossible to achieve absolute certainty in
human knowledge. This is because Descartes' "Method of
Doubt" is far more effective at dismantling the grounds of
human knowledge than his proofs are at rebuilding those
grounds. You end up with a feeling of being swindled by the
"In a single bound he was free" nature of Descartes' proofs
of a truthful God.

And do we need absolute certainty at all? Why can we not
be satisfied with thinking it overwhelmingly likely that our
perceptions are broadly correct? Well, for most people that
would be enough, but for centuries philosophers dreamed

of building a perfect, mathematical system of human knowledge, and for this they needed absolute certainty. Descartes
was a fascinating and eloquent example of this tendency,
even if we can see from a distance how his religious convic-
tions made it hard for him to carry through his system of
doubt to its logical conclusions.

In retrospect, Descartes' attempt to build a system of
mathematical certainty is flawed, but can be seen as the
moment of transition from the medieval to the modern
period of philosophy, if only because Descartes was so
honest in exposing out how much of our knowledge is open
to doubt.

Another notable aspect of Descartes' *Meditations* is his
clear exposition of mind and body dualism. He reasons that
since mind and body can be conceived independently, it is
possible for God to create either one without the other. So
we consist of both physical processes (we are a "Cartesian
machine," in that everything our bodies do can be explained
physically), but simultaneously we exist as minds or souls.
Descartes concludes that animals are mere machines, lacking
souls, unlike humans (an aspect of his work that might rile
modern animal lovers).

This rather paradoxical dualism was at the heart of much
subsequent philosophy, and questions about how mind and
body interact have been at the heart of the philosophy of
knowledge (called *epistemology*) and psychology ever since.
Descartes even considered the rather modern question of
whether or not a machine that perfectly resembled a human
could be counted as human. He concluded that because it
would not have a soul, it would not be able to interact in a
genuinely soulful way. This early echo of later ideas such as
the Turing Test shows Descartes at both his best and worst.
Once again he is unable to escape the straitjacket of his religion in the conclusions he reaches, but as ever we can admire
the rigor and curiosity that lie behind his initial ideas.

Many academic philosophy courses start with Descartes because he introduces so many elements of philosophy in a clear and easily digested form. The problems of knowledge and of mind and body are perennial subjects of western philosophers and Descartes is a good place to start understanding why these problems are so vexing.

*Meditations on First Philosophy*

# The Speed Read

To beat the sceptics at their own game, let's doubt absolutely everything we know, in order to discover what knowledge we can be certain of. If I were dreaming, or even being deceived by a devious demon, I could be certain of nothing at all. Oh dear, the sceptics win . . . But wait, I would still be thinking, so I'd know that I existed. And my clear and distinct idea of God could only be placed there by God, so God exists. And a perfect God wouldn't lie, so hurrah, I can trust my clear and distinct ideas. From here I can build up a perfect mathematical system of knowledge that bears an uncanny resemblance to the prevailing Christian orthodoxy of the seventeenth century.

## *The Leviathan*, 1651

### Thomas Hobbes

*"The praise of ancient authors proceeds not from the reverence of the dead, but from the competition and mutual envy of the living."*

Thomas Hobbes is largely remembered for his rather brutal view of human nature as "red in tooth and claw."

In fact he was one of the first British philosophers to really confront the difficulty of reconciling a physical view of the universe with concepts such as free will, and the soul. He was also influential in the language that he used. He believed that clarity in expressing ideas was of great importance to rationality, and for this reason he used many anglicized terms translated from Greek or Roman in *The Leviathan*. Many of these would become standard philosophical terminology for subsequent writers.

Hobbes took a *mechanistic* view of the universe. This means that he felt that everything, including human thought, could be explained by physical cause and effect. Thus sensations and thoughts could be completely explained by an accurate understanding of their physical action, by describing the ways in which nerves transfer the physical stimulation into a mental reaction. Where Descartes propounded a dualistic view, suggesting that mind and body were separate but concurrent aspects of the world, Hobbes took the idea that everything has a physical explanation and developed a philosophy based on this viewpoint.

From this starting point, Hobbes considered the nature of human will. He saw our desires as being essentially motivated by the need to relieve ourselves from discomfort – so a desire such as hunger leads us to seek out food in order to relieve ourselves of the discomfort of feeling hungry. Human will is therefore no more than our attempt to fulfil our desires and needs. As a result he emphasized our animal nature. He also suggested that this idea was compatible with free will, as we are not under constraint to act in the way we do.

Since our actions are governed by our base desires, he saw human nature without society as a "state of war," an existence that would naturally be "solitary, poor, nasty, brutish, and short." So the only way that we achieve a life that is better than this is by making "contracts" with our fellow human beings, in order that we can exchange things of value, and agree not to use force on one another under certain conditions. The net result of our making individual contracts is that society becomes a "commonwealth," in which we give up some of our individual freedoms in order to create a society which benefits all. So we give up our ability to act in a purely self-interested way in the service of the greater self-interest of freedom from being subjected to others brutish needs, and to create the opportunity to enrich and improve our lives.

Hobbes felt that the creation of the commonwealth effectively creates a new, conglomerate person, the *Leviathan*, who is entrusted with social order and responsibility. In order for society to function effectively we need a decision-making body to act on behalf of the Leviathan. Hobbes did not rule out the possibility that this decision-making body could be some kind of parliament or group. But he believed that the best possible option was for a single person to exercise the will of the Leviathan as this person can choose the best advisors and can rule in a consistent manner. He therefore concluded that the ideal society was one run by a hereditary monarch.

It is not unusual in philosophy to find fascinating arguments marshalled in favour of the political status quo. One might therefore imagine that many philosophers start out with the desire to prove that the beliefs they already hold are in fact fully logically justified. However, in many cases, the philosophers of the past would have risked imprisonment or worse had they reached conclusions that were too politically or theologically unacceptable. We have seen how hard Descartes found it to escape from Catholic orthodoxy in his thinking. In a similar way, Hobbes started his philosophizing with some radical and extraordinary beliefs but ended up with a very conservative endorsement of the existing political system. But most contemporary justifications of monarchy started by arguing that the monarch was the earthly manifestation of divine power, and Hobbes did at least risk undermining this to a degree by arguing that the monarch's power was essentially an arbitrary one, assigned by the society at large.

Some of the most interesting writing in *The Leviathan* comes when Hobbes considers how the will of the sovereign body is to be transmitted to society. He suggests that in a society of sufficient size, "bodies politic" will inevitably be required to convey the sovereign's will into detailed policy. He also considers the ways in which a society might fail – if, for instance, individuals acquire too much private wealth, or if religious enthusiasms undermine people's obedience to the sovereign, or if too many individuals make their own private judgments of right and wrong, rather than accepting the sovereign will. With this last point, Hobbes is emphasizing that the rule of the sovereign is essentially an arbitrary one, which we may disagree with. But at the same time he believes that the interests of society are served by our submitting to that authority, as that is the basis on which society has agreed to govern itself, to escape from the "state of war."

A century after Hobbes, Rousseau would offer up a theory of the "noble savage" that expressed opposing views to *The Leviathan*. In Rousseau's view, humans were born good and innocent, and it was society that corrupted and poisoned human nature. These two polarized viewpoints still separate many irreconcilable political divides to this day. Communists believe society needs to be tightly organized in order to restrain and channel people's instincts, while anarchists believe that society should allow people to get on with their lives, on the assumption that they will live better lives without the regulation of society. Many political liberals tend to take Rousseau's view that people are essentially good, while many conservatives take the Hobbesian viewpoint that people are essentially selfish and that we need a strong system of regulation and punishment in order to create a good society.

One could go into further detail on these oppositions, since both "left-" and "right-wing" positions contain sub-strands that take opposing views of human nature. But the long-term influence of Hobbes has been to succinctly express the viewpoint that human nature is essentially selfish and that society exists to civilize us.

---

### *The Leviathan*

## The Speed Read

The universe can be explained in physical terms. Our base desires drive our wills, and left to our own devices we will brutishly endeavour to satisfy those desires, no matter how much we harm other people. We overcome this by making contracts with others, giving up some freedom for the greater good of living in a well-organized society. The commonwealth thus created gives life to a new being, the Leviathan, and it is necessary that someone is entrusted with acting on behalf of the Leviathan. The best person for this role is a constitutional monarch, although other models of government are also possible.

---

## *Discourse on Metaphysics*, 1686

### Gottfried Wilhelm Leibniz

*"In whatever manner God created the world, it would always have been regular and in a certain general order. God, however, has chosen the most perfect, that is to say, the one which is at the same time the simplest in hypothesis and the richest in phenomena."*

Following in the footsteps of Descartes and Baruch Spinoza, Leibniz was the last of the great continental rationalists. (A *rationalist* is someone who, as Descartes had done, attempts to develop a system of knowledge based on pure reason and contemplation, rather than from observation, as an *empiricist* would.)

Leibniz was also a mathematician (he made a significant contribution to the development of calculus) and like earlier philosophers such as Descartes and Augustine, he saw a parallel between the necessary truths of pure mathematics and the immortal truths of God and the soul. His system, based on logical analysis was rather complicated, and the following digest can only offer a very brief guide to his conclusions.

First, he claimed that all true propositions must consist of a subject and predicate, as in a sum where the two sides of the equation $x+y = z$ are identical. But he divided truths into truths of fact (contingent facts that happen to be true, such as "My cat is black") and truths of reason (necessary truths such as "$2 + 2 = 4$").

In order to convert this logical idea into matters of fact, Leibniz proposed that all true propositions about the world consist of a *monad* and a quality. By a *monad,* he meant a single individual substance such as a person. He regarded space and time as not being necessary aspects of reality, and described a monad as being an individual substance irrespective of time. Thus anything that happened in the past or will happen in future to me is true at all times, and my monad possesses all the qualities it ever will. The baby born forty years ago and the old man of the future are the same monad as the person sitting typing this page, and all three possess the same qualities.

It is interesting to note that while Descartes had described a mechanical universe with a dualistic mind-body division, and Spinoza had described the universe as an indivisible whole, Leibniz saw the universe as consisting of a larger number of monads, individual substances, which were separate to one another. This is interesting firstly because each claimed to be deriving a system from first principles, yet reached very different conclusions. And secondly because to a large degree they were simply echoing the debates that the pre-Socratics had had two thousand years earlier about the nature of reality itself.

Leibniz went on to consider the nature of the world in which we live. Having put forward his view that the world is essentially defined by a collection of monads with specific qualities that relate to one another, but do not interact with one another, he had to explain why we live in this particular world rather than another. He also had to explain the role of God in his universe. It is interesting that he came up with a logical analysis based on alternative possible worlds, an idea that would be taken further in the twentieth century by David Lewis among others, including many science fiction writers.

Leibniz regarded God as the only necessarily existing being, and all of reality as flowing from his being. He pictured God considering every possible alternative world, with various numbers of monads and qualities. He concluded that a perfect God would choose the world with the most possible monads (because of Leibniz's principle of plenitude, which basically asserts this to be the case, for no very clear reason). He also claimed that an omnipotent, benevolent God would necessarily choose the "best of all possible worlds" and that this must therefore be that world. On this theory, it would be impossible to make this world better by making any single set of monads and qualities slightly better, because this would upset the balance of the world and make something else worse. This conclusion drew derision from other writers, in particular Voltaire who scoffed at the idea that this world is the most perfect possible. It is perhaps even harder to believe this to be true after the bloody wars and pogroms of the twentieth century.

Finally, since Leibniz's theory of monads required him to believe that all monads were self-contained, windowless entities that did not affect one another, and he had also stated that time was not a necessary feature of reality, he had to reject the principle of mechanistic causation. Instead he suggested that God's role in creation was to form a world with a pre-arranged harmony, meaning that the monads are like perfectly timed clocks, that just happen to synchronize with one another. This means that everything happens in such a way as to make it appear to us as though a process of cause and effect is making things happen, living as we do in the temporal world. This also solved the problem of dualism in Leibniz's view – he proposed that our mental and physical perceptions synchronize simply because of God's pre-arranged harmony. This theory of *parallelism* may be logically sound, but seems deeply problematic nonetheless.

If it were true, Leibniz would once again be up against the old problem of free will, but he settled this by assuming that some monads are able to have a perception of themselves. And as we live our lives in a temporal way, perceiving only forward motion through time, we are aware of ourselves, but cannot know what will happen in the future. Thus free will is genuine, yet at the same time it is a kind of benevolent illusion.

Leibniz's theories really stretch our credulity, but we have to remember that he passionately believed that he had deduced them from pure reason alone. When he states that this is a kind of clockwork universe, and the best of all possible worlds, his ideas seem far-fetched, but there is an internal consistency to his reasoning. He is mathematically brilliant and his arguments are superbly constructed, but as readers, we can't help feeling that they are neither correct nor useful.

As much as anything, Leibniz demonstrates the limitations of pure rationalism. No matter how hard we try to forget all our assumptions and received ideas, in order to discover the eternal, pure truth, we seem to be unable to truly leave behind our mental baggage. And the simple fact that "pure reason" can be used to discover universes that seem as different as those of Descartes, Spinoza, Leibniz and others suggests that there are serious problems with trying to create a system for understanding the universe from pure reason in the first place.

---

### Discourse on Metaphysics

## The Speed Read

The world consists of true propositions, linking monads and qualities. A monad is an indivisible substance such as a human soul, and all qualities that apply to it are eternally true – the past and future are contained within the present monad. Possible worlds are defined by a collection of monads and qualities. God's role is to choose the best possible world, which is the one with the most possible monads and qualities and the one containing the least amount of evil. As time is not real, causation between monads is not real either. Events happen because God has pre-arranged that all the monads will work in harmony. So the monads that make up the world are like a lot of little synchronized clocks, all working in unison.

---

## An Essay Concerning Human Understanding, 1690

### John Locke

*"If we will disbelieve everything, because we cannot certainly know all things, we shall do muchwhat as wisely as he who would not use his legs, but sit still and perish, because he had no wings to fly."*

John Locke was a pillar of the British intelligentsia, who could boast friends such as Royal Academy contemporaries Isaac Newton and Robert Boyle. In a period when science was making great strides forward in helping us to understand the world, his great project was to try and provide a philosophical basis for the pursuit of knowledge.

In *An Essay Concerning Human Understanding* he put forward a large part of his philosophical ideas. At the root of his thinking was the theory that all knowledge is gained from experience. He described the human mind at birth as a *tabula rasa,* a blank tablet on which all subsequent experience made an impact. This *empiricist* viewpoint led him to the conclusion that we are only capable of a limited knowledge of the world, although he believed that the knowledge we are capable of is sufficient.

He saw human thinking in terms of relations between ideas (an *idea* being whatever we have in our minds in terms of sensory impressions, thoughts or beliefs). He described the process of how ideas come to us from the external world by dividing the qualities of objects in the world into primary and secondary qualities. There is a problem for any philosophical theory that assumes that ideas represent objects in the real world (*representational realism*). This is that objects can be perceived very differently in different circumstances (for instance a red box will look very different in different light conditions, but will also look very different depending on whether we have previously been in a dark room or a dazzlingly bright room).

Locke chose to describe an object's real, unchanging qualities (such as bulk, texture and motion) as primary ones whereas he saw qualities such as colour, sound, smell and taste as secondary qualities. The primary qualities of an object may cause us to perceive the secondary qualities, but we cannot directly know the primary qualities by observing the secondary qualities – we can only infer and deduce the real nature of the object we are observing. This way of describing the qualities of objects in the real world provided one solution to the problem of how we perceive objects in the real world. While allowing that we may perceive the real world incorrectly, Locke nonetheless asserted that there was a chain that led from the real object to our idea of that object.

From this simple start Locke went on to build up a theory to explain all the ideas we have in our heads. In response to philosophers who had suggested that some of our ideas (such as mathematics, infinity or God) must have been innate, as we could not possibly have derived them from experience, Locke suggested a theory whereby all our complex ideas are derived by comparison and analysis of the simple ideas that we receive from the world. This would mean that our idea of a unicorn is a complex idea based on a combination of different real animals, infinity is an extension of simpler ideas of number, and so on. He also carefully delineated various ways in which we might derive new ideas from experience. In the process he contradicted Descartes' notion of animals as mere machines without souls, by suggesting that the only faculty we had that animals didn't have was the capacity for *abstraction*, by which we form ideas of morality.

He went further than this in his analysis of morality, looking closely at how we might form ideas of volition, will, liberty and power. He rather cleverly stepped round the problem of freedom of will by describing it as a category mistake. In his view it is irrelevant to ask if we are free to will whatever we want – as the whole notion of free will is simply based on whether or not we feel able to achieve our natural preferences. This led him to a rather hedonistic account of human freedom, in which we principally act to seek pleasure and avoid pain. (This kind of thinking was given a more moral twist by the later advocates of utilitarianism, such as John Stuart Mill, who asserted that we could measure the morality of an action by the overall happiness and pain that it caused to others.)

One interesting aspect of Locke's philosophy was his work on the meaning of words. For Locke, the meaning of a word was defined by the idea that it creates in our head. The names we use for objects in the world are created by general agreement that we are referring to the same object. So even though we can't be sure of the essential nature of the object to which we are referring, we can agree on the meanings of the words, and careful use of words can help us to eliminate confusion.

Locke is here prefiguring one of the essential splits between the Anglo-American and continental strands of philosophy in the last century or so. For both, the fact that the link between words, meaning and the objects to which they refer was of great interest. However the Anglo-American tradition has tended to take a viewpoint closer to Locke – a pragmatic acceptance of the gap between *signifier* and *signified*, coupled with a determination to find common-sense ways to talk about language nonetheless, and an attempt to be precise and unambiguous in use of language. On the contrary, the continental school has tended to take a more anarchic approach to this subject, reveling in the relativistic freedom that is created once we accept that the path from signifier to signified is opaque, and playing games with language rather than trying to "mend and make do." Of course this is too simplistic a way of dividing the two traditions and there are voices taking either approach in both traditions. But it is interesting to see Locke tussling with such a modern problem in the course of setting out his philosophy, over three centuries ago.

In the end Locke's conclusions about the scope of human knowledge are rather staid. His theories lead him to the conclusion that our knowledge is severely limited. He more or less accepts Descartes' theory that we have an intuitive knowledge of our own existence. And he accepts that we can have certain knowledge of necessary truths because they are clearly true simply from a comparison and analysis of the ideas that present themselves to us. But once it comes to the "real world" he is forced to conclude that we can't have any real certain knowledge, but must instead be content with probable knowledge, which is made more acceptable by the fact that we share the same theories or suppositions with other people. But he believes that this is adequate for us to live our lives, and that we are able to make moral decisions. And he also accepts that we can have faith in God because we can accept a rational proof of God's existence based on the ideas in our mind.

Locke isn't a bundle of fun to read, but he does produce a lot of interesting ideas. At times he identifies a problem (as in the case of his account of the meaning of words) more precisely than many of his contemporaries. And even when his solutions don't fully satisfy, his reasoning is always intriguing and worth thinking about. He gave the empiricist view one of its clearest expositions and as a result many philosophers who followed took his work as a starting point, whether they agreed or disagreed with his conclusions.

## *An Essay Concerning Human Understanding*
# The Speed Read

We are born with no knowledge at all – our minds at birth are blank tablets. Our knowledge comes from experience. The ideas in our head are representations of reality. However the objects of which we have knowledge have primary and secondary qualities. We can be subject to illusions about the secondary qualities and do not have direct knowledge of the primary qualities. But we can nonetheless attain a reasonable level of knowledge by using language very carefully and by analyzing the simple and complex ideas in our minds.

# A Treatise Concerning the Principles of Knowledge, 1710

George Berkeley

*"Esse est percipi."* ("To be is to be perceived.")

The empiricist views of John Locke were very influential in their time. George Berkeley, an Irish clergyman, was disturbed by this influence. He believed that the *representationalist* view that objects in the world were reflected by ideas in the mind created a problem. Since it is impossible to give a reliable explanation of the link between objects and ideas, Berkeley felt that Locke's philosophy led naturally to atheism and scepticism.

To counter the doubts that were left by Locke, Berkeley proposed the radical alternative theory that matter doesn't exist at all, only ideas. This theory (known as *immaterialism*) seems strongly counterintuitive on first reading, but is in fact quite a subtle and interesting idea.

Berkeley started *A Treatise Concerning the Principles of Knowledge* with an extended critique of Locke's writing. In particular he focused on Locke's suggestion that real objects have primary and secondary qualities. He started by accepting Locke's description of secondary qualities, such as colour, temperature and smell, and by adopting the point that these qualities are unreliable guides to reality, because they are subject to illusion. For instance imagine that you have both hands in a bucket of lukewarm water. If one hand was previously in an ice pack while the other was in a hot bath, the two hands will give us quite different perceptions.

However Berkeley went on to demolish Locke's theory that primary qualities are any more certain. He pointed out that shape and size are dependent on the position of the observer, and solidity is merely a function of our sense of touch. As a result he concluded that all our ideas are unreliable as a guide to the nature of "reality." But rather than allowing this point to lead to scepticism, he took a quite different direction. For Berkeley, the problem with representationalism was that it assumes there is a chain going from object to idea to perceiver. The suggestion is that the object causes an idea which is then manifested in the mind of the perceiver. But Berkeley claimed that it is literally inconceivable for material substances to exist without being perceived. So he proposed that we simplify the chain to the two things we can be certain of – the perceiver and the perceived. We know that we are thinking entities and we know that there are ideas in our mind. We need know no more than this to understand the universe.

This rather startling theory (which is also a kind of *idealism,* as compared to the *realism* of Locke) has some further consequences and difficulties to overcome. For instance if ideas are the only thing that exists, what can we say about a tree that falls in a distant forest, with no one observing it? Is it real or not? And does reality disappear every time we close our eyes?

There are two answers to the problem of the tree in the forest. The first is that as soon as we ask the question of whether or not it is real, we are picturing the tree, so it does exist as an idea in our mind. The second, more substantial point comes from a consideration of the difference between what is real and what is imaginary. If I imagine something and then stop thinking about it, it does disappear. However a real object will be perceived by more than one observer, and thus when my attention is elsewhere (or my eyes closed), someone else may be observing the object. We can know what is real by comparing our ideas.

And above all, the world exists because of God, and anything real in the world is being perceived by God. So he is the final observer who gives reality to the tree that falls unseen by human eyes in the forest. For Berkeley the persistence and regularity of the objects we perceive is an everyday proof of God's existence. Since God has an orderly mind and has created a world which follows rules, we are perceiving the effects of the mind of God in the world around us.

Berkeley developed his attack on Locke in great detail, including a strong attack on Locke's description of abstract ideas. Locke had accepted that an abstract idea such as a triangle could be perceived by the human mind. But Berkeley pointed out that this was a failure to take empiricism to a logical conclusion. Since we only perceive an instance of a triangle, the only ideas we have are of specific triangles, and we can identify a resemblance between those ideas (rather than perceiving the form "triangle").

In the end, Berkeley felt that his idealism was the only way to preserve common sense and to protect philosophy from atheism. His system places God very clearly at the centre of the universe. He believed that when we attempt a scientific understanding of the world, we are merely exploring the mind of God.

It is, however, hard to accept Berkeley's assertion that material substances are not real. It seems that traditional science could only progress by assuming that there are real objects in the world and then attempting to discover the truth about them. Berkeley put forward a coherent argument for his theories, but is it relevant to us today?

In fact idealism turns out to be a rather modern idea. Scientists such as Schrodinger and Einstein rejected the division between subject and object by proposing that the nature of reality is dependent on the observer. The debate as to whether reality is composed of waves or particles, or if these are merely alternative metaphors, demonstrates the degree to which modern science has left behind any certainty about the notion of "material sub-stance." And the solidity or otherwise of matter is generally held to be merely a function of our physical constitution and perception.

So as Berkeley would have suggested, modern physics tends to assume that our perceptions of reality are imperfect, but that we can advance by making comparisons between the perceptions of different observers. One can make all these points without believing in a God. However without Berkeley's religious faith one is left with an alternative kind of idealism in which we assume there is a universe that is independent of our perceptions – it is just that the only possible knowledge we have is dependent on our perceptions. So rather than saying that "matter doesn't exist" we might now say that it is not of any great significance whether matter exists or not.

Berkeley puts forward ideas that are difficult to accept in their entirety, but which are nonetheless coherent and useful. His critique of Locke is extremely powerful, and is a forensic demolition of the elements of Locke's philosophy that seem to be a bit of a fudge. Surprising though it is to appreciate a philosophy that asserts that matter is unreal, and that everything exists only in the minds of spirits and the mind of God, his writing puts forward many fascinating ideas that are hard to refute, especially when considered in the context of recent scientific theories.

*A Treatise Concerning the Principles of Knowledge*

## The Speed Read

Locke's philosophy is wrong because "primary qualities" are no more reliable than "secondary qualities." It is inconceivable for material substance to exist without being perceived. The only real things are perceivers (spirits and God) and the ideas in their minds. When we perceive the world we are exploring the mind of God, whose existence explains the persistence of objects in the world. This kind of idealism is the only way to defeat atheists and sceptics, since it allows us to explain the world without resorting to unknowable entities such as "matter." Instead we are exercising a truer form of empiricism by building a system on the only certain knowledge we have, the ideas in our minds.

# *An Enquiry Concerning Human Understanding*, 1748

## David Hume

*"Be a philosopher but, amid all your philosophy, be still a man."*

In the story of philosophy, it is not surprising that many writers were reacting to what they perceived as the problems and errors of their recent predecessors. Aristotle suggested revisions to Plato's system, while Berkeley was responding directly to Locke in his work. In this way philosophical theories tend to be progressively tested and modified by those who come later.

David Hume is best understood in the context of the philosophers who came before him. The European rationalists (such as Descartes and Leibniz) had attempted to create systems based on pure reason. Locke had suggested an empirical approach, while Berkeley had identified several difficulties with Locke's system and, rather than give in to scepticism, had proposed an approach based on idealism. Hume responded to this great tradition by arguing that scepticism is unavoidable, but by suggesting that we should nonetheless attempt to study the way we understand the world in a spirit of mitigated scepticism.

Hume first put his theories forward in the *Treatise of Human Nature.* The book was initially unsuccessful and Hume only came to public attention with a very different project, his extensive history of England. In 1748 he published *An Enquiry Concerning Human Understanding*, in which he gave a more compressed version of his theories. This is probably the best place to get a flavour of Hume's ideas.

Hume's starting point was to consider how it might be possible for us to learn about the world from our experience. He pointed out that we cannot reason from our current perceptions of the world to a knowledge of what will happen in future. This is because in order to do that, we would have to rely on either causal reasoning (the idea that events are related as cause and effect) or induction (the idea that because something has always happened in the past, it will continue to happen in the future). As Hume pointed out, we cannot even know with certainty that the sun will rise tomorrow, even though it always has done in the past. He saw our belief in cause and effect as basically a habit of thinking – we are used to a constant conjunction between certain events, so we suppose them to be necessarily connected. But we cannot truly know that there is such a necessary connection.

Seeing our rational thinking as a matter of habitual practice, Hume went on to hold that there is no fundamental
way to distinguish imagination and reality, apart from the
fact that we believe in one more strongly than the other.

He also applied his sceptical approach to the self. Hume
was one of the first philosophers to doubt that our idea
of self (or soul) is self-evidently true. He pointed out that
whenever we think about ourselves ("I am thinking," "I am
acting" etc.) we are actually thinking only about perceptions
and ideas. We are not directly experiencing an "I" – instead,
we are experiencing a range of sensations and thoughts,
which we assume there must be an "I" to experience. He
described the idea that we have a unitary self as a category
mistake – preferring to see the self as a bundle of perceptions. It is interesting that this train of thought undermines
Descartes' assumption that "I think, therefore I am" is a
certain piece of knowledge. Since we cannot be sure there
is an "I," the only reasonable assumption Descartes could
truly have made is that "there is a thought."

Finally Hume also accepted that we cannot have certain
knowledge that an external world even exists. He followed
Berkeley in his critique of the representationalist ideas put
forward by Locke. The representationalist view was that
rather than directly experiencing external objects, we experience ideas which are caused by qualities of objects in the
external world. But since we cannot know with any certainty how those objects cause the ideas in our mind we
cannot have any certain knowledge of those objects.

At this point Berkeley had retreated into idealism, and
put his faith in an omnipotent God. Hume was not an
atheist, although he subjected various attempted proofs
of God to a fierce interrogation in *Dialogues Concerning
Natural Religion.* Elsewhere in that book he has one of the
characters joke that if a sceptic wants to leave a room on
the second storey, he tends to choose the door rather than

the window. (Hume is a drily humorous writer, with a clear style that is relatively enjoyable for a modern reader.)

This comment is key to understanding Hume's resolution of the problems he had identified. He had shown that a rigorous scepticism shows how limited our empirical knowledge can be. However he felt that we had no choice but to believe that it is overwhelmingly likely that the world we perceive is real, and to act on our understanding of that world. We have to accept that there is no ultimate rational justification for much of what we believe, including ideas such as causation and induction. But nonetheless in Hume's view it is reasonable for us to act on those beliefs. This kind of mitigated scepticism means that the only certain knowledge we have is necessary truths such as the truths of mathematics. Beyond that we can only have our empirical observations of the world, and experimental theories that we will test in a scientific way, without assuming that our ideas necessarily relate to "real objects and substances" in the external world.

In the end Hume's scepticism serves a positive purpose – he aims to show that we have to leave behind our pursuit of absolute certainty, but suggests that it is nonetheless possible for us to act in a rational way based on our ideas of the universe.

Hume offered a solution to many problems that had been revealed by previous attempts at system building. Where the rationalists had failed to build systems of pure reason, and the empiricists had failed to fully explain how we can rely on our experiences to build knowledge, Hume proposed a common sense approach that accepted that much of what his predecessors had attempted was simply impossible. Not everyone could accept his scepticism and many contemporaries felt that his views encouraged atheism. In the end his suggestion that, even though we can't have absolute certainty, we can nonetheless aim to learn from what we perceive seems simple and obvious. But it was far from simple and obvious to many who came before him who had sought after the holy grail of absolute certainty, so Hume deserves appreciation as a voice of reason within the philosophical tradition.

---

### An Enquiry Concerning Human Understanding

## The Speed Read

So you want to be a sceptic? When you leave the second storey, do you leave through the window or the door? Rigorous scepticism shows us that we cannot know anything beyond the content of our current perceptions. Every attempt to reason from these will be unreliable because we can't assume that there is such a thing as cause and effect. Nor can we assume that the sun will rise tomorrow, even though it always did before. We can't know that we have a self or soul, and we can't know that the external world exists. But we need to put aside the quest for certainty and take an empirical approach to learning what we can about the world, limited though that knowledge must be.

---

## Critique of Pure Reason, 1781, 1789

### Immanuel Kant

*"Science is organized knowledge.
Wisdom is organized life."*

Kant is an extraordinarily difficult philosopher to summarize briefly. All we can do here is give a brief flavour of his work. The material covered here is from the three *Critiques* (*of Practical Reason,* and *of Judgment* as well as *of Pure Reason*), in which Kant created one of the most far-reaching and detailed systems of philosophy ever known.

It is hard to recommend Kant as a fun read. He writes dense, turgid prose, and relies on an array of newly coined philosophical expressions to express his ideas. Some would say that continental philosophy has never fully recovered from his love for jargon. However he was a subtle and complex thinker who succeeded in capturing and precisely describing many of the intractable problems of philosophy. He did not always provide solutions to these problems. One major conclusion of the *Critique of Pure Reason* is that genuine metaphysics is not possible.

Kant was partly inspired by Hume's writing (his enthusiasm helped to establish the Scot's posthumous reputation). In his writing he spoke of the distinction between *phenomena* (our ideas) and *noumena* (the real world of things-in-themselves). He essentially accepted Hume's conclusion that we cannot have direct knowledge of *noumena*. But he was interested in exploring what happens at the bounds of our reason, the point at which we fail to translate our understanding of *phenomena* into certain, detailed knowledge of *noumena*.

In order to do this he suggested a new way of distinguishing our judgments (or beliefs) about the world. Most philosophers before Kant had accepted a simple distinction between necessary truths (those which must be true, such as "2 + 2 = 4") and contingent truths (those that need not be true, that we learn only from observation (such as "This grass is green"). Kant used the Latin terms *a priori* to mean necessary and *a posteriori* to mean contingent, then added a further distinction between *analytic* and *synthetic* judgments. By analytic judgments he meant those in which the predicate is already contained in the subject – these add nothing to our knowledge because they are mere identities. Synthetic judgments are genuinely informative because, according to Kant, these are judgments in which the predicate is quite separate to the judgment – the fact that the judgment is true is dependent on a real connection between subject and predicate. Now, where Hume had seen mathematical truths as *necessary*, Kant was able to define a truth such as "The three angles of a triangle add up to 180 degrees" as a *synthetic a priori* judgment. This is because the concept of a triangle does not implicitly contain the information about what size the angles will be.

Whether or not this distinction is defensible or not has been the subject of much scholarly debate. Many suspect there is a degree of sleight of hand at this stage of Kant's system. But it is hard to deny the cleverness of Kant's categories. And from this start he went on to build a complex system, much of which was reliant on the idea that synthetic a priori judgments do exist.

As well as asserting that the most fruitful part of human knowledge comes from this source, Kant acknowledged that knowledge is only possible when the human mind shapes the conditions for that knowledge. So when Kant wonders how it can be possible for us to have synthetic a priori knowledge (which is both informative and necessary) he answers that we are able to have this knowledge because the human mind imposes conditions that make it true. The mathematical truths of a triangle hold because of the nature of space and time. But the human mind imposes a particular concept of space and time which allows us to make certain judgments about a triangle.

So where the rationalist Leibniz had asserted that space and time don't exist, and the empiricist Newton had claimed that space and time are absolute, Kant was able to say that both were correct. And he could also make the *transcendental* argument that we know that we make synthetic a priori judgments, so therefore we know that the conditions for us to make those judgments must be satisfied. The fact that we have knowledge of a certain sort proves that the preconditions for having that kind of knowledge are satisfied.

This seems a circular argument, but it is hard to argue with (if only because it is so confusing to think about . . .). A later example of the same kind of argument comes when Kant argues from the fact that we do have experience of the natural world to the conclusion that the preconditions for having such knowledge must be satisfied (these conditions being that it is possible for a thinker to impose order on sensory perceptions and that there must be a thinker to carry out that activity).

It is important to note also that Kant's system means that we have knowledge only within the phenomenal world of ideas. It is this aspect of his work that led on to the absolute idealism of Hegel and Fichte. Kant emphasizes this point when he considers whether or not we can have knowledge that transcends the noumenal realm. He considers whether or not we can have any knowledge of our persistence as souls, whether we can be sure that we are free agents acting in a world of causal determination, and whether we can know anything about God. In each case he concludes that we cannot have certain knowledge.

Our synthetic a priori judgments can only take us to the bounds of reason where the phenomenal realm reaches towards the noumenal realm. However our existence as rational beings compels us to act as though it is possible for us to have such transcendental knowledge. Otherwise we would have to confront the intolerable possibility that life is meaningless. (Later philosophers including Kierkegaard and the existentialists were fascinated by Kant's juxtaposition of the fear of essential meaninglessness and our reasoned choice to make a leap of faith.) One might simplistically say that while Berkeley suggested that human knowledge is an exploration of the mind of God, Kant proposed that it is merely an exploration of the mind of man.

Kant also extends his systematic philosophy to ethics. Again he uses synthetic a priori judgments to establish that all our morality is based on a single *categorical imperative* – that you should "act only according to that maxim whereby you can at the same time will that it should become a universal law." Of course this is simply a reiteration of Christ's simpler assertion that you should "do unto others as you would have them do unto you" but it is interesting to see Kant's laborious establishment of how this principle can be derived from his philosophical system.

Kant can't be faulted for the careful detail of his thinking. But it is probably only serious philosophy students who will want to attempt to read his books. They do provoke serious and difficult thought, although they also tend to provoke headaches in many readers. But he can't be ignored in any attempt to summarize Western philosophy and he has had a powerful influence on both the Anglo-American and continental schools of philosophy in the last two centuries.

### *Critique of Pure Reason*

## The Speed Read

Speed reading Kant? It's absurd to even try but . . .

The possibility of human knowledge must presuppose active participation from the human mind. Synthetic a priori judgments are a new brand of knowledge – beliefs that are informative but also necessary. Through them we can learn a great deal about the structure of the phenomenal world (of ideas). We cannot get beyond the bounds of reason to certain knowledge of the noumenal world, but as rational beings we act as though we can, in order to avoid believing that the world is meaningless. (Oh, and Jesus was right about morality, but why say it in one sentence when you can take a hundred pages to say the same thing?)

# *Science of Logic,* 1811–1816

## Georg Wilhelm Friedrich Hegel

*". . . profounder insight . . . into the dialectical nature*
*of reason demonstrates any Notion whatever*
*to be a unity of opposed moments . . ."*

Hegel's influence has been widespread on writers of widely varying positions. His predecessor Fichte, noting that Kant's system means that we only have knowledge within the noumenal world of ideas, had propounded a system of absolute idealism, in which objects only existed as the objects of consciousness. Hegel produced an even more comprehensive version of this approach. Where Berkeley had used idealism to emphasize that we need to have faith in God, Fichte, Hegel and other nineteenth-century absolute idealists had a more positive, humanist view that we could achieve a real understanding of the world through an analysis which focused more on the thinker than the thought.

One of Hegel's lasting influences was the way he used the idea of historical progress in thought to try to escape the circle of *"philosophia perennis"* (the perennial problems of philosophy). Also, for the first time in the history of philosophy he talked about the importance of the "Other" in the formation of self-consciousness. (This was expanded in his idea of the slave-master dialectic, in which he stated that the self generally appropriated the other.)

Hegel's writing style is notoriously difficult to read. This is partly because Hegel, in response to Immanuel Kant's challenge to the limits of "Pure Reason," tried to develop a new form of thinking and logic, which he called "speculative reason." The purpose of this was to try to overcome what he saw as the limitations of both common sense and of traditional philosophy at grasping philosophical problems and the relation between thought and reality.

Today, "speculative reason" is popularly called "dialectic." In the volumes of *Science of Logic*, modern philosophy, culture, and society, seemed to Hegel fraught with contradictions and tensions, such as those between the subject and object of knowledge, mind and nature, Self and Other, freedom and authority, knowledge and faith, the Enlightenment and Romanticism. As in the Socratic dialectic, Hegel proceeded by making implicit contradictions explicit: each stage of the process is the product of contradictions inherent or implicit in the preceding stage. Hegel's main philosophical project in *Science of Logic* was to take these contradictions and tensions and interpret them as part of a comprehensive, evolving, rational unity that, in different contexts, he called "the absolute idea" or "absolute knowledge."

According to Hegel, the main characteristic of this unity was that it evolved through and manifested itself in contradiction and negation. This was the process of the dialectic. Contradiction and negation have a dynamic quality that at every point in each domain of reality – consciousness, history, philosophy, art, nature, society – leads to further dialectic development until a rational unity is reached that preserves the contradictions as phases and sub-parts by lifting them up (*Aufhebung*) to a higher unity. For Hegel, this whole is both mental and rational. It is mental, because it is mind that can comprehend all of these phases and sub-parts as stages in its own process of comprehension. It is rational because it is the same, underlying, logical, developmental order that underlies every domain of reality and is ultimately the order of self-conscious rational thought.

The theory becomes more complicated when Hegel notes that it is only in the later stages of development that this dialectical process comes to full self-consciousness.

It is important to stress that the dialectic is itself a process, it does not end in a final solid consciousness of self. The rational, self-conscious whole is not a thing or being that lies outside of other existing things or minds. Rather, it comes to completion only in the philosophical comprehension of individual existing human minds that through their own understanding bring this developmental process to an understanding of itself. The recognition of self and other is then brought together as a process.

Central to this conception of knowledge and mind (and therefore also of reality) was the notion of identity in difference. According to Hegel the mind externalizes itself in various forms and objects that stand outside of it or opposed to it, the idea of "Other." Through recognizing itself in them, the mind is "with itself" in these external manifestations, they become at one and the same time mind and other-than-mind. This notion of identity in difference, which is intimately bound up with his conception of contradiction and negativity, is a principal feature differentiating Hegel's thought from that of other philosophers. It is an idea that was later taken up by philosophers such as Jacques Derrida and the psychoanalyst Jacques Lacan.

Hegel was trying to introduce a system for understanding the history of philosophy and the world itself, often described as a progression in which each successive movement emerges as a solution to the contradictions inherent in the preceding movement. For example, the French Revolution for Hegel constitutes the introduction of real freedom into Western societies for the first time in recorded history. But precisely because of its absolute novelty, it is also absolutely radical: on the one hand the upsurge of violence required to carry out the revolution cannot cease to be itself, while on the other, it has already consumed its opponent. The self appropriates the "other." The revolution therefore has nowhere to turn but onto its own result: the hard-won freedom is consumed by a brutal Reign of Terror.

History, however, progresses by learning from its mistakes: only after and precisely because of this experience can one posit the existence of a constitutional state of free citizens, embodying both the benevolent organizing power of rational government and the revolutionary ideals of freedom and equality. In some accounts of Hegel's dialectic it is often characterized as a three-step process of "Thesis, antithesis, synthesis." Namely, that a "thesis" (e.g. the French Revolution) would cause the creation of its "antithesis" (e.g. the Reign of Terror that followed), and would eventually result in a "synthesis" (e.g. the constitutional state of free citizens). In fact, Hegel used this classification only once, (on the subject of the French Revolution) and he attributed the terminology to Immanuel Kant.

Today it is widely admitted that the old-fashioned description of Hegel's philosophy in terms of "thesis-antithesis-synthesis" was always inaccurate. More recently it is thought, that in Hegel's language, the "dialectical" aspect or "moment" of thought and reality, by which things or thoughts turn into their opposites or have their inner contradictions brought to the surface, is only preliminary to the "speculative" aspect or "moment," which grasps the unity of these opposites or contradiction. The process does not end in stable unity but in unstable moments of "recognition." It could be said, therefore, that reason is ultimately "speculative," not "dialectical." Synthesis does not occur as there is always a "remainder" or anomaly beyond the "moment."

Hegel has sometimes been interpreted as saying that the process of dialectic would lead to an "end of history," an idea which has been taken up by other schools of thought since, including some Marxists and also some neo-Conservatives. In fact it is probably fair to say that this wasn't Hegel's intention. If history fully learnt from its mistakes, then, at the end of history there would be nothing left to learn, which seems impossible. However it is perhaps fair to say that Hegel took a rather complacent view of his own age (and the Prussian nationalist, protestant state in particular) as being the culmination of all previous history. Hegel was never short of self-belief (many subsequent writers including Nietzsche and Schopenhauer mocked his pomposity) and he certainly believed his own system of philosophy to be the culmination of all previous philosophical thought.

Hegel's theory of the dialectical process is important historically because it influenced the work of Marx and Engels. Marx appropriated Hegel's dialectic to create his own, claiming that his dialectic was the direct opposite of Hegel. For Hegel, the life-process of the human brain, the process of thinking, is an independent subject and the real world is only the external, phenomenal form of "the Idea." Whereas, to Marx, the idea is nothing else than the material world reflected by the human mind, and translated into forms of thought.

### Science of Logic

## The Speed Read

The structure of reality can be understood by analyzing human thought. No matter what the issue, the invisible dialectic aims to control both the conflict and the resolution of differences, and then lead everyone involved into a new cycle of conflicts. History is an inexorable process in which the dialectic leads towards higher levels of civilization and great intellectual achievements . . . such as Hegelian philosophy.

# The World as Will and Representation, 1818

## Arthur Schopenhauer

*"If I were to say that the so-called philosophy of this fellow
Hegel is a colossal piece of mystification which will yet
provide posterity with an inexhaustible theme for laughter
at our times, that it is a pseudo-philosophy paralyzing
all mental powers, stifling all real thinking . . .
I should be quite right."*

Schopenhauer is a philosopher who is often omitted from mainstream accounts of Western philosophy. He is frequently misrepresented and it is easy to find anecdotal facts that make him sound ludicrous. For instance he was a pessimistic ascetic, and an anti-semitic misogynist who became involved in a ludicrous lawsuit with a woman who made too much noise outside his apartment. He was also a bitter opponent of Hegel from the time when he became a university lecturer and, having scheduled his lecture at the same time as the much better known Hegel, was disappointed that no one turned up. After this experience, he never taught again. These kinds of snippets of information tend to make him appear a rather tragicomic figure.

However, he is an interesting figure in the history of philosophy, as much for the influence of his ideas on aesthetics and psychology as for his overall system of thought. Schopenhauer opposed Hegel for a number of reasons, both personal and rational. He regarded Hegel's politics as vacuous and "respectable" (in that he believed Hegel desired respect more than he desired truth). Instead he followed in Kant's footsteps in starting from the division of the world into *noumena* and *phenomena*. Both defined phenomena as ideas (or representation) but where Kant referred to noumena as "things-in-themselves," Schopenhauer defined noumena as "Will." By this he meant that representations, our ideas, were simply the way in which we experienced the basic drive of the world, which is will.

To explain this a little further, Schopenhauer took issue with David Hume's assertion that we had no experience of external bodies, asserting that we do have direct knowledge of our own body, which gives us an understanding of the concept of bodies or objects in the real world. In our own bodies we experience desires and drives, which we interpret as ideas, without fully understanding those desires. For Schopenhauer we live our lives being carried along on a river of will, simply rationalizing and trying to understand our own actions.

The will to live which we thus experience is for Schopenhauer a cause of suffering. We can only escape from this suffering either through ascetic living (denial of the will), which will not be an option for everyone, or through universal compassion for the human condition.

The latter idea led on to Schopenhauer's aesthetics. He saw tragedy as the highest form of art because, in a world that essentially causes us to suffer, tragedy attempts to understand and communicate the nature of the universal human condition. This is a concept of tragic art that has subsequently been hugely influential. Schopenhauer also described music as a direct interpretation of will. For these reasons he saw aesthetic contemplation as a third way of temporarily escaping the suffering imposed by the will.

Schopenhauer's concept of will also lay behind his fascinating writing on psychology. He wrote extensively about love. (His own love life was rather disastrous which may have been an influence here.) While most philosophers had given a fairly anodyne interpretation of love, based largely on aesthetic consideration of beauty, or ideas of companionship and family, Schopenhauer took a far more passionate approach. He saw love as another expression of the basic driving force of will. He described us as being carried along in love by forces that we do not truly understand.

In this respect, Schopenhauer was a harbinger of both the psychology of Freud, with its notions of libido and unconscious motivation, and the Darwinian idea of natural selection, which posits that our reproductive instincts are largely created for the good of the species. He was also ahead of his time in another way – his concept that the will creates suffering, and that we can only alleviate this through asceticism was a direct reflection of Buddhist thought, and Schopenhauer claimed to be influenced by the Upanishads as well as Buddhism. It was not common at this stage of European history for a philosopher to look to the East for inspiration, whereas it would become much more common in the twentieth century.

Schopenhauer's politics were his weakest point – he looked down on women, seeing them as essentially inferior, and described Jews and races other than northern Europeans in derogatory terms. It is impossible to defend these views but it should be noted that in many respects he was merely voicing commonly held prejudices of his era. Nonetheless these aspects of his work are uncomfortable to read now.

One philosopher who was very strongly influenced by Schopenhauer was Friedrich Nietzsche, although much of that influence consisted of provoking Nietzsche into opposing points of view. For instance Nietzsche proposed the "will to power" as a driving psychological force, but regarded denial of the will as a weakness that led to what he saw as Schopenhauer's corrosive pessimism. Nietzsche also developed a theory of tragedy that started from Schopenhauer but led to a very different interpretation of the role of aesthetics in life. At the same time as Nietzsche respected Schopenhauer's thinking he despised his fondness for Eastern asceticism and saw him as part of the establishment thinking based on Christianity, *ressentiment*, and passivity that Nietzsche opposed so passionately. Nonetheless the fact that such a spectacular thinker as Nietzsche found so much inspiration, both positive and negative, in Schopenhauer's writing should alert us to the fact that Schopenhauer is a more interesting writer than he is sometimes remembered as.

Nietzsche is more satisfying than Schopenhauer in one particular respect. While Schopenhauer sees the idea that the forces of will and desire underpin our conscious thought as a reason for pessimism, Nietzsche sees this as something to revel in. Instead of endorsing Schopenhauer's self-denial, Nietzcshe exhorted his readers to seek self-affirmation and to "overcome themselves." Schopenhauer's pessimism is a major part of his writing and seems to spring from a rather gloomy personal disposition. But for an understanding of the birth of modern psychology and aesthetics, he is well worth serious study.

## *The World as Will and Representation*

# The Speed Read

The world is made up of representation (our ideas) and will (our underlying drives and desires). Because of this, we live in a world of misery and suffering, with little hope of escape. Our only salvation lies in ascetic self-denial, sympathy with the universal human condition and aesthetic contemplation. Tragedy is the ultimate form of art because it captures the essence of human existence and provides us with a suitable subject for contemplation.

## *On Liberty,* 1859

John Stuart Mill

*"The only purpose for which power can be rightfully exercised over any member of a civilized community, against his will, is to prevent harm to others."*

In modern terms, John Stuart Mill could broadly be described as a liberal thinker. For instance, he was passionate about women's rights and the rights of minorities. And his utilitarian philosophy can be parodied as a hedonistic ideal of the good life. But his classic work *On Liberty* could also be seen as a libertarian text as it is a passionate defence of the freedom of the individual as opposed to the state. As such he is an interesting political thinker, representing a period modern enough to be very relevant to modern thinking, but sufficiently remote to give us interesting perspectives on the way that liberal and conservative, and left and right wing thinking mutated through the twentieth century.

Mill had a slightly weird upbringing. His father James Mill was a philosopher who, together with Jeremy Bentham, was an early advocate of the political philosophy known as utilitarianism. John was given a hothouse education by his father, which left him highly advanced in intellectual terms, but somewhat repressed and physically weak. As a result he suffered a period of severe depression in his early twenties.

Nonetheless he went on to become a passionate and eloquent advocate for utilitarianism. This is the belief that all actions can be judged (morally and politically) by their results. So the actions that cause the most happiness are by definition the best actions – the final moral arbiter is what action would bring the "greatest happiness to the greatest number of people" (or in later revisions, the least pain). In this respect Mill defined happiness as resulting from the maximization of pleasure and the minimization of pain. This seems a simple enough idea, but it of course leaves many complicated questions unanswered. For instance, how do we judge what is the best action? How do we measure happiness?

In *Utilitarianism*, Mill did his best to answer these questions. He fine-tuned a fascinating system of political and moral thought, derived from the utilitarian ideal. He faced up to the basic flaw in the theory as bequeathed to him by his father and Bentham – that it seems unreasonable and impossible to expect moral agents to stop and make a complicated calculation as to which people will be affected positively and negatively by any given action. This kind of "happiness sum" surely can't be the basic golden rule of human behaviour. Mill recognized that we develop moral rules from individual cases that lead us to make rule-based judgments later on, but insisted that in difficult or confusing cases the full calculation of the greatest happiness is still the appropriate guiding principle. (This is an interesting point when one considers the difficulties faced by judges in complicated legal cases to this day.) Later theorists formalized this insight as a distinction between "act utilitarianism" and "rule utilitarianism" – with the latter meaning that the rule is derived from an accumulation of observation of individual instances.

Utilitarianism is an interesting principle, even if it seems hard to vindicate as a general rule. But *On Liberty* is perhaps the more interesting book to a modern reader. Here he gives a very clear, early elucidation of the idea that a government should restrict its interference in the freedom of individuals to an absolute minimum. He held that this was especially true in a democracy because of the danger that democracy could turn into "tyranny of the majority." He argued that minority opinions should always be given the right of expression, firstly because they might turn out to be true or partially true, and secondly because it was a basic attribute of a good society that it should respect the freedom of expression of individuals. He argued that no matter how strongly we believe that our opinions are true, we should not censor or ban opposing views, because if we are right, the truth can only be strengthened by open debate.

Mill argued that the state was only justified in restricting the liberty of individuals if their actions would cause harm to others. One interesting consequence of this is that the state should not intervene to protect individuals from themselves. So in Mill's view the state should not intervene to prevent an individual harming themselves with drugs, but should when their behaviour is likely to harm others, either directly or by encouraging them to harm themselves.

It is interesting to note some of the other caveats that Mill allowed to his general libertarianism. He regarded a degree of interference in economic affairs as reasonable in the general social good, even though the economy might operate better in some respects with a laissez-faire attitude. And contrary to the general opinion of his contemporaries, he believed that it was acceptable for the state to interfere in family life, for instance to prevent child or spousal abuse.

Many of the issues that Mill confronts in *On Liberty* are still live issues in modern societies. The USA has traditionally defended free speech, to a greater degree than European democracies. However this freedom of expression has come under increasing pressure as a result of the "war on terror." Many individual freedoms have come under attack from conservatives, who have traditionally been libertarian in the USA, as a result of shifting priorities in the modern world.

Meanwhile in countries that have developed a more social democratic system of government, the degree to which a government is or isn't justified in intervening in private lives is an ever-increasing issue. For instance, if the taxes paid by the majority go to pay for the healthcare of a minority of smokers, is it acceptable for the state to intervene to restrict smokers' freedom to harm themselves? These questions are directly related to ideas that are examined in Mill's work, and reading the book 150 years after its publication one can see both surprising parallels and obvious differences between the preoccupations of the mid-nineteenth century and the current day. One need not agree with every conclusion that Mill reaches to find this a thought-provoking read.

*On Liberty*

**The Speed Read**

Governments should only restrict the freedom of individuals where the actions of those individuals are likely to harm other citizens. If individuals are harming themselves, that is not the business of government. And where an action could be performed either by an individual or by a government, it is in the interests of society that the individual's freedom should be respected, as a society based on liberty and freedom of expression is a stronger society than one that allows liberty to become compromised.

# On Formally Undecidable Propositions in Principia Mathematica *and* Related Systems I, 1931

## Kurt Gödel

*"For any consistent formal theory that proves basic arithmetical truths, it is possible to construct an arithmetical statement that is true but not provable in the theory. That is, any theory capable of expressing elementary arithmetic cannot be both consistent and complete."*

In this book we are mostly not attempting to explain works of mathematical logic – and there is a limit to how technically detailed our discussion of this crucial paper by Kurt Gödel will be. The obscurity of the title alone is enough to convey a flavour of the complexity of Gödel's work. However it represents a hugely important moment in twentieth-century philosophy, so it seems important to attempt to briefly describe its significance. Some have even described it as the end of classical philosophy.

The paper itself is a rather detailed logical proof, incomprehensible to all but advanced mathematicians. Gödel was looking at the foundations of logical systems or languages. In particular he was addressing a problem that had been raised by Bertrand Russell and Alfred Whitehead in their monumental book *Principia Mathematica*. This was an attempt to provide a formal logical basis for the whole of mathematics. Russell had noticed some problems in the earlier work of Frege, who described a logical system based on sets (where for instance the number "3" is defined by equating it with the set of all sets of three objects). The problem that Russell saw was raised by "the set of all sets which are not members of themselves". (Well, we did say this one was going to be a bit complicated . . .) Put more simply, there were inconsistencies in Frege's theories and Russell and Whitehead addressed this by not allowing such recursive constructions as the "set of all sets" in their logical system.

Their detailed work produced an advanced logical basis for mathematics which appeared to contemporaries to create the possibility that all of mathematics could be exhaustively proved from a limited set of axioms. But there remained some doubt as to whether or not this system could be complete and consistent – whether it could either lead to contradictions, or whether a mathematical statement might exist which could not be proved or disproved from these basic axioms.

This was the question that Gödel addressed. His two incompleteness theorems (the first of which is given above) showed that any consistent formal system which is powerful enough to contain arithmetic must contain at least one proposition whose truth or falsity cannot be proven within that system. For instance the statement "the *Principia* system contains no contradictions" could only be proven true or false in the Principia system if there were contradictions in the system (in which case it can be proven both true and false). If there were no contradictions, it couldn't be proved true or false.

So why is this rather arcane sounding problem of such significance? There are two major areas in which Gödel's work can be seen to be significant for philosophers. Firstly, a large part of the story of philosophy had consisted of a search for certain truth, derived from first principles. The work of Descartes, St Augustine and many others had started with mathematical truth as necessary truth, from which we might or might not be able to move on to more certain knowledge of empirical truths.

But Gödel's work struck a fatal blow to the whole concept of mathematics as a necessary, completeable system. Instead, mathematicians and logicians had to conclude that any system of mathematics is dependent on the axioms we choose to derive it from, and that we can never prove that any given system is complete or true. Of course this doesn't affect our basic ability to count or calculate. But in the further reaches of mathematical knowledge, different axioms produce different logical systems. So the whole idea that mathematics is a first principle from which we can derive perfect knowledge seems far less certain after Gödel. This is one reason why modern philosophy has, from mathematical logic downwards, become more focused on relativism and interpretation than on certain knowledge. Wittgenstein was one of many philosophers who took Gödel's proofs to mean that mathematics could not reveal absolute truth.

The second area in which the incompleteness theorems are relevant is in the study of the human mind. Gödel's theorems apply only to a logical system that could be computed from its axioms. The mathematician Alan Turing built on Gödel's work when he developed the idea of "Turing machines." These are notional, formal machines – Turing suggested that a Turing machine could solve any mathematical problem so long as it could be represented as an algorithm. This was an important piece of work in the development of computation, as it suggested that any machine that could calculate simple algorithms (such as for instance the calculations of binary code) could be used to solve far more complex problems. However the question of whether or not a Turing machine will halt on a specific program was shown by Turing to be undecidable, for reasons that mirror Gödel's theorems.

The question philosophers have often addressed is whether or not the human mind could be explained as a Turing machine. Many have attempted to prove that the human mind cannot be explained in purely mechanical terms. Gödel himself considered the philosophical implications of his own work in his 1951 Gibbs lecture. His conclusion was that the human mind could not be a consistent finite machine, but he acknowledged that this was unproven as it was based on a conjecture as to whether or not there were certain types of equation that the mind could not decide to be true or false. Some have argued that it is impossible for the human mind to be inconsistent, and find it hard to accept the idea that a human mind can be explained in such mechanistic terms. Others have reached opposite conclusions. But whatever the conclusions reached in the work of philosophers such as Hilary Putnam, J. R. Lucas or Roger Penrose, it is clear that the mathematical work of Gödel (and the related work of Alan Turing) casts a long shadow over the philosophy of mind in the last century.

*On Formally Undecidable Propositions in*
**Principia Mathematica** *and Related Systems I*

## The Speed Read

Mathematics cannot be reduced to a system that is complete and consistent. Does this mean that it is also impossible to have a consistent complete system of philosophical belief? If mathematics is not absolute truth, does that mean that there is no such thing as absolute truth? Can the human mind be explained in mechanical terms, or is it a consistent finite machine?

# *Philosophical Investigations,* 1953

### Ludwig Wittgenstein

*"Whereof one cannot speak, thereof one must be silent."*

The high regard in which Wittgenstein's philosophy is held is at least partly the result of a personality cult that developed around him in the first half of the twentieth century. Within the rather dry, academic world of English (mostly Oxbridge) philosophy of the period, Wittgenstein stood out as a fascinating and charismatic figure. After a childhood in Vienna, Wittgenstein arrived on Bertrand Russell's doorstep unannounced in 1911, and proceeded to study with both Russell and G. E. Moore. After a few year's study and a traumatic war (fighting in the Austrian army), Wittgenstein returned to Cambridge and published his remarkable *Tractatus.* He believed that this book had solved all the problems of philosophy, and so returned to Europe, giving away a family fortune, living first in isolation in Norway, then working as a rather erratic school teacher and monastery gardener as well as designing and building a house for his sister.

He discovered rather belatedly that he had become a famous philosopher, both in England and elsewhere, due to his influence on the well-known Vienna Circle, and returned to England having concluded that he perhaps still had some work to do. He refused to publish his ideas for many years, so infatuated students circulated notes of his lectures (in the *Blue Book* and *Brown Book*). Throw in hints of homosexuality, the suicide of several members of his family, and his love for westerns and detective stories and you have all of the elements for an extraordinary cult figure.

None of this should be allowed to detract from the fact that Wittgenstein's philosophy is both remarkable and influential.

It is best to divide it into the early and late phases in order to give a brief explanation. The *Tractatus* (full title *Tractatus Logico-Philosophicus)* is an elegant attempt to reduce all of philosophy to a simple, lucid system. In a series of crisp propositions, Wittgenstein describes a world made up of facts. Basic atomic sentences we use to describe the world bear a "picture" resemblance to these facts. Propositions of mathematics and logic are tautologies, merely describing the structure of thought, while anything else of which we might speak (including all matters of aesthetics, ethics and metaphysics) is simply nonsense. Wittgenstein ends the *Tractatus* rather magnificently dismissing all such nonsense with the quotation above, suggesting silence is the only response to such "nonsense." (In a letter Wittgenstein also wrote that "all of that which *many* are *babbling* I have defined in my book by remaining silent about it.")

It is fair to point out that one can interpret sections of the *Tractatus* as suggesting that these matters of nonsense, such as art and morality, are in fact the most important things in life, that we simply can't expect ever to speak of them with philosophical precision. To a degree, Wittgenstein is simply putting philosophy in its place, admonishing it for attempting to speak with certainty and clarity in areas where it cannot do so.

The *Tractatus* was enormously influential, leading many philosophers of the period to reject metaphysics and focus on logical analysis, in particular the interpretation of language and rejection of anything deemed nonsensical – although many did this with a less forensic brilliance than Wittgenstein. When Wittgenstein encountered the logical positivism of the Vienna Circle, he regarded it as a misinterpretation of his work, and this was what reawakened his interest in philosophy.

After his return to England in 1928 Wittgenstein gradually developed new ideas which both complemented and replaced large parts of his earlier work. It was many years before the publication of *Philosophical Investigations,* which can be regarded as his masterpiece, although parts of the book were compiled from his notes and published posthumously. He takes a much more thoughtful and less dogmatic approach in his later work. He now regarded both the logical atomism and picture theory of his earlier work as flawed.

Wittgenstein was still concerned about the imprecision of language and the way that it can befuddle us. He continued to think that many apparent problems of philosophy arise from the confusions introduced by language. But he had come to see language as *vague,* as a series of interconnecting games, with no fixed and certain meaning. "Language games" are played both in small and large communities – the meaning of words is created by consensus and can be unstable and varying. Controversially, he argued that even the rules of mathematics are no more than a language game, though a more stable one than others.

This led to Wittgenstein's assertion that there is no such

thing as a private language. He pointed out that traditional ideas of meaning tend to assume we have private language that describes our sensations (for instance the feeling "pain"), which we then "translate" into the public language that other people can understand.

But the words we use for pain would have no meaning, according to Wittgenstein, if they had not been created by the consensus of other people. We can only observe behaviours associated with pain, and imagine that they respond to a similar sensation to the way we behave when we feel "pain." The concept of pain is only created in the language game, but it is impossible to verify (or even make sense of attempting to verify) that different people have the exact same sensation when they talk of pain.

So Wittgenstein urges us to abandon the traditional ideas of meaning that rely on a private language, and accept that meaning is simply located in the language games that we use. This is interesting for a number of reasons. Firstly, Wittgenstein is once again undermining a great deal of the traditional Western tradition, by refusing to allow that we can match the subjective world of what we perceive, to any kind of objective truth. Pain is simply whatever gives someone the disposition to act as though they are in pain. The same applies to other sensations such as seeing the colour blue or hearing a sound. So subjective meaning is all that we can talk about. We can analyse meaning in so far as we can try to cut through the bewitchment of misunderstanding and confusion, but we are not reaching objective certainty, just a clearer understanding of the language game. This comes very close in spirit to the subjective approaches later adopted by, for instance, Derrida and the deconstruction-ists. But Wittgenstein is much clearer and less obfuscating in the way he approaches these difficult ideas. He is still aiming for clarity of thought even if he has to acknowledge that absolute clarity and certainty are not possible.

*Philosophical Investigations* is a challenging book. But it is also intriguing, and thought-provoking – and mostly written in a simple, direct style that reflects Wittgenstein's desire to clarify meaning and banish confusion. Much of the book consists of close examinations of the way in which language is used, and the ways in which philosophical problems are generated by confusion and vagueness and by language's unsuitability for doing the work to which philosophers have attempted to put it. For such a "difficult" book, it is, in the end, a rather enjoyable read.

### *Philosophical Investigations*
# The Speed Read

The *Tractatus* didn't abolish all the problems of philosophy after all. The connection between thought and facts is mediated by language. However there is no such thing as a private language – all meaning comes from the language games we use to establish and modify language. Language is innately vague, so while we can analyse and attempt to reduce confusion we can't discover certain, objective truth. Nor can we assume that what we feel as "pain" is the same as what someone else feels as pain.

# Wild and Crazy Guys:
# Outsiders and Gatecrashers

## *Introduction*

The title of this section is slightly tongue-in-cheek. All of these writers can be described in one way or another as being outside of the mainstream of philosophy that we looked at in the previous section. However, we felt it was important to include a few "outsiders." We might even say "gatecrashers," by which we mean those who weren't invited to the philosophy party, but have thankfully turned up anyway.

A number of the writers included in this section have been regarded as being slightly mad, or at least a bit odd. Nietzsche eventually became genuinely insane, Huxley ended his life by indulging in a massive acid trip, while Philip K. Dick was periodically convinced that he lived in the first century AD and that an alien intelligence was beaming messages into his brain. But as one contributor commented, rather than describing these writers as wild and crazy guys, we could just as easily say that some of them write about a "wild and crazy world."

Kierkegaard and Nietzsche could have been included in either the previous section, or in the section on continental philosophy and these summaries should be read with that in mind. Both are fascinating philosophers, but both suffer from slightly odd reputations. Both were at one point co-opted as being "proto-existentialists" though it's unlikely that either would have happily accepted that description. But whether for this reason, or because they take a more psychological view of human nature than some philosophers, both are sometimes treated with suspicion by the mainstream.

Also included here are authors who, because they write fiction, cannot be simply described in terms of the standard philosophical tradition. In the writing of authors as varied as Dostoevsky, Borges, Camus and Philip K. Dick, philosophical ideas are given fascinating treatments. These authors do not always answer the questions that they address, but they challenge us to think about the world in new and interesting ways.

The fact that Ayn Rand's "objectivism" has generally been treated as suspicious by the analytic philosophy establishment leads us to also include her here, as an outsider of sorts. (This also means we have had to make her an honorary "guy." In our defence, Rand would probably have been considerably less offended by this description than some of the feminist authors such as Naomi Wolf and Julia Kristeva who are included later in the book.)

Overall this section represents a first step towards making a point that we will address more fully in later sections – that philosophy is not just about formal academic papers and theories. Many writers of fiction, psychology or even self-help books have produced work that addresses profound philosophical ideas. Rather than focusing only on elitist academic philosophy we have intentionally tried to broaden the net to show how philosophy has interacted with other fields such as psychoanalysis or mysticism. The hope is that by doing this we can also aim to reflect the genuine breadth of enquiry that exists outside of the philosophical mainstream.

# *Fear and Trembling,* 1844

## Søren Kierkegaard

*"Anxiety is the dizziness of freedom."*

*"I begin with the principle that all men are bores. Surely no one will prove himself so great a bore as to contradict me in this."*

Kierkegaard, like Schopenhauer, is an example of a nineteenth-century philosopher who was fascinated by Kant's suggestion that we choose to embrace the unknowable, and who also reacted against Hegel's monolithic systems. He reacted to Hegel's notion of the dialectic by pointing out that the synthesis could only contain what had already been present in the thesis and antithesis. In his view, Hegel's claim to be able to bridge the problems of philosophy through dialectic was an empty promise – there would still be inevitable gaps in our knowledge. And the only way we can bridge such gaps is through a *leap of faith*.

Kierkegaard appeared to his contemporaries to be an outgoing sociable man, but privately he was tormented by depression. His family history was turbulent, with several early deaths in the family and an imposing father who had "cursed God" for his misfortunes. He despised people's desire for recognition and respect and chose to write his books under pseudonyms, cloaking his message in layers of irony and understatement. In this respect his work is decidedly literary. Books with such gloomy titles as *Fear and Trembling* or *The Sickness Unto Death* are perhaps closer to the works of Dostoevsky than any of the philosophers who had come before him.

Having concluded that we cannot bridge all the gaps in our knowledge when we stand at Kant's "borders of reason,"

Kierkegaard went on to consider the condition of human freedom. He saw Hegel's "world-spirit" as a nonsensical proposition, arguing against it that the crowd of ordinary humanity is often utterly wrong and that the only responsible human action can come from the individual acting alone. But as a result we are entirely self-reliant and alone in the world and this is a terrifying thing. In *The Concept of Dread* he uses the term *angst* (literally translated as anxiety, but here implying a more powerful fear) to describe the state of a human confronted with their own freedom.

Kierkegaard's overall message is dispersed between his books, and can be hard to discern on a casual read. It is difficult to pick out an individual title as a suggested starting point. We have chosen *Fear and Trembling* because it is a fascinating and relatively readable example of his style. In the book, Kierkegaard examines the story of God asking Abraham to sacrifice his son Isaac. He uses this biblical text as a starting point for exploring matters of theology and morality. Abraham personifies the difficulty (and angst) involved in making an apparently irrational and immoral choice based on faith alone. Kierkegaard depicts the individual contemplating making a leap of faith to overcome the paradoxes he has identified. The title of the book refers to the angst that the individual feels in the moment of making a free decision to act.

Elsewhere, in *Either/Or* Kierkegaard wrote about different spheres of existence. The aesthetic life consists of living for the moment, in having beauty and aesthetic truth as one's goal. The ethical life consists of trying to live in accordance with eternal verities of morality. Kierkegaard details the ways in which each of these spheres of existence are incomplete – and how they cannot be fully rationally grounded or justified, and therefore fail to satisfy our wills.

Kierkegaard was a Christian, but one who thought intensely about the foundations of faith. In proposing the religious life as an alternative to a merely ethical or aesthetic life, he first acknowledges that Christianity can't be a fully rational, objective choice. Objectively, there are other religions, and the ways in which Christianity (or any other religion) bridge the spiritual realm and the physical world do not make "rational sense."

At this stage of Kierkegaard's thinking, he makes a distinction between objective truth and subjective truth. When we seek for objective truth we try to achieve a state in which our internal beliefs match the real world. But we live subjective lives, so for Kierkegaard we must search for subjective truth, an internal truth in which the relationship between the knower and the object is part of the system. To believe in Christianity we need to accept objective contradictions, such as the idea that Jesus is both God and man. In making this leap of faith we are seeking after a subjective truth. But this is the only way to escape from the angst which our freedom has caused us. On one level the argument here is about how we believe. Believing in God simply because we are told to by society would seem quite inadequate for Kierkegaard. We have to make a passionate leap to that belief in order to approach fulfilment as individuals.

This focus on the self and the passionate will was a great influence on the twentieth-century existentialists. Some would argue that it is an empty ideal because it basically legitimizes a relativism in which it doesn't matter what we believe so long as we do so with passion. This is certainly a problem in trying to come to terms with the consequences of Kierkegaard's thought. His writing almost implies that it would be better to have a passionate belief in the palpably false or immoral than to have a lukewarm rational belief in the true and good. But the intense nature of Kierkegaard's thinking allows us to temporarily forget this objection – his writing is always at least fascinating, even though it is at times hard work.

As well as his obvious impact on existentialism, the "game-playing" aspect of Kierkegaard's writing was an important antecedent to some of the more intriguing philosophers who would follow him, including Derrida, in whose work irony and humour became part of the project of trying to describe the opacity of meaning. Shortly after Kierkegaard's early death in 1855 aged 42, Friedrich Nietzsche's writing would take a similar tack, using a paradoxical and occasionally contradictory style to demolish the very idea of truth as a single, monumental system. In such philosophy the very act of writing, and the varying styles used to express difficult concepts becomes part of the process of mapping out a complex idea.

At first reading, Kierkegaard can seem rather depressing and introspective, but the complexity and depth of his thought does repay repeated reading for those who have the patience. In the end he is arguing for a passionate, individual form of Christianity, while acknowledging and clearly describing the underlying difficulties in making the necessary leap of faith.

### Fear and Trembling
# The Speed Read

"Life must be lived forwards, but understood backwards." Abraham had to make an apparently absurd choice that we cannot possibly understand, in obeying God's order to kill his son. We cannot understand his choice except from the standpoint of faith. As free individuals we must make choices, but we suffer from angst and fear on the brink of freedom. The gaps in our understanding, and the inevitably unsatisfactory nature of life mean that we must make a leap of faith to embrace a personal, passionate religious faith, even though choosing that faith is different from seeking the "objective truth." We need passion as well as reason.

# *The Brothers Karamazov,* 1879–1880

Fyodor Dostoevsky

*"Did you forget that man prefers peace, and even death, to freedom of choice in the knowledge of good and evil?"*

The *Brothers Karamazov* is probably the greatest novel of all time. Fyodor Dostoevsky was a writer of extraordinary intensity who broke new ground in narrative style and technique, and this was his final novel, the pinnacle of his life's work. There is no single philosophical message in the book: Dostoevsky's characters each speak with their own voice and a variety of strands of philosophical thought are debated amongst them. But it is a book that provokes serious thought about the nature of faith and reason, and for this reason it can certainly be described as a philosophical classic.

Dostoevsky's life was strongly influenced by two major incidents: the death of his father, probably murdered by his serfs, and his own near-death experience. (He was blindfolded and left awaiting his execution for treason before being given the news that his sentence had been commuted.) He left prison with a deep fascination with matters of mortality, punishment and the state of Russia.

He is often described as the first existentialist. This seems wrong on several counts. He was in fact a mystical Christian and nationalist in his later years. He may have faced the possibility of doubt in God and a sensualist reaction to this doubt, but he would not have advocated the "existentialist" response, even if some of his characters propound views that seem to foreshadow existentialism. He also foreshadowed views that were put forward by his contemporary Nietzsche (who he couldn't have read) and the psychology of Freud in the passages where characters suffer from visions and delusions as a result of tensions in their personality.

One innovation in the book is the degree to which he foregoes the use of an omniscient narrator. His narrator is a "third person" voice, but he writes himself into the narrative and expresses uncertainty about his information to such a degree as to make the narrator a subjective voice within the book. The plot deals with the murder of Fyodor Karamazov, and with the reactions of his four sons, one or more of whom may be implicated in the murder. His characters are fully rounded personalities, but it is clear that the father (together with his son Dmitri) represents a kind of licentious sensuality, while the other sons Ivan and Alyosha respectively represent doubting reason and a fervent sort of faith. Alyosha's faith is particularly challenged by the death of the pious Father Zossima, his religious hero. The rapid corruption of the corpse is seen as evidence of a less than perfect life (because of the superstition that saints' bodies were incorruptible). One might speculate that these viewpoints represented different aspects of the author as he examined himself: in any case they throw up a fascinating friction between the different viewpoints.

There are extended theological debates throughout the book. Ivan puts forward various views on theology, which seem to come to him almost as ironic parodies of faith. At one stage he puts forward the idea that since God does not exist, "everything is lawful." One can see in Alyosha's immersion in religion and Ivan's scepticism a tussle with the problems of incipient atheism.

One of the most intense moments in the book comes with the famous "Grand Inquisitor" scene. Ivan describes to Alyosha the story of a poem he wants to write. The poem is set during the period of the Spanish Inquisition. Ivan imagines Jesus returning to earth to write, the day after a hundred heretics have been burnt to death by the Inquisition. When the Grand Inquisitor discovers that the

Messiah has returned he wastes no time in imprisoning him and promising to burn him at the stake.

The Grand Inquisitor talks to his prisoner and explains that the church doesn't need him. Jesus bequeathed to mankind the ability and right to choose between good and evil. But this responsibility brought only suffering and misery to mankind. The Inquisitor explains that mankind does not want the freedom that Jesus gave them. They are happier now that the totalitarian church has taken that freedom away and dictates all matters of right and wrong. As a result the Inquisitor intends to send Jesus to the stake to die once more. (In fact, after a kiss from the prisoner, Ivan ends the story with the Inquisitor allowing Jesus to escape.) The Inquisitor is presented as a character who has spent the greater part of his life trying to follow the path of Jesus, only to take the devil's side once he concludes that Jesus's legacy is too much for the greater part of mankind to deal with.

This rather disturbing tale has fascinating parallels with other philosophical classics. Socrates, like Jesus, can be said to have died because he urged his fellow citizens to examine their lives and consciences and choose between right and wrong. And it is worth comparing the Grand Inquisitor's message with Horkheimer and Adorno's *The Dialectic of Enlightenment*, in which the writers examine modern totalitarianism and the way that new myths are used to create the appearance of reasonableness, and to remove genuine freedom from most of the population. The Grand Inquisitor asserts that people can only be happy if they relinquish their freedom and bow down before "miracle, mystery and authority." He is basically expressing the modern authoritarian viewpoint, (also echoed in the work of Leo Strauss, which influenced neo-conservative thought) that an elite should take the responsibility of governing and use myths to govern the people and to control their freedoms.

One of the fascinations of Dostoevsky's work is that one can take very different messages from the different characters, and because the writer does not fully resolve the tensions he creates, the themes addressed linger in the mind long after reading the book. A large part of *The Brothers Karamazov* deals with the idea that mankind can achieve redemption through individual suffering. So the sons of the murdered father each suffer their own torments in the aftermath of his death, and their collective guilt points towards redemption and healing. This is a deeply Christian message although it is a passionate, personal take on Christianity. Thinkers as varied as Christians and atheists, existentialists and psychologists and critical theorists can all find challenges and meanings in the work of Dostoevsky. For anyone with any interest in questions of faith and reason in the modern world this is an extraordinary book that is worth reading and rereading.

### *The Brothers Karamazov*

## The Speed Read

Vile sensualist landowner Fyodor Karamazov suffers a tragic and gloomy death. One or more of his sons may have been guilty of murder. Saintly Alyosha, the cold rationalist Ivan, the impulsive Dmitri (as well as bastard son Smerdyakov) each suffer from guilt and horror in their own way as a result. Individual suffering may be a road to redemption of sin. And if Jesus came back to earth, would we really accept the freedom to choose between good and evil, or would we prefer to let the Grand Inquisitor burn him at the stake?

## *Beyond Good and Evil,* 1886

### Friedrich Nietzsche

*"That which is done out of love is always
beyond good and evil."*

Friedrich Nietzsche, a German philosopher whose books were mostly written in the 1880s, has a murky reputation – he has been variously dismissed as a proto-fascist, lunatic, egotist and misogynist, and is mostly remembered for declaring the Death of God. He was certainly a strange individual, a passionate, reserved loner, fond of composing his books during strenuous walks in the Alps. In 1889 his writing career ended in some kind of mental breakdown – following a period of increasingly weird behaviour, his final act before the breakdown was to fling his arms around the neck of a horse who was being beaten in the streets of Turin. He didn't recover his sanity before his death in 1900.

Reading his books, one discovers a far more complex and fascinating writer than his reputation might suggest – the experience can be likened to spending time with an extremely clever and erudite but erratic friend, who mixes flashes of sheer genius with barbed social commentary and some outrageous insults and jokes (for a nineteenth-century philospher, Nietzsche can be astonishingly funny).

Nietzsche saw the earlier work *Thus Spake Zarathustra* as his masterpiece, but *Beyond Good and Evil* is perhaps his most consistent work. Subtitled *A Prelude to the Philosophy of the Future,* the book is written as a series of aphorisms or short essays, with interludes of shorter maxims, which vary between bizarrely poetic and mordantly humorous extremes.

He starts by systematically demolishing almost every assumption of previous philosophers, making them look leaden and clodhopping in the process. He writes that it has "gradually become clear . . . what every great philosophy has hitherto been: a confession on the part of its author and a kind of involuntary and unconscious memoir." In this way, he argues that what has been previously defined as morality is no more than a psychological projection of individual desires. He views all values as being based on human drives, and mocks any attempt to base morality on truth, asking what truth is in any case, and why humans regard it as being so important. (Nietzsche's view that all truths are no more than interpretations was hugely influential on strands of twentieth-century thought from psychoanalysis to post-modernism, and existentialism to scientific subjectivism.)

Contemptuously mocking Descartes' reduction of certain knowledge to "I think," he describes this statement as no more than a grammatical accident, saying that we only believe there must be such an "I" because of the way our language works. Among others, he skewers the self-importance of Kant ("the tartuffery, as stiff as it is virtuous, of old Kant as he lures us along the dialectical bypaths that . . . mislead to his 'categorical imperative'").

Entertaining as all this is, Nietzsche's aim is not mere nihilism or academic one-upmanship. He views the drives and psychologies that have formed our ideas of truth, beauty and good as being essential human attributes. He reveals that his project is a "revaluation of all values" by which he means that free spirits such as himself (humility was never his strength) will undertake to question, examine and reinterpret the values we have inherited from the past.

In *Beyond Good And Evil*, Nietzsche's particular target is morality. He often talks in his work of free spirits or the overman – the strongest and best people who are able to act according to their drives and wills and to "overcome themselves." He aims to prove that what we have seen as "good" and "evil" are in fact the products of what he calls the slave morality, and that these "virtues" in fact work against the most natural human drives. He writes: "that which an age feels to be evil is usually an untimely after-echo of that which was formerly felt to be good." In this view, the weak in spirit, the suffering and the sick ("the herd") are envious and scared of the strong, so they define all strong virtues as being "evil" – as a result the Judaeo-Christian inheritance is one of guilt, mediocrity and inadequacy. We internalize the *ressentiment* of the weak and are dragged down by this sytem of values. Nietzsche proposes replacing "good and evil" with "good and bad," and redefining the qualities that the herd condemns (strength, will, self-creation, nobility) as "good."

One can see how the Nazis (encouraged by Nietzsche's sister who survived him and bowdlerized his books) were able to latch on to this strand of Nietzsche's thought and distort it to their own purpose. But his actual writing is closer to the romantic tradition of Blake in its vision of the free spirits of an ideal future. And while some of his rhetoric can be offensive, and some of his political views dated, in other respects his ideas still strike home forcefully today – his caricatures of democracy, religion and liberalism are at times frighteningly prescient.

With his concept of "eternal recurrence," Nietzsche talked about the idea that we should live our lives in such a way that if, at any point we were aware that we would have to live our lives over and over again, we would nonetheless make the same choices. His exhortation to us to lead lives of "creative self-affirmation" is at heart an uplifting one, and his attempt to cast off the psychological chains of history still fascinates, even if it is not always as successful as he hoped.

In *Beyond Good and Evil,* he writes, "Objection, evasion, happy distrust, pleasure in mockery are signs of health." Above all, Nietzsche despised systems and his dazzling array of suggestions, ideas and iconoclasm is better treated as an inspiration to consider the foundations of our basic assumptions in life, those received ideas we take for granted. Because, unlike most philosophers, the last thing Nietzsche would have wanted would be for anyone to take his writing as being "true" or "virtuous."

---

*Beyond Good and Evil*

## The Speed Read

Truth, value, and morality are no more than psychological projections misunderstood by past philosophers (fools, all of them). "Good" and "Evil" are illusory values by which the weak herd ensnares the strong individuals. The free spirits of the future (brilliant people like me, that is) must revalue all values and become what they will. In this way, humans can become more than human.

---

## *The Trial*, 1925

### Franz Kafka

*"If the book we are reading doesn't wake us up with a blow on the head, what are we reading it for?"*

Kafka is easily pigeonholed as a writer of absurd, hopelessly gloomy stories. Two of his best known stories are *Metamorphosis,* in which the hero wakes up one day to find himself transformed into a giant insect, and *The Trial,* in which Joseph K. finds himself accused of an unknown crime and spends the entire book trying, and failing to discover the crime of which he is accused. It's well known that Kafka asked for all of his work to be destroyed after his death (we only have his books because his friend and executor Max Brod refused to carry out this request).

However there is a lot more to Kafka than this brief description might suggest. He was certainly a writer who was keenly aware of philosophical issues – like Dostoevsky, who helped to inspire his writing, he doesn't put forward a single philosophical viewpoint, but conveys complex ideas through his characters and plot. He is also a very funny writer, albeit in a dark comedic style. It is said that when he read aloud from his work to friends, it was the humorous aspect that he emphasized, and if his reputation leads one to expect existential gloom, his humour is the most surprising aspect of his books.

*The Trial* concerns Joseph K.'s doomed attempts to prove his innocence, or at least to escape the nebulous charges that have been attached to him. In a densely bureaucratic society where the courts and church are mysterious, autonomous institutions, he meets a variety of strange characters, many of whom claim to be able to help him. But no matter whether he reacts with defiance or acquiescence, he seems to make his situation progressively worse.

Near to the end of the book, a priest relates the parable of the law to Joseph, a depressing story that parallels his own experiences. In the parable, a man comes to the courts to search for justice. A gatekeeper makes him wait outside a gate, hoping for admittance. He grows old there, never discovering how to persuade the gatekeeper to open the gate. He is told that there are further gates inside that he must pass through if he ever progresses, but in the end he never even gets past the first barrier. As he lies dying, the gatekeeper tells him that this gate was for him alone, and that it will now be closed.

Like the seeker after justice, Joseph K. is living in a nightmarish world, where the most absurd obstacles are placed in his path, yet he treats all these complications as though they are perfectly natural. The whole book is clearly a parable of sorts, in spite of the naturalistic dialogue and descriptions. Joseph K.'s situation reflects the spiritual plight of a human in a world where meaning is concealed, labrynthine or perhaps entirely absent. In spite of knowing from the start that he probably can't be released from his plight, Joseph puts his faith in a variety of ways to seek justice, before finally achieving some kind of closure by abandoning this quest altogether.

A variety of interpretations have been imposed on *The Trial*. In the heyday of existentialism, Kafka was often claimed to be a proto-existentialist, and the hopeless plight of his protagonist certainly matches the mood of some existentialist literature. Sartre gave an interesting interpretation of *The Trial*, based on Kafka's Jewish identity, in which he pointed out that anti-semitism puts Jewish people in a situation not unlike Joseph K., perpetually accused of an unknown crime, not knowing when or whether they will be attacked or punished for it. Others have given Marxist readings of *The Trial*, while Kafka's chronic feelings of guilt and social anxiety provide plenty of ammunition for those who wish to claim it as a work of psychoanalytic exploration.

In philosophical terms, Kafka is an heir to Dostoevsky, in that he represents the struggle between traditional religion and objective truth, and the modern collapse of faith and resulting subjectivity of meaning. What is the place of an individual in a world that has no ultimate or fixed meaning? Like Joseph K. we face up to a complex world where we feel that the structures of meaning and law are arbitrary yet hard to oppose. So we must absorb the norms of our society, or fail to do so and be treated as transgressors. Kafka uses a dark exaggeration of the bureaucracy of his society (he lived in Prague which was at the time part of the Austro-Hungarian empire) to convey this feeling of absurdity. Joseph K. occasionally yearns for the simplicities of objective metaphysical truth, but he is condemned to exist in a world where essential meaninglessness has been structured into a complex and oppressive human society.

*The Trial* might be seen by some who have lived under oppressive regimes in the Eastern bloc and elsewhere as being almost literary realism. Certainly the characters that thrive in Kafka's world are those who manage to assimilate themselves and their identities into the system, whereas Joseph K. fails to do this out of a mixture of defiance and sheer incomprehension. For others who live in less oppressive societies *The Trial* can nonetheless speak very clearly of a certain kind of mental apprehension that we experience when confronted with bureaucratic obstacles in the service of apparently meaningless statutes.

For all of *The Trial*'s resonance with real life situations, it is the philosophical aspect of the book that endures. Whether you read the story as a black comedy or a tragedy, Joseph K.'s bewilderment in the face of meaninglessness and forces that can't be explained tends to strike a chord with anyone who has ever wondered whether or not the world has any ultimate meaning.

### The Trial

## The Speed Read

"Someone must have been telling lies about Joseph K., for without having done anything wrong he was arrested one fine morning." In spite of many attempts to discover what crime he is accused of, Joseph K. only succeeds in making his situation progressively worse. The bureaucracy of court and church seems to exist only to thwart him in his search for justice, as a priest confirms when he tells him the parable of the law, in which it becomes apparent that the search for justice and meaning is doomed.

## *The Outsider (L'Étranger)*, 1942

### Albert Camus

*"It was as if I had waited all this time for this moment and for the first light of this dawn to be vindicated. Nothing, nothing mattered, and I knew why."*

Albert Camus was an Algerian-French author and philosopher. Camus preferred to be known as a man and a thinker, rather than as a member of any school or ideology. He favoured people over ideas. In an interview in 1945, Camus rejected any ideological associations: "No, I am not an existentialist. Sartre and I are always surprised to see our names linked . . ." Camus was the second youngest recipient of the Nobel Prize for Literature (after Rudyard Kipling) when he received the award in 1957. He is also the shortest-lived of any literature laureate to date, having died in a car crash three years after receiving the award.

Camus' first significant contribution to philosophy was his idea of the absurd, the result of our desire for clarity and meaning within a world that offers neither. He explained this in *The Myth of Sisyphus* and incorporated it into many of his other works, such as *The Outsider* and *The Plague*. *The Outsider* is a novel that tells the story of an alienated man, who eventually commits a murder and waits to be executed for it. The book uses an Algerian setting, drawn from Camus's own upbringing in the country.

At the start of the novel, the protagonist Meursault goes to his mother's funeral, where he does not express any emotions and is entirely unaffected. The novel documents the next few days of his life, in the first person point-of-view. He befriends one of his neighbours, Raymond Sintes and helps him to dismiss one of his Arab mistresses. Later, the two confront the woman's brother ("the Arab") on a beach and Raymond gets cut in the resulting knife fight. Meursault goes back to the beach and shoots the Arab once, in response to the glare of the sun. The Arab is killed immediately, but Meursault fires four more times at the dead body.

At the following trial, the prosecution focuses on the inability or unwillingness of Meursault to cry at his mother's funeral. It is argued that he must be a cold-hearted man. For Camus, the killing of the Arab is apparently less important than whether Meursault is capable of remorse. The argument follows that if Meursault is incapable of remorse, he should be considered a dangerous misanthrope and subsequently executed to prevent him from doing it again, and making him an example to those considering murder.

As the novel comes to a close, Meursault meets with a chaplain, and is enraged by the chaplain's insistence that he turn to God. He believes that we make our own destiny, and we are responsible for our actions and their consequences, not God.

The novel ends with Meursault recognizing the universe's indifference to humankind. The final lines echo his new realization: "As if that blind rage had washed me clean, rid me of hope; for the first time, in that night alive with signs and stars, I opened myself to the gentle indifference of the world." His parting wish is that, so that he feels happy, there should be a large crowd at the execution, and that they should greet him with cries of hate.

The novel is classed by various people as either existentialist or as linked to Camus's theory of the absurd. In the first half of the novel, Meursault is clearly an unreflecting, unapologetic individual. He is moved only by sensory experiences (the funeral procession, swimming at the beach, sexual intercourse with Marie, etc.). Camus is reinforcing his basic thesis that there is no Truth, only (relative) truths – and, in particular, that truths in science (empiricism and rationality) and religion are ultimately meaningless. Of course, Meursault himself isn't directly aware of any of this – his awareness of it is subconscious at best; it "colours" his actions. However Camus's basic point remains that the only real things are those that we experience physically. Thus Meursault kills the Arab because of his response to the glaring sun, which beats down upon him as he moves toward his "adversary" on the beach. The death of the Arab isn't particularly meaningful in itself: it's merely something else that "happens" to Meursault. The significance of this episode is that it forces Meursault to reflect upon his life (and its meaning) as he contemplates his impending execution. Only by being tried and sentenced to death is Meursault forced to acknowledge his own mortality that he links with "the gentle indifference" of the world. It is interesting that at the end he wishes for a crowd of hate-filled spectators to watch his execution. The imagined crowd would show the emotion that is missing in himself.

Meursault, despite being judged by many of his contemporaries as immoral or amoral, believes passionately in truth and justice. He betrays this belief through his unyielding candour; he never displays emotions that he does not feel. Nor does he participate in social conventions he finds dishonest. Although grief is considered the socially acceptable or "normal" response, Meursault does not exhibit grief at his mother's funeral. This belief in the incorruptibility of truth takes on a naïve dimension when he goes through the trial process; he questions the need for a lawyer, claiming that the truth should speak for itself. Much of the second half of the book explores this theme of the imperfection of justice. It is Meursault's belief in truth that proves his undoing – a public official compiling the details of the case tells Meursault he will be reprieved if he repents and turns to Christianity, but he stays truthful and refuses to pretend he has found religion. More generally, Meursault's love of truth overrides his self-preservation instinct; he feels that he must be punished for his actions, and refuses to try to evade justice.

Camus presents the world as essentially meaningless, which implies that the only way to arrive at any meaning or purpose is to make it oneself. Thus it is the individual and not the act that gives meaning to any given context. Camus further explores this as well as issues such as suicide and human relationships in his other works such as *A Happy Death* and *The Plague,* as well as his non-fiction books such as *The Rebel* and *The Myth of Sisyphus.*

*The Outsider*

# The Speed Read

The world is essentially meaningless. There is no God, we are responsible for our actions and for the consequences arising from them. One should remain true to oneself and not be influenced by others regardless of the consequences. The world is as indifferent to us and our own personal values as we are to it.

# *The Fountainhead*, 1943

## Ayn Rand

*"My philosophy, in essence, is the concept of man as a heroic being, with his own happiness as the moral purpose of his life, with productive achievement as his noblest activity, and reason as his only absolute."*

Ayn Rand is the founder of the philosophy known as *objectivism*. She is a controversial figure for a number of reasons, but her books have sold millions of copies, and have been influential. Her later novel *Atlas Shrugged* gives a fuller statement of her conception of objectivism, but it is a notoriously long and difficult novel, and the earlier work *The Fountainhead* is probably a better starting point for those who are interested in finding out about her ideas.

Rand was an immigrant from the Soviet Union, who quickly came to idealize America as the ideal society. She wrote plays, novels and screenplays in the 1920s and 1930s, but it was *The Fountainhead* which brought her true fame. It is a novel, but it was fundamentally a vehicle for her philosophical views. She had been an admirer of Dostoevsky (although she disliked his political views) and Nietzsche in her youth. Both influences show in her writing, although she came to repudiate what she saw as Nietzsche's view that the strong should exploit the weak, and his emphasis on interpretation rather than knowledge of reality. (It is possible that she was also influenced by contemporary views of Nietszche, which tended to emphasize his links to Nazi philosophy rather than giving a broader view of his work.)

The plot of *The Fountainhead* centres on the hero Howard Roark, Rand's idealized man, an architect who refuses to compromise his vision for the sake of petty gain. Rand had a rather heroic view of the individual, and believed that enlightened self-interest was the ideal driving force of humanity. She advocated the free market and the American way, and saw collectivism as immoral and degrading. Many of those who are influenced by Rand also take right-wing, libertarian views on politics and economics, although Rand herself rejected the libertarian label.

As a philosophy, objectivism starts from a rejection of Kantian metaphysics and scepticism. Rand believed that there was an objective world, and that human reason was perfectly capable of coming to an understanding of that world. Against Kant's distinction of the noumenal and phenomenal world, and against the enlightened scepticism of Hume, she argues that we can come to an adequate knowledge of the real world. In detail, this becomes a less radical opinion than it might first seem, as Rand is clever enough to admit that there is some complexity in our relationship with reality. But it is nonetheless a robust rejection of a large part of philosophical tradition, in that Rand simply refuses to accept the standard degree of philosophical doubt about whether or not we can have real knowledge of the world.

Rand's reputation is a strange one. Many still revere her and objectivism retains a certain popularity, although this is mostly within the United States rather than elsewhere. However the analytic philosophy tradition mostly ignores her work. This may be partly due to a stuffy refusal to believe that there can be anything interesting in the work of a woman who conveyed her ideas through the medium of novels rather than through the traditional philosophical channel of peer-reviewed academic papers and dry books of analysis. But there may also be a degree to which objectivism falls into the same pigeonhole as existentialism. Both are philosophies that have a surface appeal, particularly to young people at a certain phase who are excited by a bold, passionately stated total theory of the world. But both have obvious logical flaws that on further reflection make them seem a little embarrassing.

Rand's reputation also suffers to some degree from the soap opera that her life became. A famous and successful author, she continued to propagate the importance of her own philosophy throughout her life. But the objectivist movement suffered many schisms, some of which were based on Rand's own fallings out with previous acolytes. When her affair with Nathaniel Branden (a prominent figure within the movement) ended messily she excommunicated him, without publicly acknowledging the cause of their rift.

But there is something else going on here. Rand was sexually open and had provocative views on the nature of sexuality. In the overpoweringly male world of philosophy, the idea of such a strong woman, who was not only unashamed of her sexuality but was even prepared to incorporate it into her philosophy, may have been uncomfortable. Feminists have also been uncertain how to deal with Rand, because of her hero-worship of the "ideal man" and the elements of her novels which seem to take a power-based view of sex (including the passage in *The Fountainhead* in which the heroine is apparently "willingly raped"). While some feminist writers have been prepared to take a revisionist view of her legacy, Rand's position in culture is such that there are not many schools of thought who will defend her – other than a subsection of the libertarian fringe.

Is *The Fountainhead* a good novel? Is it good philosophy? You will get different answers to these questions from different people. A personal view is that it can be an intriguing novel at a certain age (ranging from adolescence to the early twenties), but that it is nonetheless a novel that doesn't really hold water because the characters are so clearly set up as puppets that represent specific viewpoints. So *The Fountainhead* probably only stands up to scrutiny as a vehicle for Rand's political and philosophical views. If you agree with her views, you are likely to enjoy the novel far more than someone who doesn't. But at the very least it is a philosophically challenging read, and it will be interesting to find out whether or not objectivism is remembered in another fifty years' time.

### *The Fountainhead*

## The Speed Read

The free market is the only moral system. Individuals should act from self-interest. Collectivism is corrosive to the human soul, and the great men of industry are the heroes of our age. Kant's metaphysics was morale-sapping and wrong because he denied we could really know the world, whereas objectivism states that the world is real and we can have knowledge of it. Rational egoism and individual rationality are the foundation stones of a healthy society.

# *Fictions*, 1944

## Jorges Luis Borges

*"Reality is not always probable,
or likely."*

The Argentinian author Jorge Luis Borges is one of the most intriguing figures of twentieth-century literature. He is hard to classify – as well as a writer of fiction he was a lecturer, prolific translator, poet, ex-librarian and writer of non-fiction. His greatest work came in surprisingly slender collections of short stories. His two greatest original collections *The Garden of Forking Paths* and *Artifices* were collated in one volume as *Fictions,* and this is probably the best place to start reading his work. (Although there is a great deal of interesting material in more extended collections of fiction and in his other published work.)

Borges writes in a variety of styles, so it is difficult to summarize his work. He frequently invents other books and writers, whose work he then comments on, and many of his stories deal with fantastical versions of the world, or labyrinths and mysteries within a version of this reality. He was fascinated by philosophy and weaves into his narratives paradoxical and challenging ideas about truth, mirrors, mazes and madness.

The easiest way to give a flavour of his work is probably to give brief accounts of the plots of a few of the stories. In *Tlon, Uqbar, Orbis Tertius,* a fictional version of Borges himself embarks on a literary detective story. First intrigued by a few fragmentary references in obscure literary works to a land called Uqbar, he gradually starts to uncover a vast, centuries-old conspiracy by an elite of intellectuals (including the philosopher George Berkeley) to insert fake pieces of information into the world's literature. These bogus pieces of information point to a land called Uqbar, in which all the literature tells of an imaginary land called Tlon.

Having established this complicated chain of imagination to Tlon, the heart of the story consists of Borges discussing the language and epistemology of Tlon. The people of Tlon are depicted as believing in a version of Berkeley's idealism, in that they only believe in the reality of ideas, not in a "real world." Borges puts forward various types of languages that might be spoken in Tlon, in which certain parts of grammar are missing, such as a language completely devoid of nouns. He points out that these different languages would entail completely different ways of conceptualizing the world. The plot of this shortish story therein becomes even more dazzlingly Byzantine with the suggestion that real objects from the imaginary Tlon are somehow infiltrating the real world. This extraordinarily dense, experimental story manages to pack a remarkable amount of philosophical speculation into a bizarre and entertaining yarn.

In *Pierre Menard, Author of Don Quixote*, Borges pursues a different literary conceit. The story is in the form of a review of an imaginary book (a common device in Borges' work) in which Pierre Menard is an author who has reproduced *Don Quixote* word for word. But rather than simply being a facsimile, this is presented as being the work of an author who has absorbed himself so fully in Cervantes' work that he has been able to produce a verbatim version that is *his own act of creation*. In exploring the meaning of this idea, Borges puts forward fascinating thoughts about the meaning of a literary text and its interpretation.

One more story, *The Library of Babel* creates yet another dizzying literary conceit, an infinite library in which for every possible combination of letters there is a book somewhere containing that combination. This library will contain every possible work of literature, as well as its translation into every possible language. There will also be an infinite number of meaningless or worthless works, although for every book that is apparently gibberish, it is possible to imagine a language that would make it into a meaningful book. Finally it will contain every possible useful piece of information, including the complete and finished biography of every living person.

The library is haunted by seekers of truth undertaking the hopeless search for their own biography. Meanwhile librarians, driven mad by the sheer flood of information, tussle with the problem of whether or not to destroy books that are apparently worthless, when doing so would take the risk that these are books of great value in some possible future language. Finally Borges toys with the idea of regressive infinity by imagining a single book hidden somewhere within the library that contains the essential truth of every other book in the library.

One can only speculate as to how fascinated Borges would have been by the internet, but surely the invention of a worldwide web of computers, endlessly reiterating information of every sort, true and false, useful and fatuous, would have been a source of wonder and wry amusement to him.

Borges' work has hypnotized many subsequent writers who operate in the literature of ideas – in the work of authors as varied as Salman Rushdie and Paul Auster one can clearly see his influence. In the context of this book, it is the philosophy contained in Borges' work that is of interest. Borges doesn't express one particular viewpoint, but his fascination with philosophical thinking shines through in many of his stories. As the brief plot outlines above demonstrate, he often explores the ways in which meaning shifts and changes as it is translated into text, and the ways in which rationality is influenced by language and context. His writing is erudite and absorbed by ideas rather than plot, but it is extremely enjoyable and throws up interesting and puzzling ideas on almost every page.

---

### Fictions

## The Speed Read

"It is a laborious madness and an impoverishing one, the madness of composing vast books – setting out in five hundred pages an idea that can be perfectly related orally in five minutes. The better way to go about it is to pretend that those books already exist, and offer a summary, a commentary on them." (Quoted from the introduction to *The Garden of Forking Paths*)

---

## *The Doors of Perception* and *Heaven and Hell*, 1954, 1956

### Aldous Huxley

*"If the doors of perception were cleansed every thing would appear to man as it is, infinite. For man has closed himself up, till he sees all things through narrow chinks of his cavern." (William Blake)*

Plenty of writers have written about the use of drugs to create an altered state of mind. In the sixties, the hippies latched on to writers such as William Burroughs, Carlos Castaneda, and Timothy Leary, to name but a few of those who advocated or described the use of psychedelic drugs for metaphysical or religious purposes.

Aldous Huxley was however one of the first to write on the subject (these two books were published in 1954 and

1956 and are commonly published together), and in some ways one of the most interesting. This is partly because the clichés of the 1960s were not developed at that stage, so he comes to the drug experience with less baggage than some of his later followers. Huxley was an English intellectual and writer who emigrated to California in 1937. His early writing focused on humanist and pacifist concerns and the effect of technological progress (in novels such as *Brave New World*, which presents a dystopian view of a mechanized future).

He became increasingly interested in mystical ideas and religious practices (such as meditation) after his move westward, and wrote extensively on related topics. In the early 1950s, he was introduced to psychedelic drugs by a friend. These two short books combine speculation of the possible metaphysical consequences of drug use with personal accounts of the effects the drugs had on him. In *The Doors of Perception* he writes about his experiences of mescaline, while by the time of *Heaven and Hell*, he had also experimented with LSD.

The titles of both books are references to William Blake's *The Marriage of Heaven and Hell*. The quote above demonstrates Blake's mystical idea that man's perception of the universe could somehow be enhanced by religious experience, thus opening the doors of perception. Of course, one of the central images of philosophy comes from Socrates' parable of the cave, in which the human mind is presented as perceiving only shadows of the real forms that lie beyond. This idea that there is a greater reality than the one we perceive is a crucial driving force in philosophies of very different kinds. For analytic philosophy, the question is "how can we understand the relationship between our perceptions and that greater reality?" Whereas for a more mystical mind such as that of Blake or Huxley, the question instead becomes "how can we open the doors of perception to cast more light on reality?"

Huxley believed that drugs were capable of doing this. He based his analysis on the fact that psychedelic drugs are believed to remove the brain's "reality filters." This means that a huge amount of information is received by the brain, but in order to process this information and function effectively, we acquire the ability (or limitation) of being able to filter most of this information out. He believed that the drug experience removed these filters, and that we were therefore experiencing a more overwhelming and total sensory perception while under the influence. In *Heaven and Hell* in particular, he goes beyond this to a more religious interpretation of the drug experience, suggesting that there is a sense in which we can "see God" through drug use.

Huxley is very honest in writing about his own experiences of the drugs he used, at times admitting to a degree of confusion and uncertainty. There are many criticisms that can be made of his ideas, and we will come to those shortly. But the first thing to acknowledge is that these are fascinating books, replete with connections between ideas of mystical and physical perception and religious understanding. These kinds of connections would become more commonplace in the 1960s, but at the time Huxley wrote these books, they were breaking new ground.

However, it is very clear fifty years later that there was a serious level of naïvety in this kind of rhetoric. Firstly, Huxley was an intellectual who had spent many years pondering mystical ideas. His drug experience was rooted in his own mental faculites and proclivities, and seems very different to many other reports of both drugs. Secondly, he was writing at a time when the potentially harmful psychological effects of psychedelic drugs were not understood, when the fallout from an illegal trade in these particular drugs was relatively limited, and when they seemed like harmless, innocent experiments. From this point of view, his writing makes a lot of sense. But in retrospect it seems irresponsible to make some of the claims that Huxley makes in his writing. And it should also be recognized that some of the experiences that Huxley describes can be approached through other means, such as meditation, while other aspects of the psychedelic experience come closer to simulating or causing madness than they do to allowing us a more profound understanding of reality.

Huxley's parting gesture of taking a huge dose of LSD while on his deathbed now seems part of a very remote and different world. In general he seems far too casual in his recommendation that everyone could do with a mescaline holiday and other similar exhortations.

So these books come with a health warning, and have historically been more revered by the drugs counterculture than they have by mainstream thinking. Nonetheless they remain fascinating personal documents of some strange experiences. And they do contain interesting philosophical ideas, however much we may disagree with some of Huxley's interpretations and proposals.

### *The Doors of Perception* and *Heaven and Hell*

## The Speed Read

Let me tell you about the times when I took some mescaline and acid. The doors of perception in my mind seemed to open, and I perceived the universe in a different way. The filters of the mind were bypassed and I perceived reality all at once, without it being shaped by human words and notions. Maybe I could even see God this way. Wow! You should really try it some time . . .

# *Do Androids Dream of Electric Sheep?* 1968

## Philip K. Dick

*"Reality is that which, when you stop believing in it, doesn't go away."*

Philip K. Dick is best known through the film adaptations that have been made of his science fiction novels, including *Blade Runner* (which is based on *Do Androids Dream of Electric Sheep?*), *Total Recall* and *Minority Report.* But the crash-bang approach of these films rarely does justice to the strange yet subtle thinking that underpins his novels.

Dick was a prolific writer. He aspired to be a "serious novelist" but first found success in the pigeonhole of science fiction. He spent many years churning out short stories and novels, writing through the night while working at a variety of day jobs. The writing is often slapdash as a result, but there are always fascinating ideas at the heart of his novels. More than any other science fiction writer, his obsession was the nature of the reality in which we live. He was fascinated by pre-Socratic philosophers, for instance Heraclitus, who claimed that all of reality is in flux.

His books often feature aliens, spaceships, and possible futures. But within this context he explores questions such as whether or not we can know that the world we live in is real, what would happen if time ran backwards (*Counter-Clock World*), the nature of alternative realities (especially in *The Man in the High Castle*), and the nature of our self-identities (for instance in *A Scanner Darkly* where he creates a nightmare world in which a disguised law operative keeps his own drug-addicted alter-ego under observation, unaware that they are the same person). He creates societies where humanity is organized into tribes according to their mental state, or in which each character is forced to experience the world through the consciousness of others, or in which all the characters are dead, but haven't yet realized this. He doesn't generally answer the philosophical questions he poses, preferring the ambiguity of creating a scenario that raises difficult questions, and then allowing the absurdities and complexities of that situation to play out through his plot.

*Do Androids Dream of Electric Sheep?* is one of his best known books, because of Ridley Scott's remarkable film adaptation. The question it asks is a deceptively simple one. What makes us human? Dick imagines a future society in which organic androids, robots so advanced that they are indistinguishable from humans, are widely used as labourers or slaves in the service of "real" humans. He wonders how we could tell the difference between androids and people, and, more subversively, if there is an ultimate difference at all. In addition this debate takes place against the background of a semi-populated radioactive future world, where humans who stay on earth can at any time become downgraded to the non-person status of "specials" if they become too contaminated. One of the central relationships in the novel is between an android (Pris) and a special (J. R. Isidore), two very different types of "non-person."

The book directly addresses some of the most fundamental questions of philosophy. What is a person? Do humans have souls? An android, as imagined by Dick, has essentially the same physical constitution as a person, being made up of artificial flesh and blood, with an artificial brain. So does this make them "human" or not?

British philosopher Gilbert Ryle coined the term "the ghost in the machine" to criticize the notion expressed by Descartes and others that the soul is something non-physical. In Descartes' view, it may well be that every mental process we have is explicable in physical terms, but there must nonetheless be a non-physical soul – this being the place where the "I" of "I think therefore I am" resides.

The idea of the soul is central to religious philosophy – the soul is the non-physical part of our body in the same way that God is the non-physical part of the universe. The idea that we have no soul, that all our mental processes have physical explanations is threatening to traditional religion and to the dualistic philosophy that tends to underpin it.

In *Do Androids Dream of Electric Sheep?* the hero Deckard has the job of hunting down and killing runaway androids. Humans have developed progressively more complex ways to identify androids as they become more and more sophisticated. Dick was clearly aware of the Turing Test, the idea put forward by Alan Turing, whereby a human-like level of intelligence would be attained by a computer at the stage when someone conversing with a computer would be unable to tell if it was computer or human. Turing suggested that this was a better test of a computer than the emotionally charged question "Can a machine think?"

In Dick's world, humans have to resort to an even more complicated version of the Turing Test, an empathy test. This is a series of questions and answers designed to reveal the androids' lack of "empathy."

One complex element of Dick's book that was omitted from the film, was the imaginary religion Mercerism. Most real animals are extinct in this world (a few revered examples remain, while many people, including Deckard, resort to keeping animal androids), and killing them is utterly taboo. The daily religious worship of Mercerism is a strange process whereby the participants use an "empathy box" to view a mythical figure (Wilbur Mercer) climbing a hill, and merge with him in religious empathy.

The empathy tests used on the androids largely work by revealing their lack of empathy. For instance they are not revolted by the idea of killing animals, and do not find human children endearing. One clear subtext is that these are quite artificial distinctions. Mercerism is an artificial religion, and it is not necessarily an innate human instinct to find killing animals taboo. And the androids are unable to breed because of their short life span, so they do not react to children as a human might. So while proposing the idea of this test, Dick deliberately encourages us to doubt if it really is testing humanity or an artificially constructed distinction between the androids and the humans.

At one stage in the novel, Deckard questions whether a bounty hunter like him can really be human since he feels no empathy for the androids he kills. He is also put in the position of having to wonder if he would pass the empathy test himself, when an android asks him to take one, although he ends up realizing that he actually does feel a kind of empathy for androids (if only for the attractive female variety).

These unsettling thoughts are not entirely resolved. But by raising them Dick creates an intense meditation on the nature of human identity and the soul. Like all of his work this is a fascinating philosophical read. The fact that it carries the label science fiction, a supposedly lowly genre, should not be allowed to obscure the fact that he was one of the more remarkable, thought-provoking writers of the last century.

---

### *Do Androids Dream of Electric Sheep?*
## The Speed Read

Deckard is a human whose job it is to hunt androids. But how can we tell the difference between humans and androids? If we apply an "empathy test", are we proving that humans have souls and empathy while androids lack these attributes, or are we merely using artificial constructs to create an unreliable identification? Is a human a flesh machine – or a flesh machine with a soul? Is religion real, or a program of social control? Are you a human or an android? And which am I? Are you sure?

# Meditations:
# Contemplation as Philosophy

## *Introduction*

In compiling the list of titles we wanted to cover in this book, we felt it was important to range beyond traditional philosophy to include books that are philosophically interesting or inspiring without necessarily being the books that would be covered on an academic philosophy course.

Of course there is a vast range of titles that could be included here, and the choice is inevitably somewhat arbitrary. But we have tried to include a few of the books that have gained the reputation of being philosophical, such as *Zen and the Art of Motorcycle Maintenance*, *Jonathan Livingston Seagull* and *The Little Prince*. The actual philosophical value of these books may be variable, but they are all interesting books in their own ways. We have mostly veered towards bestsellers in this selection simply because we felt it was preferable to discuss books that readers are likely to have encountered or read.

In *The Prophet*, *One-Liners* and *The Tao of Pooh* we nod towards the influence of global (and especially Eastern) religion on philosophical thinking. It is impossible to deal with all the different kinds of theological and mystical strands of thought that have had an influence on modern thought, but each of these books in their own way shows how disparate types of thinking can be assimilated into a philosophical tradition.

*Moominpappa at Sea* might at first sight appear an odd selection. It could be argued that many children's books contain genuine wisdom. We are attuned to thinking that a philosophical book must be "difficult" or "grown-up" to be of any value. But, just as *The Tao of Pooh* finds wisdom in the works of A. A. Milne, many adult readers will find food for thought in "simple" children's literature. The folk tales of the Brothers Grimm, with their savage and vengeful view of human nature, convey one view of humanity, whereas the more liberal tales of Hans Christian Andersen carry a very different message. Laura Ingalls Wilder's books have significant political and personal content, dealing as they do with childhood and adolescence and the early days of a new nation. C. S. Lewis's *Narnia* books notoriously convey the author's theology although this is often upstaged by the sheer strength of the storytelling. *Alice's Adventures in Wonderland* has a great deal to say about imagination and dreams.

Rather than deal with any of these better known books, we have chosen *Moominpappa at Sea,* because of the sheer wealth of psychological insight it contains and the strangeness of its narrative. We hope by discussing this book to express the view that it is acceptable to find philosophical meaning in books that would not generally be regarded as "philosophical."

Also included here is Primo Levi's extraordinary *If This Is a Man*, in which he questions what humanity is, given that humans were responsible for the terrible events of the Holocaust. However we start the section with William Blake's enormously influential work *The Marriage of Heaven and Hell.* Again it is the sheer weight of interesting ideas that makes this a work we wanted to include. Like the other books in this section it is perhaps best approached as a thought-provoking meditation or contemplation of existence, rather than as anything more prescriptive.

If there is one thing in common between these books, it is that they all invite you to think for yourself, rather than telling you what to think.

## *The Marriage of Heaven and Hell*, 1793

### William Blake

*"All Bibles or sacred codes, have been the causes of the following Errors.*

1. *That Man has two real existing principles Viz: a Body & a Soul.*
2. *That Energy, call'd Evil, is alone from the Body, & that Reason, call'd Good, is alone from the Soul.*
3. *That God will torment Man in Eternity for following his Energies.*

*But the following Contraries to these are True.*

1. *Man has no Body distinct from his Soul; for that call'd Body is a portion of Soul discern'd by the five Senses, the chief inlets of Soul in this age.*
2. *Energy is the only life and is from the Body and Reason is the bound or outward circumference of Energy.*
3. *Energy is Eternal Delight."*

Mystic, poet, artist, and spiritual writer, William Blake was one of the extraordinary figures of his time, although his contemporaries mostly regarded him as rather eccentric, and his fame only grew after his death.

*The Marriage of Heaven and Hell* is one of his most concentrated works, expressing some of his most interesting ideas in a startling mixture of poetry and prose. While his prophetic works expressed huge sweeps of ideas in complex narratives, and his simpler poetry such as the *Songs of Innocence and Experience* might be considered a greater achievement on purely poetic terms, *The Marriage of Heaven and Hell* is a powerful expression of complicated and unexpected ideas. Drawing on predecessors such as Dante's *Inferno* and Milton's *Paradise Lost*, it tells the story of the author's meeting with a devil and an angel, and his visits to both heavenly and infernal settings. Blake was fascinated by Christianity, but fiercely opposed to most organized religion. So there is a degree to which his "devil" is expressing the viewpoint that the organized church has perverted true spirituality. Blake asserts that all gods and morals are created in the human heart, but that "angels" (or the organized church, or authority figures such as the Priesthood) have over time co-opted the ideas of religion to create an oppressive morality.

Blake includes a selection of "proverbs of Hell" in the poem, as well as some rather incendiary references to the fact that the world will eventually adopt the "bible of Hell". The angel he speaks with in the poem ends up becoming a devil and good friend.

Blake was writing in a time of great turmoil, in the years immediately following the French Revolution (1790–1793). There is a degree of revolutionary fervour in the way he considers the possibility of a "world turned upside down." The infernal printing press that he visits in the poem could be seen as having a parallel in the small presses across Europe that were turning out pamphlets of radical ideas in this period.

At the heart of Blake's thought is the idea that Hell, rather than being a place where sinners are punished, is a source of great creative and subversive energy. The lengthy quotation above is spoken in the voice of the devil, and expresses several fascinating ideas based on this notion. Firstly, Hell is seen as a source of Dionysian (meaning wild, or primal) energy, challenging the oppressive system of the church and state. (Nietzsche would later write about a similar contrast between Dionysian and Appolonian ideals in works such as *The Birth of Tragedy*.) As noted, this is both a theological and political argument, when taken in the context of Blake's time. He makes the point that much of what is seen as "Evil" is simply that which is contrary or difficult for the current order to assimilate. Good and evil are thus constructions of society rather than absolute values.

Secondly, Blake is making a telling philosophical point when he asserts that body and soul dualism is not only flawed, but also misleading. In his view, body and soul have been falsely separated by philosophers of the past. As a result, reason and the soul are seen as belonging together, and as naturally good. Whereas energy (for which we might substitute phrases such as "will," "primal urges," or "desire") has been relegated to being a merely physical concept and as such has been seen as evil. Blake identifies Good as being the passive that always obeys Reason, whereas Evil is identified with Energy, which is "Eternal Delight." (There is also an echo here of Blake's classic poem *The Tyger*, which starts "Tyger Tyger, burning bright.")

Here Blake is prefiguring a number of important philosophical ideas. The way in which both Schopenhauer and Nietzsche would come to talk of will is clearly related to Blake's approach. The unity of body and soul contradicts the dualism of rationalists such as Descartes. The suggestion that Energy and Reason are inseparable is a first step towards a more psychoanalytic view of rationality, in which our wills and drives need to be considered as well as "pure reason." And Blake's focus on the idea that man should follow his energies is also reminiscent of the Freudian idea of repression, wherein drives that are not acted on will simply be redirected within the psyche, often in harmful ways.

Going further into the future, one can see a certain kindred spirit between Blake and abstract artists and the situationists of the last century, in the belief that pure creativity and energy are in themselves revolutionary impulses that have the power to change the world. Of course Blake was writing in the shadow of a very different revolution, and was also fascinated by movements of his time such as mysticism and romanticism. But his ideas have a genuine resonance with many interesting philosophical ideas of the subsequent two centuries.

There is far more packed into this short poem than we can possibly do credit to here – the "proverbs of Hell" alone contain an extraordinary density of ideas. There is a feverish intensity to Blake's best writing. In *The Marriage of Heaven and Hell*, it seems as though the ideas are just pouring out of him, at the same time as he manages to find a memorable way of expressing some of his most profound spiritual and philosophical thoughts.

---

### *The Marriage of Heaven and Hell*

## The Speed Read

All gods are conceived in the human heart as poetic ideas. But the priesthood has formalized the deities and oppressed desire and passion. Energy, which is called Evil, is in fact the creative genius and eternal delight, as I was told by my friend the devil while I walked in the fires of Hell. The weak restrain desire until it becomes passivity and is called Good. But in the end the bible of Hell, and pure Energy will prevail . . . "For everything that lives is Holy."

## *The Prophet,* 1923

Kahlil Gibran

*"The teacher who is indeed wise does not bid you to
enter the house of his wisdom but rather leads
you to the threshold of your mind."*

Kahlil Gibran was born in Lebanon in 1883, but his family
emigrated to New York in 1895. (He Americanized his
name from Khalil to Kahlil on the advice of a teacher.) He
first became well known as an artist, studying in Boston and
also with Auguste Rodin in Paris, and exhibiting in New
York and elsewhere. He gradually became known for his
writing as well as for his art, and *The Prophet,* written in
1923, is still his most popular work.

The book is a compilation of poetic essays. The narrative aspect of the book concerns a prophet called Almustufa
who has lived away from his home in a city called Orphalese
for many years. He decides to return home. As he is on his
way to board the ship he meets a group of people and stops
to discuss his ideas with them.

Gibran had thought deeply about religion and spirituality. He was especially interested in specific issues of religion
such as the schism between the Eastern church and cathol-
icism, in Baha'ism and in ecumenical ideas and similarities
between the different religions of the world. Almustufa's
teaching in the book ranges over a wide range of ideas,
including religion and the human condition, as well as
more everyday thoughts on love, work, and marriage. His
thoughts are clearly a condensed version of Gibran's ideas
about the world. It is a deeply thoughtful book, but also a
poetic and intriguing one.

The book gained great popularity in subsequent decades.
One reason for this is that it seems to find ways of pointing

towards spiritual truths, but without the objective dogma of organized religion. Some of Gibran's observations are clearly derived from (or in reaction to) scriptural sources, such as "An eye for an eye, and the whole world would be blind," in which he concurs with Jesus's reaction to Old Testament doctrine.

Elsewhere he explicitly makes the connection between different religions, making statements such as "I love you when you bow in your mosque, kneel in your temple, pray in your church. For you and I are sons of one religion, and it is the spirit." Such statements give this book the feel of a new poetic scripture that could follow on from any one of the world's religions.

Gibran also suggests a more sensual understanding of the world, suggesting that we should "forget not that the earth delights to feel your bare feet and the winds long to play with your hair." The mixture between this kind of poetic understanding of the world we live in and a semi-religious approach is beguiling and gives the book the feel of an extended meditation on human existence. The fact that Gibran also stressed the overwhelming importance of love in our existence also contributed to his popularity with the 1960s advocates of "love and peace" – Gibran's book underwent something of a revival in this period, and has remained popular since. John Lennon adapted a line from *The Prophet* in his song *Julia* ("Half of what I say is meaningless . . .") and other artists and poets have drawn on his work (a more recent example being Sting's use of Gibran's line that if you love somebody you should set them free).

From a philosophical viewpoint, what is Gibran's message? It is hard to reduce *The Prophet* to a few simple propositions. To a large degree it is best read as a meditation. It contains many inspiring or challenging thoughts, without setting out a specific set of prescriptive beliefs. One could point to Gibran's attempt to condense the essential truths of various religions as a philosophical challenge. Also Gibran describes the way in which perplexity is a first step towards knowledge. This implies that our confusion as we view the world should be taken as an incentive to seek after truth and knowledge. So by meditating upon the world in all its messy complexity we are also taking a first step towards under-standing and enlightenment.

Gibran sees the highest aims of life as being "truth and beauty." Philosophy in general has always sought after truth, but has a more complex relationship with beauty. Aesthetics is a difficult subject, but philosophers have rarely been as unequivocally on the side of beauty as Gibran. Yet the creation of beauty and order in our everyday lives is clearly one of the goals we aim towards as we live our lives. Perhaps *The Prophet* is best taken as a reminder that truth is not the only possible goal of philosophical enquiry. Beauty and love are also important, and it would be sad if we were to forget this in our intellectual endeavours.

## *The Prophet*
# The Speed Read

The prophet Almustafa stopped on his way home to give us the wisdom of his heart . . . "Love . . . It surrounds every being and extends slowly to embrace all that shall be." "Of life's two chief prizes, beauty and truth, I found the first in a loving heart and the second in a laborer's hand."

# *The Little Prince,* 1943

## Antoine de Saint-Exupéry

*". . . the little prince went away, puzzled. 'Grown-ups really are very, very odd,' he said to himself . . ."*

The *Little Prince* is a bitter-sweet fable, which can be read to (or by) children, but which has also had an enduring appeal to adult readers. After a disappointing career in business in his youth, the author Antoine de Saint-Exupéry became passionate about aviation. He flew for freight and mail companies in North Africa and South America in the 1920s and 1930s, was involved in many airborne exploits during the war, and finally disappeared mid-flight in 1944. Most of his writing was on the subject of flying. He had several crashes, including one in the Sahara in the 1920s, following which he had to walk several days through the desert to safety. This experience eventually provided the background story for *The Little Prince.*

In the book, a pilot has crashed in the desert and is stranded far from safety. The character of the pilot is sketched to us in the opening chapters. As a child, he became disillusioned by the failure of adults to understand the truly important things in life (such as being able to recognize that a drawing that appears to resemble a hat is in fact a picture of an elephant being digested by a boa constrictor). As an adult he has spent a lot of time with "serious people" and has found them wanting, and lacking in imagination.

In the desert he meets a charming young boy, who turns out to be a little prince who has travelled to the earth from a miniature planet far away. The prince's story emerges gradually through a series of curious and humorous conversations. On the planet he has several volcanoes, and a flower, which he believes is a unique and special flower. The prince's relationship with the flower seems rather touching to a child reader, although as an adult it seems like a romance in which the female flower is depicted as something of a moody diva. The one slightly sour note in the book is struck by a misogynistic undercurrent in this portrait of the flower. Nonetheless there is a wry humour in the account of how she bewitches the prince, and has him running circles around her to try and keep her happy.

Depressed by this romance, the little prince has flown away from his planet, visiting a succession of other small planets, where stereotypes of various grown-ups reside. For instance he meets a drunkard; a businessman who is obsessed with owning the stars; a king with no subjects; a geographer who knows nothing of the places to which his maps are guides; and a lamplighter who slavishly follows his instructions to daily light and extinguish the lamps on his planet. The prince learns much about the strangeness of human nature. Finally he visits the earth, landing in the desert. Amongst other encounters, he meets a snake, and then visits a garden, where he discovers that the flower he thought so unique is merely a common-or-garden rose.

He then meets a fox, who asks the prince to tame him. As a result, an attachment grows between them, and both are sad when they have to part. This experience teaches the prince that his relationship with the flower is indeed special. He has tended to her needs, and provided for her, and as a result they have a special love. He sees that even though she is not unique, he still wants to return to her.

Without wanting to spoil the ending, the final pages are deeply ambiguous, and leave a sad, but affecting impression of the prince's departure from earth, while the narrator finally manages to repair his plane, and lives to tell the tale.

The most obvious philosophical message of *The Little Prince* is about the way that our perceptions of the world change as we grow older. While the narrator's story about his picture of an elephant and a snake being mistaken for a hat is a comical one, it also says a great deal about how children's imaginations construct the world they perceive. And in the little prince, de Saint-Exupéry gives us an unforgettable portrait of an innocent, someone who sees everything in life with completely fresh eyes. There are scenes where the narrator comforts the crying prince, and carries him towards a distant well, where we perceive the prince as a child. But at other times there is a real wisdom in his simple comments on the world, and we see the absurdity of various "grown-ups" through his eyes.

So *The Little Prince* is a reminder of how many of the perceptions and beliefs that we take for granted are accumulations of received ideas, with the suggestion that every now and then we need to take a second look at our lives with the eyes of a child. There are also numerous passing comments in the books which seem profound as one reads (although the emotion of the narrative may mean that these comments are less deep than they seem on first reading).

The taming of the fox demonstrates two points. First, that much of what is important in our lives is not immediately visible, as it develops over time through our emotional attachments. And second, the prince comes to realize the transformative power of love. He sees that his love for his flower is not the encumbrance he thought, but an important aspect of his life, one that he should treasure.

It is hard to identify why such a simple fable has endured so long. The book still sells today, over sixty years after publication, and has been translated into many languages. Perhaps its real power comes from the fact that, even within a very simple story, the author leaves room for ambiguity and uncertainty. I remember as a child being frustrated and upset by certain aspects of the story, but rather than putting me off, it made me want to reread it, and "argue" over these points again in my head. As one grows older, especially if one becomes a parent, the book takes on further resonance. Children always ask such acute, unexpected questions about the world, and this is echoed accurately in the character of the little prince. If the mark of a philosophical classic is that it makes one ask questions and reconsider one's views of the world, *The Little Prince* deserves to be recognized as such, just as much as many weightier tomes.

## *The Little Prince*
# The Speed Read

As a child I came to realize that adults are lacking in imagination and understanding. I became a pilot, a solitary wanderer. After crashing in the Sahara, I met the little prince, a beautiful innocent who taught me about how he saw the world. He had left his beloved flower behind on his planet to travel the planets and to meet the many foolish grown-ups of the universe. In the end a fox and a snake helped him to find the best way to love his flower. If you ever meet him, let me know because I miss him terribly, and remember him whenever I look at the stars.

# *If This Is a Man,* 1947

## Primo Levi

*"The future of humanity is uncertain, even in the most prosperous countries, and the quality of life deteriorates; and yet I believe that what is being discovered about the infinitely large and infinitely small is sufficient to absolve this end of the century and millennium. What a very few are acquiring in knowledge of the physical world will perhaps cause this period not to be judged as a pure return of barbarism."*

Primo Levi survived imprisonment in Auschwitz. In a century of widespread barbarism, he experienced one of the most horrific episodes in mankind's history first-hand. Out of this he managed to create a thoughtful memoir which, rather than giving in to anger and recrimination, focuses on the philosophical meaning of the way that man treated his fellow man in the Holocaust.

Born in Turin in 1919, Levi graduated from his chemistry training in 1941, at a time in Italy when he could only do so with a degree certificate that identified him as Jewish because of the edicts of the Mussolini government. In the later stages of the war, Levi attempted to fight against the fascists but ended up being captured and, because he was Jewish (although he was not especially religious), he was deported to Auschwitz.

He was lucky to survive. His scientific training helped, as he was given work in a laboratory that was working with synthetic rubber. He was also perversely fortunate to catch Scarlet Fever as the Soviet forces approached in 1944, as the camp guards abandoned those who were too ill to march, while taking the other inmates on the notorious Death March on which so many met their deaths.

The Nazi concentration camps are far from being the only crime against humanity in the last century. But they are iconic, and astounding in the scope and level of evil that they represent. We have a variety of sources of information as to what went on in the camps, all of them heart-breaking. Primo Levi published his own memoir, *If This Is a Man* shortly after the war, and it was later republished and translated into many languages. In the United States, the book was published under the title *Survival In Auschwitz* – we prefer to refer to the book here under its original title because it seems to capture more of the philosophical content of the book.

On one level, *If This Is a Man* is a simple and honest account of Levi's time in Auschwitz. On this level it is a painful but valuable read. Levi doesn't go out of his way to pillory the German nation in general, although it is clear that he cannot forgive what happened. Much of his focus is on what happened between the inmates, and the ways in which being treated in an inhuman manner makes it hard to maintain your humanity.

And this is where the real philosophical content of *If This Is a Man* becomes apparent. Elsewhere in this book, we look at works that have dealt with the question of "How should we live our lives?" Primo Levi asks a subtly different question. "What is a human?" In other words, how do we react to inhumanity?

The book deals both with the behaviour of the camp guards – who are clearly behaving in an inhuman manner, regardless of how and why this came about – and also Levi's experience of life in Auschwitz living among people for whom all the basic aspects of life that create a sense of humanity had been removed. And he looks forensically at the ways in which this affected their behaviour through the little daily triumphs and disasters upon which they had to focus in order to deal with the utterly inhuman way in which they were being treated.

The twentieth century is not alone in being a bloody and violent period in the history of mankind. But the horrors of the two world wars, and of the many local conflicts that have marred lives around the world raise many serious questions about the meaning of being a human. Is violence and degradation a natural part of being a human, or an abominable aberration? Is there any way of ensuring that the future is less horrific than the recent past? Anyone who thinks seriously about the history of the twentieth century must conclude that these are real and serious questions.

The great power of Primo Levi's writing is that he has the moral authority to tackle these questions head on. But he still manages to discuss them with a degree of optimism, and even humour. *If This Is a Man* is an extraordinarily powerful book, because it refuses to wallow in the misery of the Auschwitz experiences, but describes the details of being treated as a non-human unflinchingly and honestly.

It is unfortunate that Levi's death in 1987 leaves some doubts about whether or not he committed suicide. (He fell from the stairway of his home, in a way that might equally have been caused by a moment of faintness brought on by his medication.) Many find it hard to reconcile his apparent optimism and positivity (both in this book and in the rest of his fine body of writing) with the idea of a final suicide.

But even if it were the case that Levi had finally chosen death over life, why should it undermine the message of his life? He had lived through extraordinary horrors and had managed to turn this experience into a philosophical and even positive approach to his subsequent life. Clearly his writing grew out of a refusal to completely give in to the nihilism and depression that might have been caused by his experiences. Personally I believe that Levi did not kill himself, but even if he had done, I can't accept that one moment of self-destruction should outweigh a lifetime's work. Levi spent his post-war life trying to translate awful experience into teaching and nurturing those aspects of mankind that he thought were worthwhile, in spite of having experienced the worst aspects of mankind.

Philosophically he has left us a record of his meditations on some of the most difficult questions we can possibly think about. And on a human level, he is a remarkable figure, simply because of the way that he transmuted a terrible experience into great and inspiring writing.

---

### If This Is a Man

## The Speed Read

Here is an honest account of my time at Auschwitz . . . If man can do to man what he did there, then what is "humanity"?

---

## *Moominpappa at Sea*, 1965

### Tove Jansson

*"Sometimes there was something about family life that Moominpappa didn't like. His family wasn't sensitive enough at times like these, although they'd lived with him for so long."*

Moominpappa at Sea is one of the oddest and most fascinating children's books ever written. Through the 1950s, Tove Jansson's creations had taken on their familiar characteristics, apparently with a marked resemblance to Jansson's own family, and this was the last complete book in the series. The Moomins are essentially bohemian, taking in their stride the endless string of relatives, visitors and marginal wanderers who drop by to benefit from

Moominmamma's cooking, domestic stability, and from the useful items in her ever-present handbag. Moominmamma is usually happy taking in and caring for others, seemingly content in her domestic world. Moominpappa, with no visible means of support, alternates between writing his memoirs and sudden whims. In *Moominpappa at Sea* he suddenly uproots the whole family because he feels depressed.

As children's stories, the Moomin novels are funny, and beautifully drawn with strong narratives and characters. But there is also a deeper resonance for adults. Jansson gives a powerful evocation of life lived close to nature, with the gathering of foods and feasts (especially picnics), and the effects of the seasons on emotions. *Moominpappa at Sea* begins with the usual busy days and evenings around the Moomins' house in Moominvalley. Moominmamma is busy tending to her garden and getting tea ready. Moomintroll is playing with Little My, the Moomins' adopted little creature (one of the best children's characters ever created; "She was just a glimpse of something, determined and independent – something so independent that it had no need to show itself."). However, even here among the Moomin family domestic bliss, the Groke, a strange, lonely, feared character, is hovering around their idyll, casting her shadow on their happy family life. Fascinated with the light (and warmth) from their lamp, she is drawn ever closer to the house. She is feared more through legend than for any concrete reason: wherever she goes the ground freezes and nothing will grow there, yet it's always clear that she is irresistibly attracted to the warmth of the Moomin family. Moominpappa however, is depressed – it seems as if everyone has a role except for him, and he feels surplus to requirements. Moominmamma suggests he works on his model lighthouse but he dismisses this as too childish. He wants to go to the real lighthouse on a different island far away. He also wants to feel some kind of self-importance for a change. Autumn is coming, the summer has ended, and along with it comes the arrival of the melancholy season of desire and longing for things that one wished one had done and the realization that the usual daily routine will now have to change.

What follows is a strange tale of these four characters as they sail for two days across the ocean, meeting an odd, silent fisherman on the way, and eventually reach the island with the lighthouse on it. Immediately upon their arrival the characters separate from each other in a way that previously only Little My had done. The first night they sleep on the beach. Moomintroll and Moominmamma sleep in a tent made out of their boat's sails. Moomintroll is immediately struck by the way that Moominmamma goes straight to sleep without doing any of her usual domestic rituals, or even making coffee. Moominpappa stays outside to guard the tent, happy to finally have lots of projects. Little My, as usual, runs off on her own to explore. The next day, when they finally reach the lighthouse, the door is locked and they can't find the key. Moomintroll is sent across the island to ask the fisherman if he knows where it is, but only finds a small silver horseshoe belonging to a seahorse. Moominpappa finally finds the key on a tiny secret ledge beneath a cliff where he can sit and observe the sea, on his own.

Everyone begins to separate off into a world of his or her own, physically as well as mentally. On a strange and unknown island, all of them find security in solitude. Moominpappa has "broken away" from his old house and is excited at his future prospects and newly discovered independence. Meanwhile his family don't quite know what to make of it all without the familiarity of their own home in Moominvalley.

Moominpappa repeatedly tries in vain to light the lighthouse lamp. Nobody else is allowed to be involved. In the top room, which he claims as his own, he finds strange poems written on the walls, presumably by the old light-house keeper.

On this new and desolate island, Moominmamma retreats to concentrate on trying to build a garden, while Moomintroll finds a glade in the forest that he decides he wants to live in on his own. Moominmamma suggests ways they can reno-vate the lighthouse. All the characters find secret little places for themselves on the island. Little My tends to follow the solitary fisherman and sleeps outside, while Moominmamma longs for a garden so much that she begins painting one on the wall. The stormy climate of the island will not allow her flowers to grow, despite her efforts at making soil from seaweed and planting her beloved roses. She insists that the wall painting is her very own garden and no one is allowed to touch it.

There are many themes of isolation in the book. Each character seeks out their own special place of privacy away from the harshness of the island and, unknown to them, the Groke has followed them here. She sings songs of how lonely she is, sounds that are heard by others only as a strange wailing. It is as if the characters are seeking to find a new identity for themselves in this strange place, precipitated by the move away from their old cosy home. Boundaries hem them in, feeding on fears of their past lives, and yet also challenging them to overcome their difficul-ties and re-adapt. The ever-present shifting and changing of the sea closes in on their horizon and the trees in the forest are slowly moving away from the sea to surround the light-house. The sand on the beach is constantly moving and Little My traps ants with a wall of sugar only to kill them with paraffin once they're inside, a sign of the perils of allowing oneself to become "boxed in." The Groke, ever present and moving closer, challenges them all to confront their demons as they seek to find themselves. She is the conscience of the book; you can run but you can't hide.

The separation of the characters deepens when Moominpappa tires of trying to make the lighthouse work, finds a deep lake where he can fish, and decides to study the sea instead, still looking for his notion of respect and esteem. Moominmamma begins to disappear into her painting of a garden, where she can wander among her flowers and apple trees. When she is inside the garden, her family can't see her, she becomes "no bigger than a coffee pot." She pushes dirty dishes under the bed and stops talking about renovating the lighthouse. She has abandoned her usual daily domestic life. It seems that only Moomintroll has picked up on the change in personality of the people around him. They barely notice that he's now living outside, because they are so wrapped up in their own individual worlds. Moominmamma dismisses his plight as "growing pains" and it seems that Moomintroll is finally coming of age.

At night he takes his lamp down to the beach to watch and talk to the seahorses. They're flighty, flirty little creatures who always arrive in pairs, never reveal which one is the owner of his horseshoe and generally giggle and poke fun at him. Nevertheless, like an adolescent boy, he is in love with his idea of the little horse whose shoe he returned, imagining that she would be grateful to him and be his special friend. It is during these nights that he notices the Groke moving closer to shore. Eventually his worst fear is right there on the beach staring him in the face. He confronts his rejection by the beautiful seahorse, and the terrifying presence of the Groke. He notices eventually that she seems to want friendship, and that she is actually as lonely and isolated here as he is. Her song is no longer simply sad, it is now "defiant" too. Moomintroll stops feeling scared of the Groke and comes to some understanding of her. On the whole island, it seems that he is the only one capable of any empathy with another.

Eventually, Moominpappa's study of the sea begins to

frustrate him. The sea is cruel and not easy to get to know. The island similarly has a life of its own. The trees continue to move inland to get away from the sea. The trees are moving from what scares them in the same way as the Moomintroll family are fleeing or denying what is frightening or upsetting them. Moominpappa eventually begins to notice his fragmented family and visits Moomintroll's little home in the glade. Moominpappa talks about the sea as if he is talking about a person and indeed throughout the book the sea is represented as another character, symbolizing the fickle, fluid and sometimes harsh nature of behaviour and emotions. The sea comes to represent our need to understand this, that we may not always understand or agree with others, but sometimes we do have to just accept them. Moominpappa and his son have come to an appreciation of the difficulty of being with, and understanding, other people. Moominmamma also eventually realizes that she has to stop trying to change the island and accept it for what it is. After this, she discovers that she can no longer get into her garden on the wall because she is no longer homesick.

Moomintroll comes to terms with his fear of the Groke and eventually goes down to the beach to watch her but without the now empty lamp. Nevertheless she's there looking happy and dancing. She's no longer frightening and Moomintroll is amazed. After she's gone back into the sea, the sand where she's been isn't frozen at all, it's just as normal as before. When he thinks of the Groke he realizes that she was no longer afraid of being disappointed. The light and warmth that she sought seems to have been within her all along, and she just had to realize it.

As the sea gets wilder, the fisherman's hut is destroyed. The Moomins are concerned about him, and go to see how he is. Although his home is gone, he refuses to come into the lighthouse but he does tell them that it's his birthday tomorrow. Moominmamma insists on having a party for him.

The fisherman is terrified of going into the lighthouse and it takes Little My shouting at him to "behave" to get him inside. The Moomin family have returned almost to their normal selves. Moominmamma even uses the last of the candles for the fisherman's birthday cake. The fisherman is surprised by her kindness, saying that she is the first person who ever remembered his birthday. Gradually we realize that the fisherman is actually the original lighthouse keeper, and the writer of the strange lonely poems on the wall at the top of the lighthouse. He has overcome his own fears and loneliness to return to his post. He becomes more assertive inside the lighthouse, asking for more coffee and wondering about the bird's nest that ought to be in the chimney. The family is almost shy of him. He suggests that he and Moominpappa swap hats (and therefore roles) and they do. The lighthouse keeper goes to the top of the lighthouse to sleep and reassures the Moomins that all is well with the sea and the island. As Moominpappa goes out to his boat to fish he realizes that the lighthouse keeper has got the lighthouse working at last.

*Moominpappa at Sea* is a voyage of self-discovery, of facing your demons within and without and of realizing that you can't run away to be happy because what makes you unhappy will follow you unless you deal with it. The book deals with the transcending of boundaries and perceived barriers, whether that be accepting the limits of yourself and others around you or pushing yourself beyond what you feel you are capable of. It shows us that we sometimes need to accept a difficult situation in order to make it better and similarly accept the difficulties in others in order to bring out the best in them.

## *Moominpappa at Sea*
# The Speed Read

Moomins are funny little creatures with affections, thoughts, and fears just like ours. If you like someone, you can put up with the flaws in their character and if you don't like them you don't have to put up with anything. Accept yourself, warts and all, and accept what is different to you in others. Sometimes you can't change what you don't like but what you don't like shouldn't change you.

# *Jonathan Livingston Seagull,* 1971

## Richard Bach

*"Don't believe what your eyes are telling you. All they show is limitation. Look with your understanding, find out what you already know, and you'll see the way to fly."*

Jonathan Livingston Seagull was a huge success when it was published in 1971, selling two million copies within the first two years of publication. It remains in print to this day. It was a mainstream success but was also popular in the alternative culture of students and radicals. But today it is mostly regarded by the literary establishment with embarrassment, as a rather ridiculous, unworthy book. So why was this little book such a success in the first place, and why has its reputation suffered so badly over the years?

On first examination, it is a simple fable about the eponymous hero and his experiments with the art of flying. Jonathan Livingston Seagull loves flying and wants to fly higher and dive faster than the other birds in the flock. The flock don't understand his enthusiasm, as they are more concerned with the daily grind of fighting for food. So Jonathan becomes an outcast, living by himself and delighting in perfecting his flights and dives.

Thus far the story is reasonably plain and even realistic, if you accept that birds can talk. But at this stage the book becomes a bit weird as two seagulls from another plane of existence meet up with Jonathan and take him to where they live. They tell him that his enthusiasm for flying makes him a "gull in a million" which is why they have approached him. The impression given is that the relationship between these gulls and normal gulls is like that between angels and humans or between those who have achieved "enlightenment" and those who have not. The seagulls have their own god, "The Great Gull," and the new seagulls seem closer to this Great Gull than Jonathan's old flock.

In this new society, all the seagulls love flying in the same way that Jonathan does. He studies with his teacher Chiang to reach new heights of understanding and skill. He finds he can fly to anywhere in the world in an instant, if he does as Chiang tells him, to "begin by knowing that you have already arrived."

In the final section of the book, Jonathan becomes dissatisfied with his new life and returns to his old flock to pass on the knowledge he has gained. He gathers a group of likeminded outcasts around him as students and teaches them that one of the things they must do is forgive the flock for failing to understand them.

The book can be read in many ways, but at its simplest it is an allegory for outsiders who come to form their own group in society. Bach claimed that the book came to him in a series of visions (although he also admitted it was partly based on John H. "Johnny" Livingston, a barnstorming pilot of the 1920s and 30s). But as far as there is a message it seems to be that in the end the seeker of enlightenment only really achieves anything if they return to the ordinary people and try to pass on their learning rather than excluding themselves from society completely.

Beyond this, the book is a rather odd mishmash of Christian, proto-New Age and Eastern ideas. In that respect it's quite representative of its time. In the sixties and early seventies there was a great fascination with the idea of reaching enlightenment by studying with a guru or master. The Beatles had their Maharishi, Castaneda had his Don Juan. And in the work of Hermann Hesse, revered in the sixties, we have the figures of Narziss and Goldmund, archetypes of student and master. Jonathan has his guru in Chiang, and then becomes a guru to the younger seagulls on his return to the flock.

This may be one of the keys to understanding the way in which this book's reputation has changed over the years. The idea of the outsiders in society seeking out gurus to take them to enlightenment seems from a distance rather facile and smug. It relies on the notion that the student is an exceptional individual, someone that others can't understand because they are "too deep." This rather adolescent idea had great power in the sixties, when many otherwise reasonable people had an exaggerated belief in the power of youth and rebellion to change the world and bring about a new age of peace and love. Eventually many of the gurus of the era came to be seen as fake or as less reliable than they had once seemed.

Many songs and books of the era also came to seem like a relic of more naïve times. (To give one example, T-Rex sang "You won't fool the children of the revolution" at the exact moment when many youths were losing faith in the whole idea of the "revolution.") *Jonathan Livingston Seagull* perhaps suffered from the same fate. And it also seems like a book that we might be very impressed by as fourteen-year-olds who feel themselves to be "special" ("a gull in a million"), but perhaps too childish a book for an adult to love.

There is some truth in these criticisms, and one wouldn't want to overrate this book. However it is a more engaging and intriguing book than its current reputation suggests. At the heart of the story is some interesting thinking about the concept of leaving "normal society" behind in search of something more sublime. The sixties myth was partly built on a confused idea that those who "turned on" and "dropped out" would be able to build a viable alternative society. And it was widely assumed that it was acceptable for the cool and enlightened members of society to despise and shun "squares" and "breadheads."

Bach's book basically accepts one part of that elitism by showing that the outcasts are able to achieve enlightenment and move to a different spiritual plane. But at the same time he struggles with the fact that this exclusive behaviour is obviously not sustainable, and suggests that the knowledge gained by Jonathan only truly means something when he re-engages with normal society ("the flock") to pass on his learning.

So the book can be read either as a revealing sociological record of the mindset of the period in which it was written, or as a sweet fable that scatters interesting but confused ideas around, in the course of addressing some real philosophical concerns.

## *Jonathan Livingston Seagull*
# The Speed Read

Jonathan was a seagull. He loved flying and diving more than anything in the world. He was more special than the boring flock who just worried about everyday concerns like food and shelter. He became an outcast because the flock couldn't understand him. Two seagulls from another spiritual plane took him home with them because they could see he was a gull in a million. He learned many amazing, spiritual, and slightly silly things from his teacher Chiang. But eventually he realized that he should forgive the flock, and return to teach his fellow outcasts how to become as special as him.

# *Zen and the Art of Motorcycle Maintenance: An Inquiry into Values*, 1974

## Robert M. Pirsig

*"Metaphysics is a restaurant where they give you a 30,000 page menu and no food."*

If we accept that it should be described as a philosophy book (rather than as a novel) then *Zen and the Art of Motorcycle Maintenance* is the best-selling philosophy book ever, having sold well over five million copies. It is an intriguing read, which weaves together elements of auto-biography, philosophical investigations and narrative. Early on, the author warns that it is not really about either Zen or motorcycle maintenance. So what is it about? The easiest way to start explaining it is to give a brief description of the author's life before he wrote the book.

Robert Pirsig was a highly intelligent youth, later saying that he had had an overwhelming desire to have a theory that explained everything ever since he started to think. He fought in the Korean War (becoming fascinated with Buddhism in the process), studied in India, and went on to teach philosophy at an American university. He was an inspiring but eccentric teacher who developed a complex theory that attempted to utilize Eastern ideas such as the Tao to bridge the dualisms of Western philosophy. But he became increasingly unstable and after what might be described either as an episode of catatonic schizophrenia or perhaps a moment of intense "enlightenment" (Pirsig has said that he uses the terms interchangeably when talking of that time), he was hospitalized, receiving a course of electro-shock treatment. His wife divorced him and his relationship with his two sons became difficult. In 1968 he undertook a motorcycle trip with his son Chris, partly in an attempt to rebuild their relationship. He subsequently used this trip as the starting point for *Zen and the Art of Motorcycle Maintenance,* a book loosely based on his experiences and ideas, which was rejected by well over 100 publishers before finally achieving its huge success.

In the book, the narrator and his son Chris travel on motorbikes, initially with a couple of friends. The philosophical discourses and conversations that are interspersed through the book focus initially on ideas about technology with motorcycle maintenance used as a primary example. Pirsig uses people's attitudes to machinery to demonstrate a basic schism between the *classical* and *romantic* viewpoint, and also to start explaining the way that Western philosophy has been defined by the dualism of subjectivity and objectivity.

This narrative alternates with the story of a mysterious character called Phaedrus, who is a slightly manic, rebellious philosophy teacher, clearly based on Pirsig's former self. The name is taken from a Socratic dialogue, and much of Phaedrus's search for truth starts from an analysis of Western philosophy, starting from the Greeks.

Phaedrus's final breakthrough is to see that Quality (or *Arete* in Greek) is the unifying principle that links subjectivity and objectivity. He then identifies Quality with the Tao or Zen, and in this way finds a way to reconcile Eastern and Western traditions. However, Phaedrus, like Pirsig, then has a moment of mental crisis, culminating in electro-shock treatment. The conclusion of the book provides a dramatic plot twist to resolve the two strands of the story.

So, is this a philosophy book? And if so, is it any good? It is certainly an engaging and intriguing novel, and one can understand why it was such a success, even if there are elements that now make it seem very much a book of its time. But does the philosophy make sense?

There are various opinions on this matter. Some have argued that Pirsig overstates the importance of Phaedrus's breakthrough, pointing out that the system he describes comes close to the Trinitarianism of the early Christian church (in which the Holy Spirit plays a similar bridging role to Pirsig's Quality), or to mystical Islamic and Jewish writers of the same period. Others have doubted that the link he makes between the Tao and Quality really hangs together as he believes. His insistence that Quality cannot be defined is very Zenlike, but frustrating to the Western philosophical mindset. At the very least, though, Pirsig's arguments are interesting, and, for a reader unschooled in philosophy, he manages to introduce (and debate) a lot of traditional ideas in the course of telling a page-turning story.

The detail of the book is also sometimes more persuasive than the overarching theory of Quality. Some of the philosophical musings along the way are fascinating to read, although others have come to seem a little dated. There are new-agey moments in Pirsig's explanations of Eastern ideas, and in the post-computer age his opposition of technophobia and the classical temperament seems a bit irrelevant. But elsewhere he writes well about authoritarianism, education, and celebrity, and much of the detailed exposition of his ideas on Quality is thought-provoking.

In the end, as a philosophical book, it perhaps suffers from the way in which it is written. One senses that Pirsig would have liked simply to publish his ideas about Quality but was unable to, so chose the novel form to smuggle his philosophy through. He succeeds in doing this, but at some cost. When we read about Phaedrus's discoveries, we aren't sure if the breathless description of his mental processes has given these ideas a spurious air of authority and certainty. While reading the book it is hard to take a step back and assess the worth of Phaedrus's thought, because we become more fascinated by his developing psychological state. To some degree Pirsig remedied this problem by taking a more measured approach in his follow-up *Lila* – this still used a semi-narrative, semi-autobiographical form, but manages to give his ideas a calmer exposition.

Overall *Zen and the Art of Motorcycle Maintenance* is a problematic read, but a very enjoyable one. It is probably still unclear whether Pirsig should have received more credit for his philosophy than he did, as the book is generally ignored by academic philosophers. But Pirsig at least deserves credit for the fact that his book has provoked interest in some quite difficult philosophical ideas in a mass audience who might otherwise never have considered reading a work of philosophy.

### Zen and the Art of Motorcycle Maintenance: An Inquiry into Values

## The Speed Read

When maintaining a motorcycle, people fall into classical or romantic camps of thought. When you take your bike apart and reassemble it, there's often one screw left over on the floor. Quality is the bridge between objectivity and subjectivity, and is therefore the basis of a completely unifying system of philosophy. And Quality is more or less the same thing as the Tao or Zen.

## *The Tao of Pooh*, 1982

### Benjamin Hoff

*" 'You see, Pooh,' I said, 'a lot of people don't seem to know what Taoism is . . .'"*

The Tao of Pooh was a rather unexpected bestseller. The book is basically an attempt to explain the eastern religion Taoism by using the characters from A. A. Milne's Winnie The Pooh books as archetypes of various kinds of thinking. This sounds unpromising, but the book is funny, sweet and enlightening.

Whether or not it is a fair representation of Taoism is a matter of some debate. Hoff compares and contrasts Buddhism, Confucianism and Taoism in the book, identifying Buddhists as those who see life's tribulations as points on a list to be ticked off on the way to Nirvana, while Confucians are parodied as rule-bound bureaucrats. By contrast, Hoff depicts Taoists as living a life of simple contemplation, in harmony with the universe.

He uses Winnie the Pooh as the archetype of the way of the Tao. Pooh is shown as the archetypal "uncarved block," meaning that he is a blank slate who simply accepts the world as he finds it, not over-intellectualizing the world or living in disharmony with it. By contrast Owl is depicted as intellectual for the sake of it, or "too clever," while Rabbit is too hasty in his problem-solving, and poor Eeyore is simply too pessimistic to accept the world in front of him.

Hoff deploys some academic back-up to his thesis, quoting from the work of classic Taoists such as Lao Tzu as well as Chinese poets. However experts in eastern religion have questioned the accuracy of his accounts of the religions he deals with, in particular his largely negative assessments of Buddhism and Confucianism. But it seems fair to say that he has caught something of the spirit of Taoism in the book, and has done this in an essentially light and humorous way.

This is the main reason that we have included this book in our selection. It is important to bear in mind that philosophical insight can come from a variety of sources, both "heavy" and "light." It is clear that Hoff's book had a wide audience and that he has made many readers think about the ways they perceive and understand the world. His analyses of different kinds of rationality certainly ring true. When he describes the characters other than Pooh as "thinking too hard" and looking for the negatives in life, this resonates with many readers, and makes them pause for thought to consider the ways in which their mind works.

We become set in ways of thinking as we become adults, and occasional immersion in a book such as this, or the original Taoist texts (of which the sayings of Lao Tzu can be a good introduction) can remind us to try to return to a more open, even "childish" way of thinking.

In Huxley's *The Doors of Perception,* reference is made to the idea that there are filters in our mind that exclude many perceptions and ideas. There is a degree to which this is inevitable (as we simply cannot process all the information that we might receive) but there is also a degree to which we learn ways of processing information. We cease to react to information as innocently and openly as we did as children. Hoff's book reminds us of a more innocent way of understanding the world we live in, and also reminds us that the way we currently think about the world is not necessarily the only possible way of doing so.

In this respect it is a philosophical book. Perhaps one might argue that it is only as philosophical as the Winnie the Pooh books are themselves. Everything about the thought processes that Hoff describes is already present in the A. A. Milne books in a pithy and humorous way. And certainly one of the consequences of reading *The Tao of Pooh* can be a desire to revisit those childhood books.

In the introduction to this section the argument was made that children's books can contain unexpected pearls of wisdom, partly because they focus on the ways in which we perceive the world before we become self-conscious adults. As a result, the most thoughtful children's books can often be inspiring and intriguing to return to as adults. There is no sensible reason for considering Kant, Descartes and Wittgenstein to be "proper philosophy" yet to deny that there can be real philosophical wisdom contained in books as varied as *Winnie the Pooh, Alice's Adventures in Wonderland, Marianne Dreams* or *The Mouse and his Child.* Even a picture book like Maurice Sendak's exemplary *Where The Wild Things Are* can get to the heart of psychoanalytic ideas about the way we perceive the world through fantasy and projection.

So the original Pooh stories on their own might well be a source of interesting ideas for many, but Hoff's book has given those books and characters a unique and interesting twist, and has brought them to a wider audience. This book may or may not express the heart of the Tao, but it is at least a thought-provoking and surprising read.

---

### The Tao of Pooh

## The Speed Read

Winnie the Pooh is the original uncarved block, meaning that he takes a simple approach to the world and lives in harmony with his surroundings. Whereas his friends, each in their own ways, over-intellectualize the world or fail to live in harmony with it. Pooh thus represents the true path of the Tao.

---

## One-Liners – A Mini-Manual for a Spiritual Life, 2002

### Ram Dass

*"Don't take yourself so personally."*

Ram Dass was born, named Richard Alpert, in 1931. By the early 1960s he was a successful psychologist, teaching at Harvard. However he became increasingly fascinated by spiritual aspects of his research, and also with hallucinogenic drugs such as LSD. In the early days of LSD, many intellectuals were fascinated by the insights into consciousness that the hallucinogenic experience seemed to offer. Alpert worked with Timothy Leary, Aldous Huxley and Allen Ginsberg, among others, on a series of research papers and books. As a result of this controversial work, he was dismissed from Harvard.

Over subsequent years, he studied meditation, yoga and a variety of other spiritual disciplines, taking the new name

Ram Dass after travelling to study with an Indian guru. As well as his spiritual preoccupations, Dass was interested in environmental, political and sociological issues and wrote prolifically on many subjects. His 1971 book *Be Here Now* caught the zeitgeist of the times, telling his story in a quirky and stylized manner, and lauding the benefits of Eastern spirituality in a wryly amusing tone that gave the book ballast and lasting power that many of his contemporaries were unable to match.

However *Be Here Now* is very much a book of its time. In subsequent writing Dass has shown his real wisdom by continuing to question his own beliefs and pronouncements, and by being admirably prepared to own up to his own failings and mistakes. He has a refreshing ability to see his own personality clearly, and this honesty is what gives his work its power. At the age of seventy he published a charming book on the problems of ageing and the fear of death, wryly titled *Still Here*, in a nod back to his best known work. Dass can be erratic in his specific advice, and veers between genuine wisdom and weaker homilies, but he is never less than interesting and challenging to read.

We have selected *One-Liners – A Mini-Manual for a Spiritual Life* from his oeuvre because it provides such a pithy and clear introduction to Dass's work. And also because, perhaps more than any other book he wrote, this addresses one of the key philosophical questions: "How should we live our lives?"

It is essentially a collection of aphorisms – short, precise statements of ideas and thought. The tradition of aphorisms in philosophy includes such worthy writers as Montaigne, La Rochefoucauld, and Nietzsche. All of these writers shared the ability to hone a thought into a single challenging sentence or paragraph that challenged readers to think for themselves.

*One-Liners* contains a range of aphorisms, distilled from Dass's lectures and writings through his life. To give a few of examples of the one-liners in the book: "Aging represents failure in our society, so each of us looks ahead and sees inevitable failure"; "Humor is the ability to see one reality from the perspective of another"; and "Don't take yourself so personally."

These are examples of the way that Dass is able to condense a serious train of thought into a single sentence, without falling into the trap of being trite or simplistic. Instead, Dass invites us to consider our own attitudes, the assumptions we make about everyday life, and the actions we take as a result.

*One-liners* is a book that is best read in small doses, with frequent pauses for thought. Dass would feel that he has not succeeded unless he makes us want to apply a level of scrutiny and honesty to our own lives that at least approaches the level of such thought that he applies to his own. You need not share all of Dass's spiritual concerns to recognize the value of his writing.

By encouraging us to question ourselves, and by providing a good example of a teacher who does not believe that he has all the answers, Dass is encouraging the reader to live a truly philosophical life. Philosophers from Socrates onwards have taught that true knowledge starts with self-knowledge. *One-liners* is a provocation, a gentle reminder that we need to re-examine our lives on a daily basis. By providing this reminder in such an enjoyable and accessible volume, Dass gives us his message in a sugar-coating. However the fact that this is a slim, sweet book should not mislead you into thinking it is not also a profound, wise one.

## *One-Liners – A Mini-Manual for a Spiritual Life*

# The Speed Read

*One-Liners* is, in the words of its author Ram Dass, "a kind of spiritual brandy, a distillation of the lectures I've given over the course of the past decade or so." His aphorisms capture " the little 'aha!' moments," the simple but profound thoughts that crystallize some part of human existence. Dass himself recommends reading the book in coffee breaks or on bus journeys, in short bursts to help reframe the way you think about life. A sweet but profound meditation from a wise and honest man.

# Psychodrama:
# How to Live your Life

## Introduction

In the time of Plato and Aristotle, it was generally accepted that one of the goals of philosophy was to help us to understand how we should live our lives. But over subsequent centuries, traditional philosophy focused more on metaphysical and epistemological questions – "What is the universe?," and "What can we really know about it?" Obviously many writers did comment on ethical or moral issues, but what was generally known as philosophy came to be more centred on questions of rationality, meaning or certainty than on the search for a good life, or on simple advice on how to conduct oneself in daily life.

In various ways, the books included here touch on these issues from angles other than the standard philosophical avenue. *The Art of War* and La Rochefoucauld's *Maxims* are both books that give basic advice on how to understand our lives and our fellow human beings. Sun Tzu's classic is a military treatise, but has been widely used in a variety of other fields as a guide to human behaviour in situations of conflict, while La Rochefoucauld's understanding of human behaviour comes from his years of experience of devious political manouevring in the French court of the seventeenth century.

The following four titles focus more on psychoanalytic interpretations of behaviour. The fledgling science of psychoanalysis has complemented philosophy in fascinating ways in the twentieth century. While many philosophers still struggled with the idea that the self could be divided or complex, psychiatry accepted the divided self as a starting point and then tried to work out the consequences of this in understanding human behaviour. When it comes to understanding ideas such as self-deception, bad faith, or insanity, the rationalist approach of philosophy often seems to need some help from psychoanalytic theory if we are to make any sense of the human mind.

The chronological order of the books here is broken by the fact that we have placed Carl Jung after Sigmund Freud, even though *Memories, Dreams, Reflections* was published later than the books of Erich Fromm and Carl Rogers. This makes more sense as a reading order, because Jung's theories were in general well known by the time that Fromm and Rogers were writing, and it is only the fact that his memoir was published posthumously that makes it appear out of chronological order. It is also worth mentioning that the work of Lacan (included later in the book) would also have been relevant here. Of course there is a huge body of psychoanalytic work that can't be mentioned here, but by including these few books we would hope to point out the importance of psychoanalytic theory for philosophy.

Erich Fromm's *The Art of Loving* is also an interesting book because it is one of the few theoretical books we have included that deal explicitly with the subject of love. Finally we look at Alain de Botton's *Consolations of Philosophy,* a book in which the author explicitly attempts to return to the Platonic principle that philosophy should be a guide to life, helping us to make sense of our lives and decide how we should live them.

# *The Art of War,* 6th Century BC

## Sun Tzu

*"Know your enemy and know yourself."*

The *Art of War* is a sixth century Chinese military treatise. As such it might seem a strange choice as a "philosophical classic." We include it here largely because of its enduring influence on modern thought, not only in military applications, but in fields as diverse as business, sport, and even romance. An acknowledged classic in the East for over 2,500 years, the book entered the western canon via eighteenth-century translations, and within the military sphere has been shown to be an influence in the thinking of planners in campaigns as diverse as the Napoleonic wars, Vietnam and the first Gulf war. It also had a recent period of notoriety when, following references by Michael Douglas's character Gordon Gekko in the film *Wall Street,* the book had a renewed period of popularity as a business classic. There was some irony in this as the kind of self-obsessed ruthless businessmen who were satirized in the film latched on to *The Art of War* as a new sourcebook, failing to realize the irony of the reference.

The book itself consists of thirteen chapters of short, consistently organized observations on the art of warfare. These include sections on strategy and tactics, use of spies, planning, technical planning and weapons and so forth. On first reading, the material has a similar feel to classic writers of Eastern religion such as Lao Tzu or Confucius. (Sun Tzu's philosophy was directly influenced by his Taoism.) As with those writers, Sun Tzu keeps his thoughts to the simplest, most stripped down form of expression. Of course, as in the writings of Zen masters, one can often think for a long time about a single sentence. But the apparent simplicity of the work is part of the reason for its enduring impact. By taking the most simple view of how two forces opposed to each other might manage to outwit and defeat one another, Sun Tzu seems to come close to the heart of some of the most basic situations that human beings face in life.

Some of his maxims are clearly of use in both military and non-military situations. Maxims from *The Art of War*, such as "the best commander is the one who wins while avoiding battle," and the advice given about knowing one's enemy seem immediately relevant to a variety of conflicts. It is interesting to see that much of Sun Tzu's advice is centered on the idea that conflict is not the only way to win. He stresses the importance of winning without fighting, and also of achieving a full understanding of any situation before risking one's resources in conflict.

Not that Sun Tzu is a pacifist. He is writing from within a society in which he acknowledges conflict as inevitable, and as an honourable practice. It is simply that he takes the view that the wise commander will judge each situation on its own merits and will often prefer to avoid conflict rather than risk unnecessary losses. In this respect, Sun Tzu's work also anticipates modern analytical techniques such as Games Theory and the prisoner's dilemma. With this in mind, he focuses much attention on the need to control appearances – for instance it may often be necessary to persuade an adversary that you have common goals, or to pretend to be on the side of those to whom one is secretly opposed. By encouraging a clear-headed analysis of the possible gains and losses of any move, Sun Tzu is also centuries ahead of Machiavelli in seeing the state's manouevres in a cold, but intellectual light in which victory is the main aim of any action.

As with the more spiritual work of Lao Tzu or Confucius, there is a great deal of wisdom to be taken from Sun Tzu.

Some object to the modern influence of the book on the basis that not all human situations are based on conflict. It is true that it is important to remember that many human endeavours are based on common purpose and co-operation. To focus exclusively on an adversarial view of human behaviour, in business, romance, or even international diplomacy can be dangerous and degrading. But if one accepts, as surely one must, that situations of conflict are an inevitable part of human existence, then a work such as this will continue to have great value. Because it focuses on such basic principles of the circumstances of war, it is still both comprehensible and relevant even though we live in a very different world to the author. And, if only because of the wide influence it has had historically, it is an extremely interesting book to study.

## *The Art of War*
# The Speed Read

The art of war is of vital importance to the State. It is a matter of life and death, a road either to safety or to ruin. Hence it is a subject of inquiry which can on no account be neglected. One hundred victories in one hundred battles is not the most skilful. Seizing the enemy without fighting is the most skilful. If your enemy is secure at all points, be prepared for him. If he is of superior strength, evade him. If your opponent is temperamental, seek to irritate him. Pretend to be weak, that he may grow arrogant. If he is taking his ease, give him no rest. If his forces are united, separate them. If sovereign and subject are in accord, put division between them. Attack him where he is unprepared, appear where you are not expected.

# *Maxims*, 1665

## La Rochefoucauld

*"There are few sensible people, we find,
except those who share our opinions."*

François, duc de la Rochefoucauld (generally referred to as La Rochefoucauld) lived through a fascinating period of French history. He was a contemporary of Racine, La Fontaine and Molière. He was one of many players in the complex intrigues in the court of Louis XIII, and saw the machinations of Richelieu and Mazarin at first hand. He survived the Fronde (a long period of civil war in the mid-seventeenth century), a brief imprisonment in the Bastille and a few years of banishment. He also had a complex love life, embarking on several passionate affairs that foundered among the manoeuvres of court life before finding platonic happiness with the writer Mme de la Fayette in his later years.

In the 1660s he was back in Paris, and in a more peaceful period, became an established part of one of the literary salons of the city. It was in this phase of his life that he produced the book that became known as the *Maxims* of La Rochefoucauld. The literary salons of Paris often dabbled in producing word portraits of well known figures, and also in the art of the maxim. A maxim was taken to be any pithy comment that compressed wisdom in such a way as to be generally applicable (rather than any more specific comment on an individual or event).

To give an example, one of La Rochefoucauld's maxims reads "We often do good so that we can do evil with impunity." One can see that this short line is deliberately stripped of all personal or historical detail in order to express what La Rochefoucauld believes to be a universal truth. But this maxim also demonstrates one of the reasons why La Rochefoucauld's writing continued to carry weight long after his demise, unlike many other writers of his period. There is a subtlety in this simple maxim that forces us to think hard about the author's meaning. Is he implying that we consciously use goodness as a cover for wrongdoing? Or is he suggesting that we unconsciously allow ourselves indulgent acts as a "reward" for previous good acts? One could read this one maxim in a number of different ways, but it could have resonance of many sorts in our own experience.

This is typical of La Rochefoucauld's writing. He writes on a variety of subjects – for instance, on human emotion and vanity, on political intrigue and endeavour, and on love and self-knowledge. In every case (there are over 600 maxims in most modern editions, although those published in his lifetime were shorter) the maxims are deceptively simple. (La Rochefoucauld spent many years honing the maxims and reducing them to their absolute essence whilst ruthlessly editing out those which seemed false or too specific.) But it is their very simplicity that gives them such strength. In spite (or because) of the fact that La Rochefoucauld never wastes a single word, he often seems to approach universal truths of the human condition. And even when he doesn't do so, the humility and humour of his opinions is at the very least engaging.

A few more examples might help to give a flavour of La Rochefoucauld's writing:

> "Moderation has been declared a virtue so as to curb the ambition of the great and console lesser folk for their lack of fortune and merit."

This maxim demonstrates why Nietzsche was, in the nineteenth century, a great fan of La Rochefoucauld's writing. While hinting at psychological motives in the praise of moderation (that Nietzsche would describe as *ressentiment*) the author also points to the ways in which society constructs itself into a model that soothes the anger of the disadvantaged by creating a narrative that allows them to feel virtuous. In a simple line, this maxim hints at different ways of interpreting the whole idea of moderation as a virtue, and the ways in which this impacts both on the "great" and the "lesser folk."

> "At times we are as different from ourselves as we are from others."

Again, this maxim hints at psychologically complex ideas. Is the author saying that we take on different personas in different situations, or that we are in a state of self-deception or bad faith? Is he anticipating the Hegelian idea that self is constituted in the "other"? Or is he simply remarking on the fact that we are rather less consistent than we like to imagine. Either way he is making an interesting comment on human nature.

> "You can find women who have never had a love affair, but seldom women who have had only one."

La Rochefoucauld's earlier maxims were occasionally rather bitter in their views on women, presumably because of the ways in which his own love affairs had ended. (This was before the company of Mme de la Fayette made him more moderate and calm in his views, and he revised some of his most trenchant maxims in later editions of the book.) But even while some of his comments can be regarded as misogynistic, there are occasional shafts of light cast on the nature of relationships between men and women. While this maxim is a wry and slightly tetchy comment on the way that women (in his view) are attracted to the idea of romance, it is at least amusing. And La Rochefoucauld was clearly very fond of women, even if they did sometimes leave him bemused, infuriated, or broken-hearted.

In some respects La Rochefoucauld's maxims are comparable to *The Pillow Book of Sei Shonagon,* the collected thoughts of a court lady from Japan six centuries earlier. In both cases, the authors write from a relatively privileged viewpoint – we have few accounts from the point of view of "lesser folk" from these periods simply because the wealthy classes were the only ones who were both educated and possessed of the luxury of spare time. But 99 per cent of the writing of courtiers and aristocrats of such periods is of little contemporary interest, while the occasional jewel such as *The Pillow Book* or *The Maxims* stands out from the crowd by expressing universal wisdom and insights into human knowledge and life. La Rochefoucauld is by turns funny, wise, acerbic, and insightful, but in this short book he is never less than interesting.

*Maxims*

## The Speed Read

"Hypocrisy is a tribute vice pays to virtue." Human life is a little like court life. There are intrigues, fools who believe themselves to be wise, and love affairs that seem wonderful until they go inexorably wrong. What passes for wisdom is often merely having the appropriate folly for our time. Generosity is often self-interest in disguise. We are vain, weak or foolish, but we excel at forgiving ourselves for our own faults and misdeeds. We are rarely either as fortunate or as unfortunate as we believe.

# On Sexuality, 1905

Sigmund Freud

*"No one who has seen a baby sinking back satiated from
the breast and falling asleep with flushed cheeks and a
blissful smile can escape the reflection that this picture
persists as a prototype of the expression of
sexual satisfaction in later life."*

Sigmund Freud was an Austrian neurologist and the
co-founder of the psychoanalytic school of psychology. Freud is best known for his theories involving the
unconscious mind, especially involving the mechanism of
repression and his redefinition of sexual desire as mobile
and directed towards a wide variety of objects. His work has
been tremendously influential in popularizing such notions
as the unconscious, defence mechanisms, Freudian slips and
dream symbolism. His ideas are also accepted as having
made a long-lasting impact on fields as diverse as literature,
film, Marxist and feminist theories, literary criticism, philosophy, and psychology.

Many have claimed that the most significant contribution
Freud made to Western thought was his argument for the
existence of an unconscious mind. During the nineteenth
century, the dominant trend in Western thought was positivism, which subscribed to the belief that people could attain
true knowledge concerning themselves and their environment and therefore judiciously exercise control over both.
Freud's theories, however, suggested that such declarations
of free will are in fact delusions. We are not entirely aware
of what we think and often act for reasons that have little to
do with our conscious thoughts.

The concept of the unconscious as proposed by Freud
was groundbreaking in that he proposed that awareness

existed in layers and that there were thoughts occurring "below the surface." More importantly, we do not have full conscious access to those thoughts and so cannot automatically control them. For Freud, any kind of positivism and rationalism could only be approached by understanding, transforming, and mastering the unconscious, rather than through denying or repressing it. Crucial to Freud's idea of the operation of the unconscious is the notion of "repression."

Freud distinguished between two concepts of the unconscious: the descriptive unconscious and the dynamic unconscious. The descriptive unconscious referred to all those features of mental life of which we are not subjectively aware. The dynamic unconscious is a more specific construct, referring to the mental processes and contents that are defensively removed (or "repressed") from consciousness as a result of conflicting forces or "dynamics."

In *On Sexuality*, Freud argued that infantile sexuality must be seen as an integral part of a broader developmental theory of the human conscious and unconscious mind. He suggested that humans are born "polymorphously perverse," meaning that any number of objects could be a source of pleasure. From this account of instincts or drives, Freud argued that from the moment of birth, the infant is driven in his actions by the desire for bodily/sexual pleasure. Initially, infants derive such pleasure, through the act of sucking, and Freud terms this the "oral" stage of development.

The "oral" phase is followed by a phase in which the centre of pleasure or energy release is the anus, particularly in the act of defecation, and Freud therefore termed this the "anal" stage. Then, the young child develops an interest in its sexual organs as a site of pleasure (the "phallic" stage). During this time, Freud maintained that children passed through a stage in which they fixated on the mother as a sexual object (known as the "Oedipus Complex" – *see below*) but that the child eventually overcame and repressed this desire because of its taboo nature. This knowledge gives rise to (socially derived) feelings of guilt in the child, who recognizes that it can never supplant the stronger parent. In the case of a male, it also puts the child at a risk, because he perceives that if he persists in pursuing the sexual attraction for his mother, he may be harmed by the father. Specifically he comes to fear that he may be castrated. This is termed "*castration anxiety.*"

This repressive or dormant latency stage of psychosexual development preceded the sexually mature genital stage of psychosexual development. Freud hoped to prove that his model was universally valid and thus turned to ancient mythology and contemporary ethnography for comparative material. Freud named this theory the Oedipus complex after the famous Greek tragedy, *Oedipus Rex* by Sophocles. "I found in myself a constant love for my mother, and jealousy of my father. I now consider this to be a universal event in childhood."

Freud sought to anchor this pattern of development in the dynamics of the mind. Each stage is a progression into adult sexual maturity, characterized by a strong ego (self-identity), and the ability to delay gratification. Both the attraction for the mother and the hatred are usually repressed, and the child usually resolves the conflict of the Oedipus complex by coming to identify with the parent of the same sex. According to Freud, this usually happens around the age of five, whereupon the child enters a "latency" period, in which sexual motivations become much less pronounced. This lasts until puberty, when mature genital development begins, and the pleasure drive refocuses around the genital area. Freud believed this to be the sequence or progression implicit in *normal* human development. At the infant level, the instinctual attempts to satisfy the pleasure drive are frequently checked by parental control and social coercion. The developmental process, then, is for the child essentially a movement through a series of *conflicts*, the successful resolution of which is crucial to adult mental health.

Although Freud's theories were quite influential, they have also come under widespread criticism both during his lifetime and afterwards. Some have attacked his claim that infants are sexual beings, and, implicitly, Freud's expanded notion of sexuality. Others have accepted this expanded notion of sexuality, but have argued that this pattern of development is not universal, nor necessary for the development of a healthy adult. Instead, they have emphasized the social and environmental sources of patterns of development. Moreover, they call attention to social dynamics arguing that Freud de-emphasized or ignored issues such as class relations and social environment.

Some feminists see Freud's theory as claiming that women are a kind of mutilated male who must learn to accept their "deformity" (the "lack" of a penis) and therefore argue that Freud contributed to the vocabulary of misogyny. However, there are also some feminist theorists who argue that psychoanalytic theory is essentially related to the feminist project and must, like other theoretical traditions, be adapted by women to free it from vestiges of sexism. Shulamith Firestone (in *Freudianism: The Misguided Feminism*) discusses how Freudianism is essentially completely accurate, with the exception of one crucial detail: everywhere that Freud writes "penis," the word should be replaced with "power."

### On Sexuality
## The Speed Read

The human mind and thus identity are a product of a conflicting series of thoughts and urges, not all of them conscious. Identity is male, and women are only recognized as women because they don't have a penis. If women challenge the dominant male culture they are accused of having "penis envy." Similarly, men who are afraid of such dominant and argumentative women are seen as having a "castration complex." All very school playground except for the bit about "I'll show you mine if . . ." because women by definition have nothing to show.

## *Memories, Dreams, Reflections*, 1971

### Carl Gustav Jung

*"Your vision will become clear only when you can look into your own heart. Who looks outside, dreams; who looks inside, awakes."*

Carl Jung is a fascinating figure within twentieth-century culture. Some regard him as a wise oracle, while others see him as something of a charlatan. Jung's legacy is perhaps slightly obscured by his popularity among the odder fringes of the new-age community because of his interest in myths, writing on subjects as varied as Arthurian legend, flying saucers, and Eastern philosophy. For instance, his ridiculous book on *Synchronicity* (the idea that coincidences reveal some mystical underlying structure in the world) was referenced by Sting in a song and album by rock band The Police

– one of many flaky cultural references to Jung that could be listed. He is also somewhat tainted by his apparent collaboration (or at least acquiescence) with the Nazi regime during the Second World War.

However, in spite of Jung's occasional mysticism and other flaws, he is an important figure. He became well-known in the fledgling science of psychoanalysis early in the twentieth century. First a Freudian and friend of Freud, he had a notorious split with Freud in 1913, and suffered from some kind of mental breakdown in the next few years. Much of his subsequent work dealt with his own mental state during this difficult period.

It is hard to describe succinctly Jung's differences with Freud, but there are a couple of aspects which interest us from a philosophical viewpoint here. Firstly, while Freud had described the personality in terms of ego, super ego, and id, Jung took a rather different approach. He took the approach that a person's mind could effectively contain more than one personality. From observations of himself, his mother, and people such as a supposedly psychic girl he met at a young age who appeared to channel a different personality, Jung concluded that it was necessary to see the individual personality as a far more fragmented entity than was traditional. The process of individuation through someone's life allowed these personalities to interact and develop, and turning points such as a mid-life crisis might result from such unconscious conflicts.

This is philosophically interesting because it is a major step towards dismantling the standard identification of the self as a simple, obvious unity. When Descartes said "I think therefore I am," he assumed it was clear what was meant by "I." The work of Freud and Jung in particular went a long way to showing how complicated that "I" could be, and the development of theories of the unconscious further complicated the picture. In allowing that our personality was a relatively arbitrary construct, subject to split personalities and radical change through individuation, Jung pictured a self very different to the self that Descartes had assumed existed. This has other interesting implications. Philosophers have struggled to understand the idea of self-deception. Because they assumed a coherent self, they assumed that self-deception would involve "lying to oneself," in other words, knowing the truth, but deceiving oneself nonetheless. But in Jung's writing about his mother we see a more subtle definition of self-deception. He perceived her as having at least two personas – one very conventional and sensible, and one more rebellious and daring. The two could hold different and opposing beliefs, leading his mother to be in a state of effective self-deception.

A second point of departure between Jung and Freud was in the way that they spoke of the unconscious. Freud saw the unconscious largely in terms of repression – he described it as the repository for drives, ideas, and beliefs that had been repressed by the conscious mind. In this way Freud's theory of the unconscious is a largely negative one, and Freud laid a lot of stress on sexuality as a source of repression. Jung on the other hand gave the unconscious mind a more positive press. He saw it as a potential source of creativity and of the friction that drives the individuation of the conscious mind.

Some of Jung's writings on the unconscious, in particular the collective unconscious, tend towards mysticism. The collective unconscious is in fact an idea that can be valuable if one understands it as meaning that, since human beings share so much with each other in terms of early experience, physical constitution, needs and drives, it is not surprising that our mental architecture is quite similar. Different cultures independently generate similar myths for this reason, myths such as hero myths and sun-god myths. "Archetypes" (a Jungian term) such as the mother have similar connotations in most human discourse. However Jung is occasionally a sloppy thinker, and often a rather bad writer – as a result he unfortunately seems to imply that the collective unconscious is something rather more mystical than this, a kind of cosmic mind shared by all humanity. He makes a similar mistake in books such as *Synchronicity*, where he fails to distinguish clearly between the operation of the human mind when confronted with coincidence, and the idea that those coincidences are of some real cosmic significance.

But if we accept the simpler definition of the collective unconscious, there is one important consequence in Jung's writings. He sees myth-making as an essential human activity, one that allows us to create meaning and give sense to our lives when none seems to exist. This can apply both in a cultural sense (as it might in a culture that invents myths and deities related to agriculture and survival) and in an individual sense. Jung goes so far as to describe schizophrenic patients in terms of this idea. He sees them as constructing personal narratives to attempt to deal with their own worlds. The fact that their personal narrative is badly adapted to survival in society is a problem. However we all live by one myth or another (and here Jung was being brave in realizing that religion was essentially a myth of the same variety) – it is just that some of these narrative structures allow us to survive more successfully in society than others.

So the importance of myth and narrative for Jung are that they are ways in which our unconscious attempts to channel creativity in our lives. It is perhaps fair to say that modern psychoanalysis has been more influenced by Freud's theories of repression than Jung's theories. However Jung's ideas were influential in a host of other disciplines (including anthropology and linguistics) and have often appealed strongly to artists as an explanation of the way in which the artistic impulse operates.

The idea that narrative plays an important role in the way we create our personas and interpret our own lives is one that philosophers would traditionally balk at. Philosophers tend to see themselves as drily analytical, and are disturbed by theories that allow for a more creative interpretation of the individual and self. But some philosophers have grappled with ideas of narrative and creativity. Alexander Nehamas's classic study of Nietzsche (*Nietzsche – Life as Literature*) stressed a narrative interpretation of Nietzsche's work. In particular *eternal recurrence* (the Nietzschean idea that we must live our lives as though we are going to have to take each action over and over again) is interpreted by Nehamas as meaning that we view our lives as an ongoing story that we are creating. As we do this (in his view) we stress those parts of the story we wish to include, and downplay those that are more difficult. This is obviously an idea that comes closer to Jungian psychoanalysis than it does to the standard philosophical explanation of memory and the individual. Continental philosophy has generally been more receptive than the Anglo-American tradition to the idea that there are only interpretations, and that the world can be understood as a literary text.

There is a great deal more to Jung's work than we have space for here, including the development of well-known terms such as *anima* and *animus*, *complexes*, and *archetypes*. *Memories, Dreams, Reflections* is Jung's autobiography, written late in his life and published posthumously. It is effectively a classic piece of Jungian analysis applied to his own life story, and also includes reflections on many of the ideas mentioned above, as well as his extended thoughts on the existence or otherwise of God. He has been criticized for a rather solipsistic focus on the self (as opposed to relationships with others) in his analysis, and that is backed up here by the fact that he rarely even mentions his wife. However there is much of interest in the book, and it is one of the best places to start if one wishes to find out more about Jung, as it ranges across a wide range of his thinking in a relatively concentrated form.

*Memories, Dreams, Reflections*

## The Speed Read

Who am I? I fell out with my friend Freud, then had a breakdown, then spent many years pondering all this as I tried to understand the human mind. We can have different personas within a single individual, and life is a process of individuation. Myths and the collective unconscious underpin creative unconscious processes. Turning points in life, like my own mental crisis, are messages from the unconscious as we struggle to achieve our individuality.

## *The Art of Loving*, 1956

### Erich Fromm

*"Love is the only sane and satisfactory answer to the problem of human existence."*

Erich Fromm is one of those writers who was highly rated thirty or forty years ago, but who has come to be rather neglected. Sometimes this happens for good reason, sometimes it is simply a matter of fashion. There are certainly aspects of Fromm's writing that seem dated, but he also makes good sense at times. We have included him here partly because this is one of the more interesting books written on the subject of love, a subject which is dealt with surprisingly rarely by philosophers.

Fromm was born in Germany in 1900, and studied psychology, philosophy and sociology in Frankfurt from 1918 onwards, becoming interested in Zen Buddhism and the work of Freud, among other things. He was associated with the so-called Frankfurt School, and, like other writers such as Horkheimer and Adorno, he became a refugee in the Second World War, eventually emigrating to America.

His writing focused on man's alienation under the modern systems of capitalism and communism. He propounded a humanistic socialism as an alternative to either of these. His first book *Escape From Freedom* (also known as *Fear of Freedom*) dealt with the ways in which humans deal with freedom. He asserted that we often fail to deal with the responsibility that freedom gives us and seek escape mechanisms. He identified specific ways in which people escape from freedom – through an automaton-like conformity with the society around us, by submitting to authoritarian control, or by giving in to destructive urges.

Fromm wrote extensively about the tensions and contradictions that he identified in Freud's writing and also in the early books of the Old Testament. He was especially fascinated by the story of Adam and Eve, identifying the shame that they felt on eating the apple of knowledge as the birth of human self-awareness and the loneliness and alienation that this can cause.

He felt that this led to us trying to deal with our alienation in various ways. We strive to develop our creative transcendence from society, we try to find groups to which we can belong, and we look for connection through love, and romantic love in particular.

In *The Art of Loving*, he looks at the various types of love that we can feel, including parental, sibling love, erotic love, self-love and love for God. He argues that our focus on romantic love is partly a flight from our aloneness and alienation from nature and our fellow man. Indeed he argues that to "fall in love" is often to misunderstand the basic nature of love. Because real love should contain care, responsibility, respect, and knowledge and the ways in which we pursue romantic love often exclude these characteristics.

Fromm describes our existence as though we are each in a kind of solitary confinement, distanced from those around us, and fearful of the responsibility that would come with real freedom. We feel afraid and ashamed and use romantic love to try to address these perceived problems.

He argues that in a saner society this would not be the case. It is a slight weakness of Fromm's work that his idea of a sane society is a bit woolly and seems to simply be a description of modern liberal democracy. As we know, modern liberal democracies do not necessarily solve all the problems of the soul, even if they do create a slightly different kind of alienation to unbridled capitalism or communism.

Fromm's critiques of capitalism and communism are thus more effective than his positive political ideas. In fact his politics are probably the weakest part of his writing, at least in retrospect, as they don't relate well to the problems of the modern world.

However Fromm's thoughts on love are extremely interesting. Love is a subject that has been dealt with periodically by philosophers since Socrates (in *The Symposium*) and earlier thinkers. But it is dealt with less frequently than problems of ethics or epistemology, and often only in passing. Fromm's book is fascinating in the light it casts on the differences and similarities between the different kinds of love in our lives. Whether or not you accept his basic premise that romantic love is often defective and a flight from alienation, this is a book worth reading for its breadth of reference and thinking.

## *The Art of Loving*
# The Speed Read

Since Adam and Eve discovered knowledge and self-awareness we have been alone, ashamed, alienated. We seek romantic love to escape from this alienation, but often the romantic love we seek excludes the crucial elements of real love – care, responsibility, and respect. "Love means to commit oneself without guarantee, to give oneself completely in the hope that our love will produce love in the loved person. Love is an act of faith, and whoever is of little faith is also of little love."

# *On Becoming a Person*, 1961
## Carl Rogers

*"This process of the good life is not, I am convinced, a life for the faint-hearted. It involves the stretching and growing of becoming more and more of one's potentialities. It involves the courage to be. It means launching oneself fully into the stream of life."*

Carl Rogers was an American humanist psychologist who became well known for his theories through the 1940s and 1950s. His *person-centered psychotherapy* has been an influential strand of psychiatry, especially in the sphere of counselling and therapy (as opposed to the deeper analysis applied by Freudians).

Rogers' work is philosophically interesting for several reasons. We've seen how traditional philosophy tended to treat the self as an undoubted, unitary object. Philosophers such as Nietzsche, Schopenhauer and Kierkegaard had questioned this viewpoint within philosophy, while the early psychoanalysis of Freud and Jung specifically rejected the idea that we could assume that self was a simple unity.

The writing of Carl Rogers takes a close look at the way that our perception of self develops. He does this by considering the ways in which our perception of self (the *self-concept*) differs from our *ideal self* or *real self*, and the problems that ensue when there is too big a difference between these three versions of self.

Rogers' view of psychotherapy was that it had to start from the perceptions of the individual being counselled. Rather than assume that the therapist or counsellor had a superior knowledge, and that clients or patients were essentially unbalanced or unaware of their own problems, he chose to start from the viewpoint that the individual is basically healthy. The question he tried to address was what makes someone into a functioning person. From his therapeutic experience he believed that the therapist needed to understand the viewpoint of the patient, to show empathy with that viewpoint and to work primarily through *reflection* (mirroring the patient's attitude back to them) and *clarification* (trying to jointly understand the patient's attitudes more clearly, through the use of empathy).

He describes the individual living in a world where they have a wide variety of experiences and perceptions. From this smorgasbord, the individual gradually marks off a portion of the perceptual field, and differentiates this portion as their self. So the self develops as a partly voluntary choice of which parts of our experience we identify with.

Problems arise when we encounter perceptual experiences that don't fit in with our self-concept. Such experiences tend to be seen as a threat to the self-concept. As a result we deal with these threats in two main ways, *distortion* and *denial*. Distortion occurs when we mentally edit or revise an experience so that it fits our self-concept. Denial occurs when we simply choose not to acknowledge the threatening experience.

Perceptions that threaten our self-concept tend to cause anxiety. Other psychologists have identified this phenomenon as *cognitive dissonance*. This is a state of discomfort that occurs when two of our beliefs are inconsistent. We prefer to maintain consistency in our self-concept so we need to downgrade or ignore one of two conflicting beliefs. Philosophers have traditionally struggled with the concept of self-deception because they assumed that the self was a unitary object and that self-deception involved knowingly lying to oneself – in other words knowing the truth but believing the lie simultaneously. Rogers' theories give a more detailed example of the ways in which people are subject to self-deception or bad faith. Because the self is a construct and one that we try to protect from threats, it is quite natural to us to eliminate beliefs that cause anxiety.

It is not in itself an unhealthy thing that we have to differentiate parts of our experience into a self. However when there is too wide a gap between our self-concept and our real selves, we can experience problems. Rogers prefers not to use labels such as neurosis or psychosis, but both can be given fairly clear explanations using this kind of analysis.

Rogers' overall theory is based on the *actualizing tendency,* by which he means that all life-forms aim to develop their potential to the greatest extent possible. He also sees positive self-regard as an important part of a functioning person (in other words, we need to see ourselves in a positive light) and this is obviously an easier thing to achieve when our self-concept is closer to our real or ideal self.

In his writing, Rogers identifies a number of attributes of a fully functioning person. Firstly he sees them as someone who is open to experience. Because we only allow a portion of our experiences to relate to our self-concept, the more flexible we are in our self-concept, the more of our experience we are able to assimilate and comprehend (rather than denying or rejecting it). He also sees it as important to live in the here and now, which again is an aspect of being open to understanding that the self is a flexible concept, and that past memories or future hopes are not always the most important guides to current experience.

Rogers sees freedom as an important concept. He addresses the philosophical problem of free will, but from a psychoanalytic viewpoint decides that the most important thing is that we feel as though we have free will. He considers the individual who acknowledges the sense of freedom and takes responsibility for their choices as being a functioning person.

Some of Rogers other views on the fully functioning person have a slightly dated feel. He sees *organismic trusting* as important, by which he basically means that we should do what comes naturally. He has received some criticism for this view on the basis that what comes naturally is not necessarily a healthy or good thing for us to do. However, Rogers would have pointed out that this idea should be seen in the context of a functioning person whose self-concept is in a state of reasonable congruence with their ideal and real self. He also considers that the fully functioning person will be naturally creative, whether this be in an artistic way, a nurturing way, or simply through striving to do one's work to the best of one's ability.

Overall Rogers is an interesting psychologist to read. One can disagree with some of his detailed points, but there is a great deal of interest to be found in his analysis of the way in which the self is differentiated and the consequences of incongruence between the self-concept and real life. Jung and Freud are more dogmatic about their specific concepts and theories, whereas Rogers is simply trying to put forward a framework for therapists and counsellors to understand how their patients construct a sense of self.

And this is something that we all share – the fact that our selves or personas are to some degree constructed, whether voluntarily or involuntarily. Understanding the process by which we do this is a first step towards understanding ourselves, whether we feel we need therapy or not.

### On Becoming a Person

## The Speed Read

From the wide variety of perceptual experiences we encounter, we carve out a portion that we label our self. When we encounter perceptions that threaten this self-concept, we deal with it by distortion or denial. Mental problems result if our self-concept is too remote from our real self and perceptions. The fully functioning person is open to experience, lives in the moment, acts naturally, and is creative and free.

## *The Consolations of Philosophy*, 2000

### Alain de Botton

*"It is common to assume that we are dealing with a highly intelligent book when we cease to understand it. Profound ideas cannot, after all, be explained in the language of children."*

We started this book by considering Bertrand Russell's *The Problems of Philosophy*, because it gives an overview of the kinds of problems that are dealt with by philosophy. Alain de Botton's *The Consolations of Philosophy* is in some ways a similar book, in that it makes a good introduction to philosophy for someone who has little experience of the subject. But it is a very different kind of book to Russell's guide because it is a much more chatty, subjective take on the subject.

De Botton was previously a novelist, and also makes television programmes based on his non-fiction books. He takes a populist approach, and has a light, entertaining tone of voice, even when dealing with difficult subjects. He previously had a success with a book entitled *How Proust Can Change Your Life,* in which he used the writings of the notoriously difficult French novelist as a starting point for a consideration of self-help and how to live a good life.

In this book he once again starts from the point of view that philosophy can be used as a tool for understanding your own existence, and learning how to live a better, more rewarding life. He does this by looking closely at the writing of six great writers of the past. At times his writing is closer to autobiography or a self-help book than it is to traditional philosophy dealing as it does with topics as varied as impotence and sexual frustration, broken love affairs and the difficulties of having less money than one would wish. But along the way he has many interesting things to say about more traditional philosophical subjects.

De Botton starts by describing an epiphany he had upon thinking about Socrates and realizing that, while Socrates' life was driven by a search for truth, his own life had been driven by a desire to conform and to be approved of. Here, as elsewhere, his self-criticism is simultaneously disarming and slightly disingenuous – somehow we never really feel that he is as harsh on himself as he might momentarily pretend – indeed his rather condescending tone tends to give the impression of a rather self-satisfied man. But this is only a minor note of dissonance in an otherwise very enjoyable read.

He goes on to give brief biographies (together with rather clever thumbnail sketches) of each of his philosophers, and to show ways in which he has been able to apply their thinking to his own life. In Socrates he finds inspiration for those who feel unpopular; in Epicurus he looks at the problems of poverty; in Seneca he finds lessons about frustration; the French writer Montaigne is used to look at feelings of inadequacy; in Schopenhauer's pessimism he finds a balm for broken hearts; while he uses Nietzsche's writing as an inspiration to overcome difficulties in life.

This is put together in a friendly package including some relevant and facetious illustrations. (These include a rather unfortunate comic Superman for Nietzsche, which doesn't help to overcome the hard work Nietzsche scholars have put into making it clear how very different Nietzsche's concept of the *overman* is to any kind of Superman cliché.) And de Botton throughout is a charming and entertaining guide. His personal anecdotes are self-effacing and witty, and help to keep our interest as he explores his subject matter.

At times one can regret that he has failed to do real justice to the philosophers he has chosen. In his desire to make them accessible to a modern readership, he often over-simplifies their ideas. For instance, we find it hard to recognize why Socrates was so hated and feared by his fellow Athenians, since de Botton presents him in such an anodyne light. But to carp too much about this would be to fail to acknowledge the book's real strengths.

The most valuable aspect of this book is that it presents a model of how to read philosophy. Rather than treat the writings of great writers of the past as "difficult" subjects of canonical study, de Botton gives us a different picture of how to read them. He shows himself in a personal debate with the ideas of these writers, applying the lessons he takes from them to his own life with varying success. He is thus taking us back to a much older concept of philosophy, which is that it should be a tool to improve one's rational faculties and, most importantly, to help one to live a good life.

*The Consolations of Philosophy* has predictably been sneered at by some academic reviewers for not being sufficiently rigorous, or for failing to give a full account of the writers mentioned. But this misses de Botton's real intention, which is to show how we can read a philosopher and apply their ideas in modern life. When a philosopher derides a book like this for being mere "self-help" rather than philosophy, they are perhaps forgetting that philosophy was the original "self-help" subject. In times past, works of philosophy were often expected to provide an enhanced understanding of one's life, and to suggest ways of living a good life. If that is no longer the role of philosophy, one has to wonder if philosophy might have taken a wrong turn – in which case de Botton's book is one that gives it a nudge back in the right direction.

---

### *The Consolations of Philosophy*

# The Speed Read

I was flying over the Atlantic recently when I looked at a postcard of Socrates and realized that while he spent his life searching for truth, I had just spent mine searching for popularity. So I thought I'd write a book about it, but it would have been too short (and you need plenty of material for the TV adaptation as well . . .) So I also wrote some stuff about Epicurus, Seneca, Montaigne, Nietzsche, and Schopenhauer. These writers can help you through difficult times, like not having enough money to pay the rent, embarrassing moments of impotence, or even a broken heart.

# Twentieth-Century "Isms": Political and Personal Issues

## Introduction

Over the last century, a number of political idealisms have been remarkably significant. Large parts of the world became governed by nominally communist regimes, and the cold war was a stand-off between capitalism and communism. Women started the twentieth century without the vote in many Western countries, but ended the century with equal rights to men in many respects, partly as a direct result of feminist political action. Anarchism and situationism have each played their part in various cultural movements, uprisings or civil wars. Each of these ideas has philosophical implications as well as political ones.

For each of these strands of thought we have included one seminal classic. Marx's original manifesto was philosophically rather different to some of the totalitarian versions of communism that would follow, but was clearly an influential work. Anarchism is represented by Emma Goldman (also a strong advocate of women's rights in her time). There are other anarchist works that might be regarded as more crucial, but Goldman is fascinating as an example of an anarchist who worked her way through many of the problems and contradictions of the anarchist ideal, and is also one of the most likeable anarchists that history has to offer, with her insistence on the importance of love, celebration, and joy. For situationism we have included Raoul Vaneigem's *The Revolution of Everyday Life* rather than the more obvious choice, Guy Debord's *The Society of the Spectacle*, for reasons that will be explained.

From modern feminism we have selected Naomi Wolf's *The Beauty Myth*. Many would argue that there are more influential classics of the feminist movement and that Wolf's book is derivative of earlier works. However we have taken the view that, since feminism is still evolving, it is important to choose a book which reflects the ways in which the earlier wave of feminism has already changed our societies, and that addresses the challenges that feminism faces now. *The Beauty Myth* may have its flaws. However it is nonetheless a good summary of feminist issues in a world where women do have the right to work and to participate fully in society, but still suffer from different pressures, via phenomena such as plastic surgery, size zero models and airbrushed fashion magazine images.

Beyond these obvious political 'isms' the twentieth century saw the growth of other interesting ideas. Jean-Paul Sartre here represents existentialism, an idea which aimed to be a philosophy, but which can retrospectively be seen more as a fashion or posture. At one time existentialism was widely regarded as an important philosophy and even if its star has faded somewhat, we felt it needed to be included here.

Finally, the twentieth century has seen a major growth in environmentalism and in the animal rights movement. The works of Peter Singer and James Lovelock here represent these respective political ideals. In the case of environmentalism, this brings us very much up to date, as issues of global warming and energy depletion look likely to be hugely important issues over the next century. Singer and Lovelock each present aspects of the philosophical underpinning of these ideas.

# The Communist Manifesto, 1848

## Karl Marx and Friedrich Engels

*"The history of all hitherto existing society
is the history of class struggles."*

Karl Heinrich Marx was an immensely influential philosopher, political economist, and socialist revolutionary. While he addressed a wide range of issues, he is most famous for his analysis of history in terms of the class struggle. He developed a critique of society that he claimed was both scientific and revolutionary.

Marx actively took part in the political and philosophical struggle of his times, writing the *Communist Manifesto* a year before the Revolutions of 1848, although the two events were unrelated. He famously asserted that "philosophers have only interpreted the world, in various ways; the point however is to change it." He disagreed with the unification of theory and practice into idealist interpretations that he saw as opposing themselves in various philosophical *Weltanschauungen* (world views).

Marx's view of history, which came to be called *historical materialism* (controversially adapted as the philosophy of dialectical materialism by Engels and Lenin, although this was a term never used by Marx himself), is influenced by Hegel's claim that reality (and history) should be viewed dialectically. Hegel believed that the direction of human history is characterized in the movement from the fragmentary toward the complete and the real (which was also a movement towards greater and greater rationality) and that it could be seen as a product of the conflict between these two opposing realms. While Marx accepted this broad conception of history, Hegel was an idealist, and Marx sought to rewrite dialectics in materialist terms. He argued that Hegelianism stood the movement of reality on its head, and that it was necessary to set it upon its feet. Marx looked for the causes of developments and changes in human societies in the way that humans collectively make the means to life, thus giving an emphasis, through economic analysis, to everything that co-exists with the economic base of society (e.g., social classes, political structures and ideologies).

Marx argued that it is the material world that is real and that our ideas of it are consequences arising *from* that reality, not that our ideas cause the world (the reality). Thus, like Hegel and other philosophers, Marx distinguished between appearances and reality. But he did not believe that the material world hides from us the 'real' world of the ideal; on the contrary, he thought that historically and socially specific ideology prevented people from seeing the material conditions of their lives clearly. Marx believed that the identity of a social class derived from its relationship to the means of production (as opposed to the notion that class is determined by wealth alone, i.e., lower class, middle class, upper class). He created the term "class consciousness" to refer to the self-awareness of a social class and its capacity to act in its own rational interests.

Marx describes several social classes in capitalist societies, including primarily the *proletariat*, which he argues is composed of "those individuals who sell their labour power, (and therefore add value to the products), and who, in the capitalist mode of production, do not own the means of production." Secondly, he described the *bourgeoisie* as being those who "own the means of production" and buy labour power from the proletariat and who are recompensed by a salary, thus exploiting the proletariat. He further divided the bourgeoisie into the very wealthy bourgeoisie and the petty bourgeoisie. The petty bourgeoisie are those who employ labour but also work themselves. These may be small proprietors, land-holding peasants, or trade workers. Marx predicted that the petty bourgeoisie would eventually be destroyed by the constant reinvention of the means of production and the result of this would be the forced movement of the vast majority of the petty bourgeoisie to the proletariat. Marx also identified the lumpen-proletariat, a stratum of society completely disconnected from the means of production, such as the unemployed and the sick or elderly.

In his view of political economy, Marx used the terms *base* and *superstructure* to refer to the means of production of society (how society is produced). The superstructure is formed on top of the base, and comprises a society's ideology, as well as its legal system, political system, and religions. For Marx, the base is the economic underpinning of society and determines the superstructure. The relationship between superstructure and base is considered to be a dialectical one, not a distinction between actual entities. Because the ruling class controls the society's means of production, the superstructure of society, including its ideology, will be determined according to what is in the ruling class's best interests. Therefore the ideology of a society is of enormous importance since it confuses the alienated groups and can create "false consciousness" such as commodity fetishism (perceiving labour as "capital" which Marx saw as a degradation of human life).

Another key term from Marx is the notion of *the mode of production*. This is a specific combination of productive forces (including human labour power, tools, equipment, buildings and technologies, materials, and improved land) on the one hand, and on the other the social and technical relations of production (including the property, power and control and relations governing society's productive assets and relations between people and the objects of their work, and the relations between social classes). According to Marx, the capitalist mode of production establishes the conditions that enable the bourgeoisie to exploit the proletariat due to the fact that the worker's labour power generates an added value greater than the worker's salary. According to Marx, in capitalist societies, class relations shape the individual. In other words, people's capacities, needs and interests are seen to be determined by the mode of production that characterizes the society they inhabit.

"Marxism" refers to the philosophy and social theory based on Karl Marx's work on one hand, and to the political practice based on Marxist theory on the other hand. There have been many different strands of Marxism linked to other writers and politicians: "Leninism" (belief in the necessity of a violent overthrow of capitalism through communist revolution); "Stalinism" (a necessary dictatorship of the proletariat as the first stage of moving towards communism); "Trotskyism" (declaring the need for an international "permanent revolution"); "Maoism" (a version of Leninism with "permission" given to markets including speculation to operate by the Party which retained final control); and the broader terms "Communism," or "Socialism" advocating either centralized state ownership of the means of production or collective/co-operative ownership of the means of production, depending on the stage of the revolution. Although there are still many Marxist revolutionary social movements and political parties around the world, since the collapse of the Soviet Union and its satellite states, very few countries have governments which describe themselves as Marxist. Even though socialistic parties are in power in some Western nations, they long ago distanced themselves from their direct link to Marx and his ideas.

*The Communist Manifesto*

## The Speed Read

Having to work for a living is a drag. You'll never earn the money needed to stop the daily grind because if you could there wouldn't be so many rich parasites relying on you to finance their luxury lifestyles.

## *Anarchism and Other Essays,* 1927

### Emma Goldman

*"Destruction and violence! How is the ordinary man to know that the most violent element in society is ignorance; that its power of destruction is the very thing Anarchism is combating? Nor is he aware that Anarchism, whose roots, as it were, are part of nature's forces, destroys, not healthful tissue, but parasitic growths that feed on the life's essence of society. It is merely clearing the soil from weeds and sagebrush, that it may eventually bear healthy fruit."*

Emma Goldman was born in 1869 in a Jewish ghetto in Russia where her family ran a small inn. At fifteen her father tried to marry her off but she refused. It was eventually agreed that the rebellious child should go to America with a half sister to join another sister in Rochester, New York. Goldman quickly realized that for a Jewish immigrant, America was not the promised land of opportunity. America, for Goldman meant slums and sweatshops where she earned her living as a seamstress.

What initially drew Goldman to anarchism was the outcry that followed the Haymarket Square tragedy in 1886 in Chicago. Because of the poor conditions in the workplace the workers held a protest rally calling for an eight-hour day. A bomb was thrown into a crowd of police during the rally and four anarchists were eventually hanged. Convicted on the flimsiest evidence; the judge at the trial openly declared: "Not because you caused the Haymarket bomb, but because you are Anarchists, you are on trial." Emma Goldman had followed the event intensely and on the day of the hanging she decided to become a revolutionary and turned her mind to anarchism. By this time Goldman was twenty and had been married for ten months to a Russian immigrant. The marriage had not worked out so she divorced him and moved to New York.

It was while she was in New York that she befriended Johann Most, the editor of a German-language anarchist paper. Because of her keen interest and analytical intelligence, he quickly decided to make Goldman his protégé and sent her on a tour to speak to workers. Johann Most instructed Goldman to condemn the inadequacy of a campaign for the eight-hour day. Rather he argued that we must demand the complete overthrow of capitalism. Campaigns for the eight-hour day were merely a diversion. Goldman duly conveyed this message at her public meetings. However, in Buffalo, she was challenged by an old worker who asked what men of his age were to do? They were unlikely to see the ultimate overthrow of the entire capitalist system. Should they also forgo the release of perhaps two hours a day from the hated work?

This encounter affected Goldman and she took the old worker's question on board. Goldman realized that specific efforts for improvement such as higher wages and shorter hours, far from being a diversion were part of the revolutionary transformation of society. From this point on she began to distance herself from Most and became more interested in a rival German anarchist journal *Die*

*Autonomie*. It was in *Die Autonomie* that she first read the writings of Peter Kropotkin. She sought to balance the inclination of human beings towards the socialism and mutual aid which Peter Kropotkin stressed with her own strong belief in the freedom of the individual. This belief in personal freedom is highlighted by an anecdote where Goldman was taken aside at a dance by a young revolutionary who told her one did not become an agitator to dance. Goldman wrote "I insisted that our cause could not expect me to behave as a nun and that the movement should not be turned into a cloister. If it meant that, I did not want it. I want freedom, the right to self-expression, everybody's right to beautiful, radiant things."

In these early days Goldman supported the idea of propaganda by deed. In 1892, together with Alexander Berkman she planned the assassination of Henry Clay Finch, who had suppressed strikes in the Homestead Pennsylvania factory with armed guards. They believed that by killing a tyrant, a representative of a cruel system, the consciousness of the people would be aroused. This was not to happen. Berkman only managed to injure Finch and was sentenced to twenty-two years in prison. Goldman tried to explain and justify the attempted assassination, insisting that true morality deals with the motives not the consequences. Her defence of Berkman made Goldman a marked woman and the authorities regularly disrupted her lectures. In 1893 she was arrested for allegedly urging the unemployed to take bread "by force" and was given a year in Blackwell's Island penitentiary.

She was imprisoned a second time for distributing birth control literature, but her longest sentence resulted from her involvement in setting up "No Conscription" leagues and organizing rallies against the first world war. Goldman and Berkman were arrested in 1917 for conspiring to obstruct the draft and sentenced to two years in jail. Afterwards they were stripped of their citizenship and deported along with other undesirable "Reds" to Russia. J. Edgar Hoover, who directed her deportation hearing, called her "one of the most dangerous women in America."

In 1919, as Goldman and Berkman travelled through Russia, they were horrified by the increased bureaucracy, political persecution and forced labour they found. The breaking point came in 1921 when the Kronstadt sailors and soldiers rebelled against the Bolsheviks and sided with the workers on strike. They were attacked and crushed by Trotsky and the Red Army. On leaving Russia in December 1921, Goldman set down her findings on Russia in two essays contained in *Anarchism and Other Essays* – "My Disillusionment in Russia" and "My Further Disillusionment in Russia." In these writings, she argued that never before in all history had authority, government and the state, proved so inherently static, reactionary, and even counter-revolutionary. In short, what was happening in Russia was to her the very antithesis of revolution.

Her time in Russia led her to reassess her earlier belief that the end justifies the means. Goldman accepted that violence was a necessary evil in the process of social transformation. However, her experience in Russia forced a distinction. She wrote in *On Anarchism*, "I know that in the past every great political and social change, necessitated violence ... Yet it is one thing to employ violence in combat as a means of defence. It is quite another thing to make a principle of terrorism, to institutionalize it, to assign it the most vital place in the social struggle. Such terrorism begets counter-revolution and in turn itself becomes counter-revolutionary."

These views were unpopular among radicals who still wanted to believe that the Russian Revolution was a success. When Goldman moved to Britain in 1921 she was virtually alone on the left in condemning the Bolsheviks and her lectures were poorly attended. On hearing that she might be deported in 1925, a Welsh miner offered to marry her in order to give her British nationality. With a British passport, she was then able to travel to France and Canada. In 1934, she was even allowed to give a lecture tour in the States. At the age of sixty-seven, Goldman went to Spain to join the anarchists' struggle in the Spanish Civil War. She told a rally of libertarian youth "Your Revolution will destroy forever [the notion] that anarchism stands for chaos." However she refused to condemn the anarchists for joining the government and accepting militarization as she felt the alternative at the time was communist dictatorship.

Emma Goldman died in America in 1940. She left behind her a number of important contributions to anarchist thought. In particular she is remembered for incorporating into anarchism the area of sexual politics that had only been hinted at by earlier writers. Goldman campaigned and went to prison for the right of women to practise birth control. She argued that a political solution was not enough to get rid of the unequal and repressive relations between the sexes. There had to be massive transformation of values and most importantly in women themselves. In the essay "On Women's Suffrage" in *On Anarchism* she argued that women could do this first, by asserting themselves as a personality and not as a sex commodity.

She also urged women to refuse anyone the right over their bodies and not to have children if they didn't want to. And she suggested that women should refuse to be a servant to God, the state, society, husband or anything else. According to Goldman, this could be done by making their lives simpler allowing their thoughts to become deeper and richer, by trying to learn the meaning and substance of life in all its complexities while freeing themselves from fear of public opinion and public condemnation. "Only anarchist revolution and not the ballot, will set woman free, will make her a force hitherto unknown in the World, a force of divine fire, of giving a creation of free men and women."

*Anarchism and Other Essays*

## The Speed Read

Anarchism urges man to think, to investigate, to analyse every proposition. Anarchism is the philosophy of a new social order based on liberty unrestricted by man-made law. All forms of government rest on violence, and are therefore wrong and harmful, as well as unnecessary.

The new social order rests, necessarily, on the materialistic basis of life. However, while all anarchists agree that the main evil today is an economic one, most maintain that the solution of that evil can be brought about only through the consideration of every phase of life – individual, as well as the collective; the internal, as well as the external phases.

## *Being and Nothingness: An Essay on Phenomenological Ontology,* 1943

Jean-Paul Sartre

*"Existence precedes and rules essence."*

Being and Nothingness: An Essay on Phenomenological Ontology (sometimes published with the alternative subtitle *A Phenomenological Essay on Ontology*) is a 1943 treatise by Jean-Paul Sartre that is regarded as a seminal moment in the growth of existentialism. The main purpose of *Being and Nothingness* was to define consciousness as transcendent.

Existentialism was highly regarded in the post-war period, especially among radicals and students, and at this time Sartre was a revered figure. It is probably fair to say that Sartre is now taken less seriously than he was fifty years ago, and existentialism in general is seen as something that was more fashionable than meaningful. However, Sartre's work still has plenty to offer.

*Being and Nothingness* is often said to have been influenced by Martin Heidegger's *Being and Time*. However Sartre was profoundly sceptical of any measure by which humanity could achieve a personal state of fulfilment comparable to the hypothetical Heideggerian re-encounter with "Being." Sartre's account in *Being and Nothingness* is much darker. He sees man as a creature haunted by a vision of "completion," what Sartre calls the *ens causa sui* (literally "a being who is the cause of his, her or its own being") that religions identify as God. For Sartre one is born into the material reality of one's body in an all too material universe. It is here that one finds oneself inserted in being (with a lower case "b"). But consciousness is in a state of cohabitation with its material body; it is no "thing" existing independently by itself. Consciousness can imagine that which is not (for instance it can imagine the future).

In the Introduction, Sartre rejects the "dualism of appearance and essence." For inanimate objects, the essence of an existent is the manifest law that presides over the succession of its appearances. The concept of "being" occupies a much more prominent position in *Being and Nothingness* than the concept of "existence."

Sartre uses the term "being" predominantly in the distinctive sense of "what grounds" something (for instance, "the being of consciousness"). He divides the concept of being into two regions: "being-in-itself" and "being-for-itself." This division is Hegelian in its origin, but unlike Hegel, Sartre thinks that the chasm is unbridgeable. He avoids the traditional

Cartesian duality of subject and object by regarding man as a concrete totality in the sense of "being-in-the-world."

Sartre claims "It is evident that non-being always appears within the limits of a human expectation." For Sartre, when we go about the world, we have expectations that are often not fulfilled. Pierre is not at the cafe where we thought we would meet him, so there is a *negation*, a void, a "nothingness," in the place of Pierre. This nothingness is experienced through human expectation. "The look" is another theory Sartre introduces. The mere appearance of another person causes one to look at him/herself as an object, and see his/her world as it appears to the other. This is not done from a specific location outside oneself. It is a recognition of the subjectivity in others. Sartre describes being alone in a park: at this time all relations in the park (e.g., the bench is between two trees) are available, accessible, and occurring for him. When another person arrives in the park, there is now a relation between that person and the bench, and this is not entirely available to him. The relation is presented as an object (e.g., man glances at watch), but is really not an object – it cannot be known. It *flees from him*. The other person is a "drainhole" in the world, they disintegrate the relations of which Sartre was earlier the absolute centre. For Sartre, "the look," is also the basis for sexual desire; Sartre declares that there isn't a biological motivation for sex. Instead, "double reciprocal incarnation," is a form of mutual awareness that Sartre takes to be at the heart of the sexual experience. This involves the mutual recognition of subjectivity of some sort, as Sartre describes: "I make myself flesh in order to impel the Other to realize for herself and for me her own flesh. My caress causes my flesh to be born for me insofar as it is for the Other flesh causing her to be born as flesh."

Sartre also discusses the notion of *bad faith*. Bad faith is a condition entered into when individuals negate their true nature in an attempt to become a self they are not. "Bad faith" is pretending to be something that you are not. The classic example is Sartre's waiter who is always just slightly too friendly, too helpful, too willing to play the part of a waiter rather than being the less friendly, less helpful and less waiter-like self he would be if he were not assuming the identity of "waiter." In assuming the role of "waiter," Sartre's character has negated himself by denying his authentic ego with all its characteristics not appropriate for a waiter. An extreme example of this would happen when you see a mannequin that you confuse for a real person for a moment.

Sartre believes that human existence is a conundrum whereby each of us remains, as long as we live, within a circuit of *nothingness*, in other words, the state of free consciousness. However, in also *being*, we are compelled to choice and therefore anguish, because choice represents a limit on the unbridled scope of our thoughts. What we can *be* is limited. We then flee this anguish through action-oriented constructs to enact visualizations or dreams of necessity, destiny, determinism, etc. We must *be*, because we are more than thinkers, we are also *actors* who must do what we must do to become what we are. We choose what to be but, for Sartre, these choices merely represent failed escape attempts from the anguish of intellectual freedom. Sartre describes these choices as *failed dreams of completion*, because they inevitably fail to bridge the dichotomy between thought and action, between *being* and *nothingness* inherent in our *self*. This is where Sartre is expressing the heart of what has commonly been understood by existentialism.

Sartre argues that *being* pales before *nothingness*. This is because consciousness is more spontaneous than stable seriousness. A *man of seriousness* must continuously struggle between the conscious desire for peaceful self-enclosure through physical constraint and social roles. This is like living within a portrait that one paints of oneself. Sartre therefore, contends that consciousness does not make sense by itself: it arises by the awareness of objects. So *consciousness of* is the proper way to qualify consciousness. One is always aware of *an object*, whether this is *something* or *someone*.

---

*Being and Nothingness:*
*An Essay on Phenomenological Ontology*

## The Speed Read

You are nothing. You are nothing, and if you are trying to be something, you are no more than a pretentious actor. You will feel this more when other people doubt the being that you are trying to be.

---

## *The Revolution of Everyday Life,* 1967

### Raoul Vaneigem

*"Suffering is the sickness of constraints. An atom of pure delight, no matter how small, will hold suffering at bay. To work on the side of delight and authentic festivity can hardly be distinguished from preparing for a general insurrection."*

The history of the first Situationist International (the small intellectual grouping that espoused *situationism* from 1957 to 1972) is so tangled and murky that it is first necessary to explain why we have chosen this title rather than the better known book, *The Society of the Spectacle* by Guy Debord.

Debord and Vaneigem were two of the major figures of the situationist movement, and Debord in particular was known for being something of a control freak, often falling out with his comrades and excommunicating them. Vaneigem eventually left the SI in 1970. He actually resigned, although Debord subsequently denounced him and his ideas.

Debord's book is probably the clearest and simplest explanation of situationist ideas. But it is rather dull and stodgy, as he attempts to lay out a coherent, rather sub-Marxist theory of society. By contrast, Vaneigem is an enormously engaging writer, full of spirit and extravagance, and often extremely funny. And situationism in general is better remembered or celebrated as an intelligent but humorously subversive strand of thought. As a result we would suggest that the very readable *The Revolution of Everyday Life* is a better (or at least more entertaining) place to start.

So what is situationism?

Well, to give a flavour of how difficult it is to pin situationism down, the journal of the SI says that "there is no such thing as situationism, which would mean a doctrine of interpretation of existing facts. The notion of situationism is obviously devised by antisituationists." In spite of this rather doctrinal view, it seems fair to describe situationism as consisting of the theories that were put forward by the most prominent situationist theorists, including Debord and Vaneigem.

The first thing to say here is that elements of the basic situationist analysis draw on both Marxism and anarchism as well as on George Bataille's visions of excess. Situationism depicts a society in which we have too much of everything and too much information and are befuddled and enslaved as a result. Essentially it is a political philosophy which emphasizes that our lack of freedom is expressed through our failure to experience authentic joy. We focus on the everyday surfaces of appearance and as a result we fail to understand the ways in which we are constrained by forces of social control.

Situationism is post-Marxist, in that it is an ideology which addressed the fact that the "masses" were not responding to their oppressed situation in the ways that the communists had predicted. Rather than rising up against capitalism, the masses were rather pleased to be sold washing machines, plastic toys and televisions. Vaneigem writes about how some have suggested that the proletariat no longer exists, "that it has disappeared under an avalanche of sound systems, colour TVs, waterbeds, two-car garages and swimming pools."

The situationists thus focused on the objects of everyday life. They also espoused various forms of direct action (or *situations*) to try to subvert the society of the spectacle. Anything from graffiti to skiving off work, being a *flaneur* (an urban wanderer) or even shoplifting or rioting could be described as an authentic situationist response to society's faults.

At times, situationism blurred the barrier between art and politics (and many of the splits in the movement centered on how this barrier should be breached). At one level, the situationists espoused the idea that any artistic gesture could be a subversive gesture (and that a non-revolutionary artistic gesture was a worthless one). In this they saw themselves as successors to the surrealists and dadaists, although it would be fairer to say that they believed that their idea of art as subversion should supersede previous notions of art. Vaneigem is particularly entertaining in describing the ways that artistic situations or festivities help to counter the boredom and suffering that we suffer in modern society – writing, for instance that "the eruption of lived pleasure is such that in losing myself I find myself; forgetting that I exist, I realize myself." He sees spontaneity, bacchanal, celebration and other forms of pure improvised joy as an essential part of the individual's attempt to find an authentic response to life.

To give an example of the way that Vaneigem can shift from a slightly warped humour into political exhortation, there is one passage in which he describes society as a state in which many people are crushed beneath a giant wardrobe, struggling to get free. He describes thinkers who either refuse to believe in the wardrobe, or who add to the weight of the wardrobe by explaining why the wardrobe is objectively inevitable, continuing "And the whole Christian spirit is there, fondling suffering like a good dog and handing out photographs of crushed but smiling people. 'The rationality of the wardrobe is always the best,' proclaim the thousands of books every day to be stacked in the wardrobe. And all the while everyone wants to breathe and no one can breathe . . . It is now or never."

There is also an obvious echo of Nietzsche in this passage (and elsewhere in Vaneigem's writing), in the way that he presents Christianity as a fetishization of passivity, and of the Christian church as purveyors of *ressentiment* to the masses. This is another strand in Vaneigem's thought. He always seeks to challenge the passivity that leads us to accept various forms of social control, from the law and religion through to the ways in which the media and advertisers seek to shape our perceptions of the world. For Vaneigem, the individual must always strive to find authentic joy in opposition to these forms of social control.

The situationists are often reputed to have been influential in the May 1968 uprising in France. It is true that situationist slogans such as "I take my desires for reality because I believe in the reality of my desires" (as well as others drawn directly from the work of Debord and Vaneigem) were scrawled as graffiti on walls in Paris during this period. But it is also fair to point out that the situationists were few in number and not especially influential, so they were fairly tangential figures in the uprising.

There are also claims that punk music was partly

inspired by situationism. There is perhaps an element of truth in this as several of the early figures in the UK punk movement were at least interested in situationism, although the influence was probably more notable on record sleeve design and in the slogans that were used, than on the music in general.

*The Revolution of Everyday Life* is still a very relevant book. The revolutionary fervour of the 1960s may have passed, but in many ways we live in the same kind of society. We have more and more passive entertainment, apparent wealth, plastic trinkets from around the world, and increasing social control (both at a government and localized level). Vaneigem's fervent declarations that we must search for creative ways to reassert authenticity give us an interesting glimpse of the intellectual environment of the 1950s and 1960s but this book can also still strike a real chord for many readers today.

## *The Revolution of Everyday Life*

# The Speed Read

Our increasingly trivial everyday lives preoccupy our minds. But behind this we are humiliated, isolated, and suffering. Today, the thinkers of tomorrow are on the streets, organizing situations that create authentic joy, to combat the crushing social control of work, religion, and organized thought. "We have a world of pleasures to win and nothing to lose but our boredom."

# *Practical Ethics,* 1979

## Peter Singer

*"In the world as it is now, I can see no escape from the conclusion that each one of us with wealth surplus to his or her essential needs should be giving most of it to help people suffering from poverty so dire as to be life-threatening. That's right: I'm saying that you shouldn't buy that new car, take that cruise, redecorate the house or get that pricey new suit. After all, a $1,000 suit could save five children's lives."*

Peter Singer is one of the most interesting and controversial philosophers to write about ethics in recent years. He is best known for his writing on ethics with regard to other species, in which he has espoused the view that it not logically consistent or morally correct to claim that humans have certain rights (such as the right to life) yet to deny those rights to animals. His work on this subject was a strong influence on the movement for animal rights (or "animal liberation"). He is also well known for his challenging views on subjects such as abortion, euthanasia, and how we should deal with world poverty.

Perhaps because he tackles such difficult subjects head on, his views are often represented (and criticized) in their most simplified form. Inevitably, given the space we have available, we can't convey every nuance of his arguments here, but the first thing to note is that Singer is a scrupulous debater who provides meticulous back-up arguments for his views. For those who are interested in what he has to say, the most complete statement of his views comes in his 1979 book *Practical Ethics*.

Singer's moral philosophy is based in a form of utilitarianism (the philosophy expounded a century or more earlier by John Stuart Mill, Jeremy Bentham and others), in which the moral value of an action must be based on its consequences.

Singer has also claimed that many of his conclusions could be based on a much simpler moral principle such as the idea that if an action that causes me mild discomfort can prevent real suffering in others then it is the morally correct thing to do. However, it must be said that at heart this is just a simplified utilitarian principle, as it is based on consequences rather than on the idea that actions can be innately more or less moral.

Singer takes Kant's categorical imperative (or Jesus's golden rule) to mean that we can't judge morality alone on our own self-interest, but that we must give equal weight to the interests of others. So he starts with the assertion that ethics must be based on an equal consideration of interests. He then looks closely at whether or not we should restrict whose interests we consider to the human race, and also whether or not we should accord every human being the same rights. Singer argues that there is no such thing as the right to life *per se*. He claims that in so far as we should recognize the right to life we should do so on the basis that human beings are *persons,* that is to say having self-awareness. Because some animals are self-conscious and rational, Singer also argues that it is *speciesism* to deny them the same kinds of rights we accord to rational self-aware humans.

Singer thus concludes that, for instance, it is worse to kill an adult chimpanzee than it is to kill a human fetus. In particular he argues that until a fetus is developed enough to feel pain, killing it is a morally neutral act – that is to say the moral argument should be decided on other grounds such as the interests of the parents and others. He also controversially extends his argument to euthanasia and to killing human infants. Because he regards a human infant under the age of one month as lacking self-awareness, he regards killing such a child as on the same moral level as killing an animal that lacks self-awareness. He argues that in, for instance, cases of extreme disability it may thus be morally acceptable to kill a child at this age.

Singer would argue (and many would accept) that rather than trying to downgrade human rights, he aimed to elevate the rights of animals by taking this approach. It is certainly true that much of his writing is effective in demolishing arguments that claim it is morally correct to have an absolute chasm between humans and animals in our ethics. However his conclusions have been widely attacked by campaigners against abortion and euthanasia and Singer added a chapter to his book after he came under heavy attack in Germany in particular for his views on euthanasia. It does seem dangerous to accept Singer's proposal that we regard some humans as persons and some as non-persons, if only because it raises the worrying spectre of scientists and politicians pronouncing on who may live or die.

On the other hand, we are currently in the middle of an ongoing debate about the use of stem-cells in which a dogmatic refusal to allow stem-cell research using cells derived from fetuses that would otherwise be destroyed anyway is putting future scientific progress, and perhaps future lives, at risk. Singer's views (and some of his conclusions) may seem obnoxious on a first viewing, but it is at least giving careful consideration to his determination to draw realistic lines about who we should treat as a person, with unalienable rights.

Another area in which Singer has made interesting arguments is on the subject of world poverty and charity. Singer argues that failing to donate money to charity can in a sense be as morally culpable as intentionally allowing a child in the third world to die of starvation or illness. Because if one is rationally aware of the fact that the $100 one didn't donate could have saved that life, it is immoral not to donate that money. Singer does live by his own edicts in this case as he donates 20 per cent of his own income to charity, although he doesn't take this to the extreme Franciscan position of renouncing all possessions.

There are many possible ways of opposing Singer's arguments. The most fundamental worry about his ethical system is the old question of whether or not utilitarianism can really make sense of moral decisions. There are various specific problems that throw up logical paradoxes in utilitarianism. For instance if all moral decisions are to be based on a balance of pleasure and pain, would it be a better world if there were ten times as many people, each one half as happy? Can morality really be reduced to this kind of calculus? And in any case shouldn't morality be based on an assessment of whether an action is right or wrong *in itself*?

Utilitarianism seems to allow a cold-hearted rationalization of morally degrading acts. For instance if the interests of the many outweigh those of the few, Singer's own arguments would support painful animal experimentation that was certain to avoid a great deal of suffering. Even worse it would seem to support such experimentation on infant babies. And one can also use versions of utilitarian arguments to justify torture or genocide. If we are to judge acts morally, would it not be better to accept that sometimes we must choose between two wrongs, rather than simply declaring that the act that causes less suffering is morally justifiable? Singer does deal with these kinds of counter-arguments in his work, in a logical and clear way, but not all readers will be convinced that he has answered the basic flaws in utilitarian thinking.

One more avenue of attack comes from Singer's thinking on world poverty and immigration. As well as the argument given above about charity, Singer argues that rich countries have a moral responsibility to accept far higher levels of refugees, up until the point where it is clear that to accept more immigrants would cause more harm than good. Both arguments are based on a single case analysis – on the analysis that to give this money may save a life, to accept this refugee will increase the balance of happiness in the world. But it can be argued that the net result of many single cases would be to make the world a worse place – huge flows of refugees might well lower the standard of living in rich countries while allowing poor countries more room to continue expanding their populations. And over-reliance on charity in the third world can cause dependency and corruption, meaning that giving to charity is a more complex decision than Singer suggests. These are complicated arguments of course, but to only consider the single case of one donation, one refugee at a time seems to overlook the wider moral and practical dimension that such decisions hold. Singer makes a good and worthy case that we should all give more to charity, but it is not clear that the logical foundation of the argument is as sound as it should be. (It should also be mentioned that Singer has written interestingly on meta-ethics, which is the whole subject of how one should choose one ethical framework, such as utilitarianism, over others.)

For all that it is possible to find ways to criticize Singer, it is easy to recommend his books to an interested reader. He gives a clear account of his own arguments, in a way that is thought-provoking and a valuable contribution to the kinds of important debates that moral philosophers have not always been brave enough to get involved in.

## Practical Ethics

# The Speed Read

Ethics should be grounded in an equal consideration of interests, wherever those interests may lie. There is nothing sacred about life per se, so we must make moral decisions about whether or not it is right to take a life, based on the consequences. It is speciesist to exclude animals from this consideration. It can be morally less acceptable to kill an adult animal than it is to kill a non-rational human lacking in self-awareness. Euthanasia or abortion can be morally neutral acts (depending on various factors) – in these cases we must judge their morality on other grounds.

# *Gaia: A New Look at Life on Earth,* 1979

## James Lovelock

*". . . the quest for Gaia is an attempt to find the largest living creature on Earth."*

The Gaia theory is primarily a scientific hypothesis, but it is one that has serious philosophical implications. James Lovelock is a scientist and inventor who worked for NASA in the 1960s. He was involved in a project that involved trying to assess the atmosphere of Mars. It was from a comparison of the atmospheres and other aspects of lifeless planets with the ecosystem of Earth that the Gaia theory originated.

The theory basically states that the Earth as a whole is a complex entity, constituting a feedback or cybernetic system which "seeks" an optimal physical and chemical environment for life to exist on the planet. This is a system which operates through the biosphere, atmosphere and through the chemical and physical constitution of the oceans and the soil. So according to the Gaia theory, the biomass self-regulates conditions on the planet such as the temperature and chemistry to make the planet more hospitable for the various species that constitute life on Earth. Specific examples of the way we might observe this in action would include the fact that, over time, the temperature and chemical constitution of the atmosphere have been relatively stable. This is in spite of the fact that the sun's heat has increased over millennia by 25 per cent or so. Another example is the long-term stability of the level of salinity of the oceans in spite of good reasons why we might expect the oceans to become more saline over time.

The theory was propagated and modified from the early 1970s onwards by Lovelock and the microbiologist Lynn Margulis, and given its most complete statement by Lovelock in his book *Gaia: A New Look At Life On Earth* in 1979. There was much early criticism of the theory on two grounds. Firstly, Lovelock's language was sometimes misinterpreted as a mystical assertion that the planet was alive or conscious, and this was unfortunately an interpretation that was taken up enthusiastically by New Age devotees. Secondly, Lovelock was criticized for giving a teleological argument – a belief that any effect must derive from an intentional cause. Lovelock later clarified that he hadn't intended to say that Gaia was consciously or intentionally seeking to create the conditions for life – simply that it acted as a whole in such a way that this was the observable outcome. (In this respect he was describing the biosphere as being in a state of *homeostasis* – a self-regulating equilibrium with no need for conscious control.)

Darwinists have also often criticized Gaia on the basis that the process by which the processes of the biosphere are supposed to have evolved is unclear. Darwinists can explain equilibria or changes in species on the basis of natural selection, but it is hard to see how such a concept could explain the development of a planetary system. The well known scientific writer Richard Dawkins has for instance said that there is "no way for evolution by natural selection to lead to altruism on a global scale."

So within the scientific community there is no agreement on the value of the Gaia hypothesis. Environmentalists and ecologists tend to accept that there is some basic truth in the theory, but agreement is far from universal even there.

The importance of the Gaia theory in the context of this book is that it introduces a different element into the philosophical arena. Most of the other "isms" we are considering in this section look exclusively at human society. At least since the idea of the "Leviathan" was put forward by Hobbes, philosophers have often talked of human society as a kind of closed system, regulated by a mass of individual actions that add up to a unified whole. But it has been less common for philosophers to extend their sphere of interest beyond the human world.

Over the past century it has become ever clearer that humans do not exist in an isolated bubble. Our actions have real and lasting consequences on the environment of this planet. Whether or not we agree with the theory that human actions are causing global warming, it is hard to deny that the destruction of rainforests, damming of rivers, mining of mountains and slow depletion of natural energy reserves are having a lasting impact on the planet we inhabit.

The Gaia theory is one approach that forces us to take a broader view. There have been other seminal environmental works, such as Rachel Carson's *Silent Spring*. And Gaia is more of a scientific theory than an environmental tract. But the approach that it takes points us towards a framework for conceiving of human existence in a different way. Rather than limiting our thinking to human society, it is often important that we take a global view, seeing human society as merely one element among others in the biosphere. Progress towards sustainable living, recycling and less wasteful ways of using our environment are all a part of this way of thinking. And it seems likely that this century will see the need for a great deal more thought of this sort, as the remaining reserves of oil and natural gas gradually start to run out.

The strongest version of the Gaia theory, which sees the Earth as a conscious being, is scientifically unsustainable. But as a metaphor it has been a powerful image, and this is another way in which the Gaia theory has affected modern thought.

Recently Lovelock has argued (against the larger part of the environmentalist movement) that more nuclear power is needed to reduce our contribution to global warming. He has also warned that we may be closer than we imagine to a tipping point beyond which the biosphere will be unable to regulate itself. In his latest book *The Revenge of Gaia* he presents a rather dystopian view of mankind's future, describing us as a fever in the biosphere that is gradually causing sickness in the planet, a sickness that will only be cured after drastic changes, which will probably reduce our numbers by a massive degree. Whether or not his most pessimistic predictions come to pass, the environmental challenge is clearly one that we will all need to be conscious of over coming years.

*Gaia: A New Look at Life on Earth*

# The Speed Read

The planet is a self-regulating biosphere (called Gaia) that aims to maximize the hospitality of conditions for life on Earth. This homeostasis operates through chemical and physical control mechanisms rather than through any conscious or intentional actions. The human race is doing its best to break the system and is close to succeeding.

## *The Beauty Myth*, 1991

### Naomi Wolf

*"The more legal and material hindrances women have broken through, the more strictly and heavily and cruelly images of female beauty have come to weigh upon us . . . During the past decade, women breached the power structure; meanwhile, eating disorders rose exponentially and cosmetic surgery became the fastest-growing speciality . . ."*

In *The Beauty Myth*, Naomi Wolf examines how beauty is used as a demand and as a judgment upon women. Subtitled *How Images of Beauty Are Used Against Women*, Wolf examines how modern conceptions of women's beauty impact on the spheres of employment, culture, religion, sexuality, eating disorders, and cosmetic surgery. Her basic thesis is that there is a relationship between female liberation and female beauty.

Wolf believes that women in Western culture are damaged by the pressure to conform to an idealized concept of female beauty. She argues that the beauty myth is political, a way of maintaining the patriarchal system. The beauty myth replaced the feminine mystique, which relegated women to the position of housewife, as the social guard over women. There are countless women who believe their thighs are too big, their breasts are too small, that their hair is boring, their skin is flawed, their body has a funny shape, or their clothes are outdated. Many women believe their life would improve if they could lose 15 pounds; if they got a nose job, a face lift, a tummy tuck, and so on. Many also feel shame or unhappiness when they ponder some part (or all) of their body. Wolf demonstrates how our culture cultivates the stereotypes of women as sex objects and men as success objects, to the detriment of all of us.

Wolf's research attempts to show that there is a cultural backlash against feminism that uses images of female beauty to keep women "in their place." This is demonstrated by pointing out how many people have succumbed to the idea of the ugly feminist activist who is only a feminist because she's too undesirable to get a man. That popular meme first showed up on the scene to describe suffragettes lobbying for the vote. Wolf shows that, throughout the years, there have been forces in culture that attempt to punish women who seek more control over their lives and their environment.

According to Wolf, The Beauty Myth is the most dangerous of a long line of "lies" concerning the "rules" of feminine attributes and behaviour. This is because it has succeeded in affecting women's internal sense of themselves. It has created a standard of femininity that is impossible to attain for most women, and women are reacting with increasingly obsessive behaviour in their attempts to measure up. Instead of expending their energy towards further positive goals for themselves, that energy is instead turned inwards leading to feelings of guilt, shame, and unhappiness.

Wolf traces these "lies" through history by pointing out that a century ago, any female political activity was classified as ugly and sick. If a woman read too much, her uterus would "atrophy." Women were simply seen as walking wombs, and anything they did to expand their usefulness in the world was attacked as a threat to this "reality," often leading to them being labelled as "sick." The idea that women could have had more to offer society beyond the children they bore was not conceivable or allowed. It should be noted here that Wolf seems to have forgotten the role of women writers from the nineteenth century and earlier who furthered the world of literature by commenting on the world they lived in, if only fictionally.

The advent of the two world wars changed the rules. It now became important to society for women to leave their homes and work for the war effort. For the sake of the economy the role of women had to change. Advertising in women's magazines jumped on the bandwagon. After each war, the propaganda in women's magazines took a different turn in emphasis. Forces in culture were concerned about finding work for the returning soldiers and fueling the consumer economy. It was important to put pressure on working women to get them back into their homes again, buying household products.

For Wolf, the ramifications of this post-war social propaganda were reflected in the television shows of the day: *Ozzie and Harriet*, *Leave it to Beaver*, *Make Room for Daddy*, *The Donna Reed Show*, and *Father Knows Best*, for example, show images of the happy housewife, who didn't seem to do anything but waltz around her beautiful home in her pretty dress, immaculately made up, looking after her family. We rarely saw her visiting with friends, we never saw her involved in school, civic or other cultural activities. She was blissfully serene in her safe, clean suburban bungalow full of modern appliances.

Still delving into history for examples, Wolf states that during the 1960s, the second wave of feminism began to make itself felt. New avenues for women outside the home emerged, and women left in droves, to go to university and carve out their own careers. However, it was in 1969, according to Wolf, that *Vogue* magazine made the break-through that has evolved into the cast-iron Beauty Myth of today. Through such magazines, we are bombarded today with images of the "perfect" woman. She may be a gor-geous blonde, or a sultry brunette. There are also beautiful redheads and exotic women of colour. The ideal is that she is tall and willowy, weighing at least 20 per cent less than her height requires, rarely looking older than twenty-five. She must have no visible flaws on her skin, and her hair and clothes are always immaculate. Wolf sees these ideal forms as a "lie" precisely because if we look back in history at images of women from fifteenth century paintings to photographs of film stars from the forties and fifties the precise dimen-sions of what is considered beautiful in a woman change.

Although most obviously fuelled by advertisers, Wolf states that there are political and economic forces that act to maintain this standard. In the workplace, a woman has no clear legal recourse if she feels that her beauty, or lack of it, is being used against her: in one 1986 case, cited by Wolf, a woman lost a sexual harassment claim because she dressed "too beautifully." In another, a woman was denied partnership in a top-ten accounting firm "because she needed to learn to walk, talk and dress more femininely." In another case, the judge ruled that the woman rightfully lost her job because it was "inappropriate for a supervisor of women to dress like a woman." Over and over, Wolf sup-plies precedents in law in which the woman is judged to be too beautiful, too ugly, too old, too fat, dressed too well, not dressed well enough. In other words, for Wolf, it seems to be legal that a woman could be hired or fired generally on the basis of her physical appearance. She does however, tend to gloss over the fact that many women today do enjoy successful careers and lives even if they don't look like *Vogue* models.

*The Beauty Myth*

# The Speed Read

Our culture judges women, and women judge themselves, against an impossible standard of the "ideal woman." Wolf calls this "beauty pornography." Magazines are full of pictures of underweight models that are usually between fifteen and twenty years old. We rarely see a picture of a woman who is not wearing make-up applied by an artist, hair professionally coiffed, clothes professionally designed or "styled." All flaws or wrinkles in her skin are airbrushed out. This is a form of social engineering to keep women competing with each other inside and outside of the workplace. It has been going on for years but the new availability of cosmetic surgery makes women turn inward to self-hatred and disgust if they cannot afford or achieve the look that is presented as standard. If you are not tall, thin, beautiful and under twenty you have little chance of success.

# Modern Philosophy: A Sampler

## Introduction

In the first section of this book we had a quickfire tour of the Western philosophical tradition. We finished at the point where Gödel's incompleteness theorems had helped to undermine the long-cherished hope for a "total theory of the world," built from mathematical logic upwards. Meanwhile, Wittgenstein's progression from his early logical positivism to the subtlety of his later thought was an example of the way that philosophy was forced to adapt. Rather than seeking for certainty, philosophy had increasingly to be about meaning and interpretation, and in studying language and rationality, one had to allow for a degree of vagueness and development.

Modern philosophy took many different paths in the latter half of the twentieth century. Rather than attempt to explain many different strands of thought, or attempt to impose a coherent narrative, we have chosen a selection of important and interesting works that demonstrate some of the areas in which modern philosophy has operated.

We start with *Dialectic of Enlightenment* by Horkheimer and Adorno, a work which demonstrates the angst created among many intellectuals by the horrors of the Second World War. The authors take the viewpoint that rationality and the enlightenment are failing projects and are thus fearful of a new age of barbarism. While their views were conditioned by the historical period in which they were writing, it is interesting to see how the certainties of the past have been replaced by uncertainty, and the search for objectivity by an acceptance of subjectivity. Indeed Horkheimer and Adorno see the doomed attempt by pragmatists and logical positivists to dispel mystery as part of a modern malaise. They suggest instead that the progress from the age of objective reason to the age of subjective reason has left us more vulnerable to barbaric behaviour because we are taken in by new myths.

In different ways John Rawls and Ted Honderich ponder the foundations of morality. The barbarities of the twentieth century unfortunately provide rich material for the study of ethics and each of these philosophers takes a view that is partially influenced by the problems of recent history. Rawls is essentially seeking to provide a basis for a theory of justice in a modern liberal democracy, while Honderich struggles with the ethical problems raised by modern warfare and terrorism.

The books by Saul Kripke and David Lewis represent different strands in modern thought. Each takes a highly technical, analytical approach, which is typical of much contemporary academic philosophy. In each case the specific problem addressed is an interesting one: the books respectively look at what we mean when we use names and the logic of possible (alternative) worlds. In each case the full philosophical package includes some rather dry logical analysis, but each author in their own way gives an insight into the kinds of problems that modern academic philosophy deals with.

Finally, we also include *Darwin's Dangerous Idea* by Daniel Dennett and *Small Pieces, Loosely Joined,* by David Weinberger, two books that deal with specifically modern scientific problems. Dennett's book takes a broad view of the significance of Darwinism in our understanding of the universe, while also making comparisons between artificial intelligence and the human mind. Weinberger considers the impact of the internet age on our philosophy of who we are and how we fit into the world.

While Rawls, Kripke and Lewis are each taking modern approaches to old philosophical problems, the books by Dennett and Weinberger show how philosophy always has to adapt to deal with new problems, as human culture and science continue to progress. The final entry, on Ted Honderich's book *After the Terror,* ends by wondering if humanity might be heading for a new dark age of unreason. This is a possibility, but it is also possible that our understanding of rationality and morality will help us to adapt and progress towards a more enlightened future. Philosophy alone cannot change the world, but it can provide valuable mental tools and strategies for dealing with whatever the future might bring.

## *Dialectic of Enlightenment: Philosophical Fragments*, 1944

Max Horkheimer, Theodor W. Adorno

*"Myth is already enlightenment, and enlightenment reverts back to mythology."*

Horkheimer and Adorno were two of the leading thinkers of the Frankfurt School, an informal group of thinkers centred on the Institute for Social Research in Frankfurt in the period before the Second World War. It brought together writers on philosophy, and critical and social theory. Most of these writers were strongly influenced by Marxism, but

alienated by the progress of orthodox Marxism as represented by the Soviet Union and communist parties, and
were seeking to use the theories of Marx, Freud and others
to analyse the world in which they found themselves.

*Dialectic of Enlightenment* was published in 1944, at
which point the authors were in exile from the Nazis in
America. It was written during a deeply pessimistic period,
in which it seemed eminently possible that Europe, and
perhaps the world, would be overrun by totalitarian politics
of the Nazi model.

Horkheimer distinguished between objective and subjective reason, suggesting that our rationality had gradually
moved from the former to the latter. In the phase of objective
truths, we act according to absolute truths, for instance the
absolute moral certainties that are backed up by religion. But
as we come to believe that our former certainties were delusions, we move to a more relativistic state of subjective reason
wherein every truth is subjective, and we judge what is right
according to what is "reasonable" rather than "correct."

In *Dialectic of Enlightenment,* Horkheimer and Adorno
return to a form of dialectic closer to Hegel's version than
the Marxist one, in order to analyse human history. The
essential aim of the work is to try to understand why the
process of enlightenment was leading the world into a state
of greater barbarism rather than to a higher state of humanity. An essential part of this process is to study the role of
myth in human reason, and to show why the banishment
of the myths of objective reason (such as religion) merely
leaves us open to new myths.

The book is written in a fragmentary fashion, with essays
on De Sade, anti-semitism and Homer's Odyssey. It is to
the latter that they trace back their dialectic of myth and
rationality, as they see the sacrifice in the Odyssey as placing
mankind on a level with the gods, and therefore as a first
step towards subjective reason.

They also write well about the "Culture Industry" (which we might call the mass media) and the ways in which it helps to shape our perception of reality. The ways in which the Nazis were able to control the perceptions of their population through propaganda was obviously in their minds in the writing of the book, but they cover the culture industry in general as part of their analysis.

Horkheimer and Adorno suggest that the process of enlightenment, of the rejection of objective reason and the myths that supported it lead to two things. Firstly we are forced to live on the understanding everything is exactly as it appears. But secondly, the culture industry is a cog in the machinery that strives to control appearances.

Pragmatism in America and logical positivism in Europe were at this time popular philosophies, each of which claimed to be able to solve all problems by focusing on the usefulness or verifiability of truths. Both are prone to logical flaws, and can be rejected on a variety of grounds. But for Horkheimer and Adorno, the fact that they complacently expressed the viewpoint that science and reason can dispel all mystery from the world was part of the essential malaise of the enlightenment. As the old myths are replaced by a subjective world of "reasonable" beliefs, there is no emancipation for the believers. Instead, the culture industry and governments seek ways to control appearances and to convince us that the status quo is reasonable. The Nazis were able to project the idea that their government was one that would appeal to all reasonable citizens. Mussolini, rather than appealing to the "workers," appealed to the "producers" and thereby made people feel that they were part of a common group.

At the same time, these regimes demonized the "other" – the non-conformist, the Jewish population in Germany, as well as the communists, gypsies, homosexuals, and anyone who was a threat to their imposed idea of "reasonableness."

So even as the enlightenment was dispelling the old myths, new myths were being propagated to take their place. Thus was the new age of barbarism being created.

Some of the deep pessimism of this book might now seem irrelevant on first encounter. The totalitarian fascists of Europe were defeated in the Second World War, and the communist regimes of Eastern Europe eventually fell. In that respect, some of the authors' worst fears were unrealized. But in this book there is much more than an analysis of an historical moment. And much of what they wrote can be applied in different ways today.

We live in a world where the old religious certainties are making a comeback. This is partly a result of the failure of the "enlightenment" as Horkheimer and Adorno defined it and partly a result of new ways of propagating information (at least in so far as the major world religions now have significant subsections which put forward extreme versions reliant on indoctrination and stigmatization of the "other").

We also live in a world where the culture factory or mass media is as strong as ever. In a world where there is a flood of information, we nonetheless see the many ways in which information and perceptions are influenced or controlled. We also see a world where national and local myths sustain public discourse as strongly as ever.

There is some dispute as to how strongly the philosopher Leo Strauss influenced the neo-conservative strand of modern American thought. What can be said is that Strauss argued firstly that many philosophers needed to be interpreted as having both an exoteric and esoteric reading, by which he meant that the true meaning of many philosophers' writing was hidden to the general reader. He also argued that relativism (which we can equate with Horkheimer's subjective reason) led to either the nihilism of totalitarian regimes, or to the softer nihilism of liberal, hedonistic regimes.

He concluded that a "noble lie" was sometimes justified on the part of the ruling elite, and that leaders might reasonably use a myth to sustain a cohesive society, and to avoid the nihilism that relativism tends to cause.

Some neo-conservative thinkers have interpreted these ideas to mean that the best course of action for modern America is to provide the myth of permanent war against enemies of the "American way" in order to provide cohesiveness and avoid nihilism and decline in modern America. This intention has partly been acted out through interaction with the mass media.

It is unfair to single out America in identifying the ways in which the worst fears of Horkheimer and Adorno continue to be a part of the modern world. Many modern regimes are based around the whole idea of "spin," media control, and appeal to the "reasonable citizen." The fact that few of these regimes are as blatantly evil as the Nazis does not mean that the interpretation of modernity put forward in *Dialectic of Enlightenment* has been proved false. To the contrary, many of the themes of the book have a serious and depressing ongoing significance in the modern world.

*Dialectic of Enlightenment* is not an easy read. The text is dense, and it is hard to follow the structure and logic of the book in places. But it is a book that repays careful study, and that puts forward an interpretation of history and rationality that will still, to many, seem all too relevant.

*Dialectic of Enlightenment: Philosophical Fragments*

# The Speed Read

Since Homer, Western civilization has been in the slow transition from objective to subjective reason. As we leave behind the objective moral certainties of religion, we think we are leaving myth behind and living in a world where everything is as it seems. But the "culture factory" and the establishment control the appearance of what is "reasonable" and instead we move into a new age of barbarism and myth.

# *A Theory of Justice*, 1971

## John Rawls

*"The principles of justice are chosen behind a veil of ignorance."*

There have been numerous attempts in the history of philosophy to explain the concept of justice. In the general problem of the relationship between the individual and society, and how to define justice, the most significant contribution in the last century probably came in the work of the liberal political philosopher John Rawls.

Of the previous attempts to deal with this issue, it is worth briefly reminding ourselves of the two theories which had received most attention in the last few centuries. Firstly, there was the theory of the *social contract*. Writers such as Hobbes, Locke, and Jean-Jacques Rousseau had different approaches to the social contract, but the general principle was the same. Prior to society, the individual starts out in a state of absolute freedom. It is however a rational decision for individuals to group together into a society, and in doing this they must agree to give up some of their original freedoms (because members of society cannot be allowed unlimited freedom to harm others in that society). So the individual takes out an explicit or implicit contract with society, agreeing to abide by the rules of that society and to give up some freedom in return for the benefits that society can provide.

A second traditional theory, best known from the work of John Stuart Mill, was *utilitarianism*. This theory focused less on the original formation of society and more on how we were to judge what is right or just in current society. The answer given was that we must judge actions according to which actions cause the greatest happiness (or least pain) to the greatest number of people.

Both of these theories are open to significant doubts. The social contract suffers from the fact that the contract is clearly not an explicit one, and gives us little guidance on how to react to those who wish to oppose or change current laws, seeing them as unjust. While utilitarianism seems a theory that is hard to apply rigorously, as the idea of the greatest happiness or least pain are very hard to quantify in actual practice.

In his ground-breaking *A Theory of Justice*, Rawls attempted to improve on both of these theories. He chose to focus on the question of how we judge what is fair in society. Seeing that any individual member of society is liable to be prejudiced by their own interests he came up with a theoretical idea that he hoped would provide the kind of blindness to individual interests that justice seems to require.

He asked us to imagine a group of citizens inventing rules of justice from behind a "veil of ignorance." For instance a group of spirits, ghosts or unborn citizens who would in future be part of the given society, but who as yet had no idea of what level of wealth, talent or luck they would be born with. He conjectured that such a group would endeavour to base their principles of justice on a real sense of fairness.

Rawls progressed from this idea of the veil of ignorance to two specific principles that he felt should underpin any fair system. The way that he did this owed a bit to games theory, in that it involved the "blind committee" making judgments based on alternative outcomes of any given situation. Firstly he looked at the concept of liberty and suggested that any restriction of liberty that should be adopted could only be justified if it strengthened the overall liberty of the society. Secondly he looked at the question of inequality, and in particular how we should judge a change in the distribution of equality. He concluded that the blind panel would only accept an increase in inequality if it made the least advantaged member better off. So if an inequality were proposed that increased the share of all members, then it would be acceptable, but if the increase in inequality were to be to the detriment of the least advantaged members then it would be rejected.

These two principles of *liberty* and *difference* were the lynchpins of Rawls' approach to a wide variety of questions of political justice. The difference principle can for instance be used to argue that a successful, wealthy capitalist society is more just than a communist society where all have equal, lesser shares. The principle of liberty can be used to closely examine questions such as whether or not we should accept restrictions on our liberty as part of the attempt to counter terrorism in the post-9/11 world.

By defining what is right as what is fair, Rawls is not denying that members of society will have different personal ideas of right or good. He is merely trying to lay down the framework of a theory which we can use when we try to judge whether the actions of a society and its individuals are right or not. By focusing on putative members of society who operate behind a veil of ignorance, he goes a long way towards providing a simple and clear rule of thumb by which we can judge the raw principles of justice.

There are of course many fine details in both the work of Rawls and of his followers, and it is clear that Rawls' theory, while basically liberal, can be put to many uses according to what assumptions are made as we interpret it. Some of Rawls' later work on international justice in particular was disappointing to his earlier liberal supporters as he seemed to be reaching rather realpolitik, conservative opinions as to how his own principles should be applied to international justice (as opposed to intra-societal justice).

There are also other inherent problems even at the root of Rawls' theory. How wide should the net be for members of the original committee? Should non-humans be included? Should members of other societies be included (on the basis that there is movement between populations)? Such questions seem arcane but would significantly affect the deliberations of the "blind" committee of justice – in these particular instances towards the treatment of animals and immigration policy. And in trying to second-guess what a blind committee would judge fair, it is always going to be hard for us to genuinely escape our real world experience and prejudice. In which case we might be tempted to use Rawlsian reasoning to justify our prejudices, rather than as a pure tool of justice.

A further question can be levelled at the second principle of difference. Rawlsian argument can be used to justify massive inequalities in society on the basis that the poorer members are therefore enriched. Is a society with such inequality really the one that a blind committee would choose, or might it take the view that there is a limit as to how wide relative inequality of wealth should be?

So Rawls' theory is not perfect. But nor is it without value simply because one can niggle at the detail. The original idea that he has endowed is that justice is defined by fairness, according to the judgment of those who do not know which role they will play in life's drama. And the principles of liberty and difference provide powerful analytic tools by which we can debate the rights and wrongs of many current and future political problems of justice and fairness.

---

*A Theory of Justice*

## The Speed Read

Justice in society can be defined as fairness. The best theoretical way to assess fairness would be to ask a committee of disembodied souls who had no idea of what part they would play in society to judge. They would conclude that restrictions on liberty are only justified if they increase the overall liberty of society, and that inequalities are only justified if the inequality means that the representative least advantaged member is better off than if that inequality didn't exist.

---

## *Naming and Necessity*, 1972

### Saul Kripke

*"It really is a nice theory. The only defect I think it has is probably common to all philosophical theories. It's wrong."*

Saul Kripke is one of the best known modern American philosophers. One of the difficulties that he presents for us in compiling this book is that his work is intensely theoretical and almost impossible to summarize in a brief and comprehensible manner. All we can do here is to give a fairly brief outline of some of his most important ideas.

Kripke was something of a child prodigy and developed most of the elements of a major breakthrough in *modal logic* while he was still a teenager. The resulting theories (which have become known as *Kripke semantics*) lay out the groundwork for understanding non-classical logical systems. This part of his work is probably the hardest to understand for anyone without a background in philosophical logic. However his work in this area has had a lasting impact, in the same way that the writing of Russell and Whitehead did earlier in the century in the field of mathematical logic.

*Naming and Necessity* is the published version of Kripke's 1970 Princeton lectures. In these he looks at some of the consequences of his logical theories, but also takes a wider look at meaning and interpretation, in the process making some weighty contributions to the philosophy of language. As we saw earlier in the book, one of the major problems of understanding language is the problem of reference. How do we know what is referred to by a proper name? A theory such as that of John Locke's took it for granted that it was clear that the language we used had a direct relation to ideas in our mind and to objects in the real world. But there are many detailed ways in which we can doubt whether or not this connection is real.

Firstly one can doubt the connection from an idealist point of view, by questioning whether or not the objective world exists or can be assumed to exist. Secondly we can wonder whether the name Julius Caesar can be taken to refer to the same entity no matter who uses it. One person may be referring to the Roman Emperor of that name, while another may be referring to a dog who has that name. And in another possible world, someone might use a version of that same name to refer to an infant Caesar who died before he became emperor. What gives us any certainty that the names we use have a clear path of reference to the people or objects we intend to refer to? And without this clear path, how does language function? Wittgenstein of course dealt with this question in his later work by talking of the impossibility of a private language and by developing a theory of language games.

Kripke raised doubts about the *descriptivist* theory of names, in which a name refers to a set of descriptions of a person (or object). For instance, a descriptivist would argue that when we talk of Julius Caesar we are referring to the man who became the first Caesar of the Roman Empire, the man who led an army against Scipio, and so on. However in a possible world where Caesar died aged six months none of these facts would be true. Yet it seems nonsensical to say that a conditional statement such as one starting "If Caesar had died aged six months . . ." does not refer to the same person as the other descriptive statements.

Kripke's solution to this problem was to propose a causal theory of reference. On this theory, proper names are not definite descriptions. Instead they are *rigid designators* that would refer to the same object in all possible worlds. There has been a great deal of discussion of the respective strengths of causal and descriptivist theories in modern philosophical literature, with philosophers such as Hilary Putnam, Gareth Evans, Richard Rorty, and John Searle weighing in with examples and counter-examples on both sides of the argument.

One consequence of the causal theory of reference is that (in Kripke's opinion) it is possible for there to be identities that are both necessary and a posteriori. What this means is that a fact might be necessarily true (for instance "the morning star is the evening star" or "Water is $H_2O$") but that this can only be discovered by observation. There is nothing in the concept of the morning star that allows us to infer that it is the evening star – only observation of their identical orbits can lead us to conclude that these are one and the same object, even though this is a necessary truth.

Following on from this, Kripke argued against a position in the philosophy of mind that is known as *identity materialism.* This is the idea that every mental fact is identical with a physical fact. So for instance the idea that pain (a mental event) is identical with some physical event (Kripke gives the notional example of C-fibers in the nervous system firing) can't be a necessary fact, because pain and its possibility doesn't have any clear relation to the firing of C-fibers.

Elsewhere, Kripke also wrote some illuminating material on the work of Wittgenstein. There is some controversy within the academic world as to whether or not Kripke's explication of Wittgenstein is true to his original ideas or not. The main importance of Kripke's work in this area is perhaps to add some detail to the scepticism about meaning that Wittgenstein espoused in his later work.

It is also important to mention that when Kripke talks about possible worlds, it is not in the same way that David Lewis would do later. In Lewis's theories, possible worlds had the same status as actual worlds. Whereas for Kripke a conditional remains a conditional – a possible world is just a world that did not in fact become actual, rather than a universe of equal status to the actual world. This is important to mention because modal logic is a term that is used in reference to both philosophers, yet each has a rather different approach to counterfactual conditionals.

Kripke is an important modern philosopher, but he is not a philosopher whose work will provide great enlightenment to a layman. His work is technical and complex and some of his key arguments are subject to intense debate in the philosophical community. Some of the arguments in *Naming and Necessity* will be of interest to a general reader, but overall it will be hard for any reader without a detailed knowledge of formal logic and of Kripke's philosophical forebears to understand or enjoy the arguments therein.

*Naming and Necessity*

## The Speed Read

A proper name such as "Aristotle" or "Julius Caesar" refers to an object by being a rigid designator pointing to the same object in every possible world, rather than through a set of descriptions that identify that object. An identity can be necessary but a posteriori (discovered by observation). It is not the case that every mental event is identical with a physical event. And modal logic and Kripke semantics are extremely interesting, but too complicated to explain here . . .

## *On the Plurality of Worlds,* 1986

### David K. Lewis

*". . . I am at a disadvantage compared to someone who pretends as a figure of speech to believe in possible worlds, but really does not . . . as I believe that there really are other worlds, I am entitled to confess that there is much about them that I do not know, and that I do not know how to find out."*

The idea that there might be alternative universes that are different to this one has been explored in a variety of contexts. Science fiction writers including Philip K. Dick and many others have set books or stories in, for instance, a world where the car was never invented, or where the Axis powers won the Second World War. *Star Trek, Doctor Who,* and *Buffy The Vampire Slayer* are just a few of the many television programmes and films that have used alternative universes as a plot device. And there has been a fascinating strand of modern historical discussion in which historians consider what might have happened in another universe, if for instance the Normans hadn't invaded Britain, or the South had won the American Civil War.

While such discussions have a certain frivolity, they can serve a serious purpose. Examining "what might have happened" can cast a great deal of light on what actually happened in the world we live in. Nonetheless it might seem a little unexpected in the dry world of academic philosophy to encounter a modern writer who not only devotes considerable time to writing about possible worlds, but also asserts that alternative universes are as real as this one.

David Lewis was an American-born philosopher who also spent a lot of time working in Australia. His early work focused on social conventions – for instance, the theoretical explanation of why we drive on the left-hand side of the road in Britain, but on the right-hand side in America, or why certain social behaviours have developed in the way that they do. In doing this he used games theory, which had traditionally been used to study adversarial situations such as the Prisoner's Dilemma, to study co-operative behaviour patterns. He also dealt briefly with possible worlds in his early book *Convention*, but it was his 1973 book *Counterfactuals* that really made his reputation. In this book he put forward a novel way of dealing with counterfactual conditionals. To explain, a counterfactual conditional is used where we say, "X actually caused Y, but if X hadn't happened, what would have happened?"

Lewis's book proposed not only that we should deal with such conditional statements in logic by assuming that there are different possible worlds in which such counterfactual events might have happened, but, more radically, that we should treat such possible worlds as real. He extended and developed this theory over subsequent years, and *On the Plurality of Worlds* provides a more complete statement of his theories, which became known as *modal realism* (although Lewis later wished that this label hadn't been applied to his theories).

Possible worlds had been a feature of philosophy at least since Leibniz, who claimed that we live in the best of all possible worlds. Leibniz's way of reaching this conclusion was to assume God's perfection and then to assume that many alternative universes could have been created by God. He believed that God's perfection entailed that any change to this universe would have made it less perfect overall, and that therefore we must live in the best possible world. This was a riposte to those who used the existence of evil as an argument against religion.

But since Leibniz, alternative universes had generally been regarded as notional, not as being as real as the actual universe in which we find ourselves. Lewis's proposal was that, for logical consistency, we must assume that all possible universes are equally real, and that actuality is just indexical. (This means that when we say that this universe is actual, we are merely making a self-referential statement of the same kind as when we say "I am here" and "the time is now").

This is a rather startling proposal, which reminds many of science fiction alternative universe scenarios, and Lewis admits that his ideas were often met with an "incredulous stare." It has to be noted that Lewis's argument for his thesis is a rather pragmatic one. He believed that the logical and ontological gains of making the assumption that possible worlds are all real, and as real as this world, are large enough that they outweigh the problem that we have in really believing in such possible worlds. In the fine detail of his philosophy, there are a lot of fascinating and powerful logical tools that did much to disentangle the logical problems of talking about counterfactuals and conditional statements. And if it were instead to be assumed that the actual world was a different kind of entity to possible worlds, he felt that his system would become untenable or diluted.

So Lewis's modal realism was not something that encouraged him to believe we could discover anything about, or explore other possible worlds. Since his assumptions led him to the conclusion that possible worlds are causally isolated, we have no way of knowing about other possible worlds directly. His focus was on the idea that we could use the existence of such worlds as a logical tool for analyzing this world and language. He was at heart a purely analytical philosopher, but a particularly imaginative and interesting one in the broad approach he took to the problems he dealt with. Non-philosophers should be warned that in spite of the interesting talk about possible worlds, his books contain a lot of rather dry logical analysis, which can be hard to follow at times.

Lewis unfortunately died at the relatively young age of sixty in 2001, having suffered from diabetes throughout his life, an early death that robbed the world of one the more interesting philosophers of the post-war period.

### *On the Plurality of Worlds*
# The Speed Read

Other possible worlds are real, and are the exact same kind of thing as this world. Actuality is as indexical as location, meaning that saying "this universe is the actual one" is the same logical class of statement as saying "I am here" – it merely marks your location in the pantheon of alternative universes. You can choose whether or not to believe this theory, but if you accept it, it provides us with some extremely powerful logical tools with which to analyse the world in which we live.

# *Darwin's Dangerous Idea,* 1995

## Daniel Dennett

*". . . I view the standard philosophical terminology as worse than useless – a major obstacle to progress since it consists of so many errors."*

Daniel Dennett is best known for his writing on the philosophy of mind, and in particular where this strand of philosophy crosses over into the fields of cognitive science and artificial intelligence. He is known for arguing that there is no good reason why consciousness can't be explained in terms of computational process, and for claiming that it is theoretically possible for a machine to attain consciousness. In making this claim, Dennett is rejecting claims that consciousness can only be attained by living, organic beings or that it is impossible to construct consciousness artificially.

This is interesting for a number of reasons. Firstly Dennett's position is a strong refutation of dualism. Secondly his theories, if true, chime closely with theorists of artificial intelligence who believe there is no essential impossibility in the theory that all human thinking can be replicated by an artificial machine.

The philosophy of mind has been a fruitful and interesting area in the last century. While many of the basic problems of philosophy have not changed over the centuries, the last century has given us some significant new tools for analyzing the human mind. Sometimes new technology can be seductive in that its importance can be overrated in the short term. But in the concept of Turing machines, the development of genuine computational machines, in psychoanalytic theory and in a variety of developments in our physical and neural understanding of how the brain works, there is a wealth of new information for philosophers of the mind to explore. Dennett is one philosopher who has written especially well on the subject but other writers such as John Searle, J. R. Lucas, Douglas Hofstadter, and Stephen Rose are also interesting to explore.

*Darwin's Dangerous Idea* is nominally a book on a different subject, the importance of Darwin's theory of evolution – although as we shall see, there are ways in which Dennett's thinking on this subject ties in with his philosophy of mind.

Dennett's starting point is the argument that Darwinian processes are a central organizing force in the universe, and that natural (or adaptive) selection is the blind, algorithmic force that accounts for far more than the development of traits in species. Dennett has elsewhere commented that evolution was a more important scientific theory than the discovery that the Earth rotates around the sun, or Newton's theories of gravity. He describes Darwin's ideas as a kind of "universal acid" that eats into all kinds of attempts to explain culture and science. Dennett uses Darwinian theories in this book to explain phenomena in fields as varied as the social sciences, theology, and psychology as well as applying it to philosophy.

In doing this Dennett mounts a spirited defence of the basic Darwinian idea. He takes swipes at several writers who have attempted to revise or refute elements of Darwinian theory, notably Stephen Jay Gould, whose theory of punctuated equilibrium is given a rough ride by Dennett.

Dennett proceeds to a detailed look at the ways in which consciousness might have developed through a process of adaptive selection. Since he regards the mind as being the same thing as the brain, and the brain has developed through a process of natural selection it is natural for him to explain consciousness and rationality itself as a product of evolution.

The fact that it might be too expensive or complicated to actually build a conscious robot does not prove that it is impossible, merely that it is impractical for science to replicate a human brain or close facsimile of it. For Dennett, atheism is also justified by this argument because the argument that the universe is too perfect to have been designed by mere chance is invalidated by the fact that it is perfectly possible to describe the ways in which the human mind has evolved. David Hume had made a similar argument (though without appealing to Darwin) in an earlier century.

Dennett writes inspiringly about the ways that evolutionary theory opens up vistas of beautiful, endless change and creativity. Since all processes are subject to adaptive selection, the universe is in an ongoing process of self-creation. Dennett also accepts some elements of Richard Dawkins' theory of *memes*. This is the theory that ideas (or chunks of information) behave in a similar way to genes, developing over time. The consequence of this theory is that cultural history and the history of language can be explained in terms of adaptive change.

Dawkins' meme theory sometimes seems a bit woolly as it's unclear why information needs to survive in the same way as a species' genes do. And, since memes are defined in various ways by different thinkers, it seems a rather loose concept. On the other hand we regularly see how popular ideas or pieces of new language are propagated and communicated through populations, and the internet gives us a clear thumbnail view of the ways information (true or false, useful or not) can be communicated and mutated. It seems that even if it is difficult to give meme theory a definitive form, it is at least a useful idea.

In general, Dennett presents a cosmos where there is no overriding teleological purpose to life. Life is simply one of many processes that develop by chance, and our idealism and religion are just superstitions that develop for their own adaptive reasons. Reading *Darwin's Dangerous Idea* one can understand why religious fundamentalists (both Christian and of other religions) are so alarmed by Darwinism. Dennett demonstrates how powerful it is as an explanatory theory of how life and the human mind function, and it is thus a very clear threat to the myths of religion. Dennett is polite enough to give consideration to theories of *intelligent design*, but he gives them fairly short shrift. Indeed the book starts with a comparison between different kinds of explanatory scientific theories – Dennett describes Darwinism as a "crane," a building tool that has its feet firmly rooted on simpler theories at ground level. Whereas he sees alternative theories and religious explanations as "skyhooks," theories that don't refer to simpler levels of theory, but instead hang from the sky as if by magic.

Dennett also helps to emphasize the slightly unfortunate fact that Darwin's theory was first propagated in an area in which it immediately impinged on religious belief by raising awkward questions about how man was created. Darwinian theory has so many other useful applications, and adaptive design is such a powerful concept, that it is a shame that its progress has been impeded by religious dogma concerning human evolution. Whether or not one agrees with every aspect of Dennett's arguments, this book is at the very least an enlightening and interesting discussion of hugely important issues.

### *Darwin's Dangerous Idea*
# The Speed Read

Darwin's theory of natural selection is one of the most important scientific breakthroughs ever. It can be applied to a wide range of fields of knowledge including cultural and scientific theory. Human consciousness and the mind can be completely explained in physical terms and in terms of adaptive selection over time.

# *Small Pieces Loosely Joined:*
# *A Unified Theory of the Web,* 2002

## David Weinberger

*"The conversation I believe we need to have is about what the Web is showing us about ourselves. What is true to our nature and what only looked that way because it was a response to a world that was, until now, the only one we had?"*

One of the ways in which the world has significantly changed in the last few decades is the advent of computers and the even more extraordinary development of the World Wide Web. It is only twenty years ago that very few of us knew what "e-mail," "websites" or "online" even meant, yet now this computer network linking a huge part of the global human community together is almost taken for granted.

There are plenty of books about the importance of the internet, many of them flawed by being breathless paeans to the online world, or else already dated by the constant changes that the web is undergoing. One of the more interesting and durable contributions to this literature is David Weinberger's *Small Pieces Loosely Joined.* Rather than focusing entirely on the internet, Weinberger looks at the philosophical implications of the new technology – the ways in which the internet is causing us to revise ideas of space and time and of human relationships and the concept of self. He also argues that our perceptions of morality are being steadily altered by the internet (although many would wonder if this is a good thing, as this often means we are becoming desensitized to the lowest common denominator, for instance with respect to the phenomenon of the internet's sexual content).

Weinberger's basic thesis is that in some respects the way we perceive our selves and others through the web is a more authentic experience than the "real world." Because certain constrictions of space and time are removed and connections between people become the most fundamental aspect of the subjective world, the web is a closer metaphor for the way our minds actually work.

There are some thought-provoking points made here about the ways in which we interact on the internet. We are able to adopt personas and disguises online, which can encourage bad behaviour, but can also allow us to feel free to express our "real selves." At the very least the experience of becoming different personas in different forums or roleplay experiences can give us a real insight into the ways in which we construct personas for our everyday lives, in work, in the family or wherever.

Philosophy has often drawn a distinction between the objective world of fact and the subjective world of what goes on in our heads. In fact there is a great degree to which we construct our own subjective worlds by choosing what we wish to allow into that world. Using the internet makes the ways in which we construct a subjective world a far more conscious experience. We choose what to search for, where to "go" and who to talk to. We choose our information sources, and from these we build up an "online world." In some respects, rather than bringing the world together in one big village, the internet thus splits us into a million little villages where people with similar ideas and tastes mingle and reinforce one another's subjective worlds.

There has always been this distinction as, even before the internet, our subjective (and imaginary) worlds were partially a conscious creation – but the web has clearly given us new ways of constructing a private reality. It has also provided us with new ways of constructing a self (and of perceiving how a self is constructed). The phenomena of personal web pages, blogs, and now the huge success of Facebook is largely about the fact that people feel a need to both construct and assert an identity.

Weinberger writes that the web "is enabling us to rediscover what we've always known about being human: we are connected creatures in a connected world about which we care passionately." Perhaps this is a slight overstatement, but it does seem fair to say that the web has given us an array of new ways of understanding what it is to be human. We can see more clearly some of the basic psychoanalytic processes of the construction of self and world, simply because having done this in the real world, we then go back and repeat the process in subtly different ways in the "second world" of the internet.

We also see how both language and identity are partially a public creation – by reacting to other people we reinforce our own intentions and the resulting personas and uses of language are partially created in the public, connected realm. Theories of language creation, including Wittgenstein's theory of language games and his denial of a private language, can be seen in interesting new lights when one considers how the language of the web is constantly reinvented and mutating.

Weinberger is occasionally bombastic or sweeping in the statements he makes and at times he may have been misled by the excitement of a new technology into overrating the ways in which it has really changed the world. But this is nonetheless a genuinely interesting meditation on the impact that the web is having on our lives and upon our understanding of our selves and the "real world."

---

*Small Pieces Loosely Joined:*
*A Unified Theory of the Web*

# The Speed Read

The World Wide Web is changing everything. In some ways, the web reveals our authentic selves. As our perceptions of space, time and self are challenged, we are forced to look at the ways in which we construct our selves and subjective experiences of the "real world." Through this process we can come to a better philosophical understanding of our world.

---

## *After the Terror*, 2002

### Ted Honderich

*"It most certainly does not follow that to be persona non grata to some people on both sides of a conflict shows you are in the right. That is weak stuff . . . You can, on occasions, infuriate both sides and be wrong."*

Mainstream philosophy has traditionally been cautious about entering into analysis of current affairs. While philosophers are happy to make abstract judgments about ethics and the rights and wrongs of theoretical situations, they are less willing to be drawn on how these judgments apply to political reality. One typical philosophical tool is the "thought experiment" in which a philosopher imagines a possible situation in order to work out the philosophical implications of that situation.

So Ted Honderich is in some respects stepping out of the philosophical mainstream when he deals directly with issues of the modern war on terror in recent work such as *After the Terror* and *Right and Wrong*. In these books Honderich attempts to use an ethical approach to analyse why 9/11 was wrong, and to consider the rights and wrongs of the Iraq War, the actions of the Israelis and Palestinians, and the acts of terrorists.

There is a good deal of controversy involved in any attempt to address these problems. Honderich has been attacked for seeming to blame US foreign policy for terrorism (a simplification of his viewpoint, although he does consider the ways in which US foreign policy has contributed to the growth of terrorist organizations) and especially for his views on Israel and Palestine.

In this area, Honderich describes himself as a Zionist, but as someone who opposes neo-Zionism. By this he means that he believes the original creation of Israel was right, but that its post-1967 expansion beyond the original borders created a new phase of neo-Zionism, which he opposes. He explores the morality of these phases carefully in his books, and bases his idea of what is right or wrong on what it was reasonable to believe at the time. (For instance he decides that it was reasonable in 1948 to believe that creating the state of Israel in that particular location was a good thing to do on balance.) He also concludes that the Palestinians at this stage have a moral right to their terrorism.

This is the conclusion which has created the most controversy, with Honderich being attacked as an anti-semite among
other things. The quote above comes from a paper in which
he wryly considers the fact that he was at the same time criticized by Palestinian speakers, simply because he is a Zionist
and accepts the original creation of Israel as morally right. In
doing this he is also prepared to consider that the occasionally
terrorist actions of the Jewish freedom fighters which led up
to the creation of the state of Israel were on a par with the
actions of modern-day Palestinian fighters. On these grounds
one might be forced to consider that it is absurd to consider
one "right" and the other "wrong." Certainly it seems fair to
make the point that unless we are to reject all violence and
renounce war of any kind, we have to attempt to engage with
the question of when we believe violence to be justified. All
too often this question is dispensed with by simply labelling
the fighters we agree with as "freedom fighters" and those we
disagree with as "terrorists."

One can agree or disagree with Honderich's specific
conclusions, and with the detail of his analysis, but it is interesting to see these issues dealt with in a way that attempts to
appeal to first principles of ethics, as they are issues that are
all too easily clouded by rival dogmas. Of course some who
oppose Honderich would assert that he is simply rationalizing his own dogmatic viewpoint. The only way to decide if
you agree with this is to read his work.

In this respect it was courageous of Honderich to publish
*After the Terror* a year after 9/11, and to question some of
the morality of the "war on terror" in that book. It was
a period in which any attempts to question the invasions
of Afghanistan and Iraq and the use of the Guantanamo
Bay prison camp were being widely attacked as unpatriotic
and inappropriate. Large parts of the media were failing
to question the detail of these actions or their moral
appropriateness. As this piece is being written one can see

all too clearly how this lack of scrutiny contributed to the problems that are now being experienced in Iraq, Syria and elsewhere.

Honderich has questioned the morality of the war, asserting for instance that it is never an acceptable defence to claim that civilians who are killed (for instance in a bombing campaign aimed at terrorists) were the inevitable victims of an essentially good action. He makes this point on the grounds that if one's action made it inevitable that those civilians would be killed, one is morally culpable for their deaths. This was not only brave of him, but valuable. The great danger in times of war and uncertainty is that our rationality will be pushed aside in favour of myth and dogma. While there are plenty of voices heard on all sides of the war on terror, it seems appropriate that philosophy should at least attempt to engage with such issues in the modern day. If the study of morality and ethics is to be of any use, it must surely create ways for us to think and write about the real world in which we live.

We saw earlier how *Dialectic of Enlightenment* by Theodor Adorno and Max Horkheimer expressed the fear of the writers, at a time when fascism looked set to triumph in Europe and elsewhere, that the end point of the enlightenment was a collapse into myth and barbarism. In the short term that pessimistic viewpoint proved apparently unjustified, although the twentieth century can be seen in retrospect as a rather bloody and dogmatic one from start to finish.

In the early years of the twenty-first century, the world faces considerable danger, especially from extreme religious and political dogmas and myths, and from natural problems such as global warming. Now more than ever it seems necessary to try to use our rationality and morality to argue against those extremists who wish to impose their viewpoint on all regardless, and to try to reach global solutions to global problems. If philosophy (and common sense) is unable to help us in this endeavour, then maybe "the enlightenment" really has failed and we are on the verge of a new dark age of unreason.

*After The Terror*

# The Speed Read

Clearly the actions of the terrorists who bombed the Twin Trade Towers on 9/11 were wrong. But what exactly do we mean by that – how do we define right and wrong when it comes to the actions of terrorist groups and governments? If we accept that it is sometimes necessary and morally acceptable to kill, how do we decide which killings are acceptable and which are not?

# Meaning and Interpretation: The Continental Tradition

## *Introduction*

In the first part of this book we focused on the Anglo-American tradition of philosophy. In the twentieth century in particular, continental philosophy followed a rather different path, and there was a degree of mutual incomprehension and suspicion between the two.

So what is the difference? A simple explanation is that the Anglo-American tradition tended to continue the search for objective truth and certainty, or at least aimed to come to a common-sense view of rationality. Whereas continental philosophy was much happier to accept that all knowledge and meaning is subjective or relative and to explore the consequences. The continental tradition has generally regarded the Anglo-American tradition as rather stodgy and bogged down in logic and analysis, while the Anglo-American school sees the continentals as relativist, airy-fairy and tending to pretentiousness.

The schism can probably be traced back to the time of Hegel. While Kant and Hegel are seen as part of both traditions, they are understood rather differently. In particular the continental tradition focused on Hegel's ideas about self and the other, and took the failure of both Kant's and Hegel's attempt at system building to mean that the traditional project of philosophy, to discover certain knowledge, had already failed. Nitezsche and Kierkegaard within this tradition were influential in the way that they dealt with the doubts and problems created by Kant and Hegel. Ideas of Marxism and psychoanalysis were also absorbed more fully into the continental tradition.

It is hard to compress an entire philosophical tradition into the space allowed here, so instead we have focused on a few representative figures, hoping to give a flavour of such disparate types of thinking as post-modernism, structuralism, psychoanalytic thought and critical theory. Some of the writers included here seem to bear out the Anglo-American suspicion that continental philosophy is pretentious, yet vacuous. Writers such as Lacan and Derrida have certainly been accused of these faults, and it is hard to recommend either as an easy read, even though some of the ideas they present are fascinating. Other writers represented here are more approachable – Bataille is an example of a writer whose philosophical contribution is often overlooked even though he put forward some interesting ideas, while Barthes and Baudrillard are enjoyable to read, whether or not one goes along with the finer points of their theory.

Kristeva, Irigaray, and Foucault are also included in this section. Each of them deals in their own way with issues of sexuality and gender. They also demonstrate some of the difficulties of reading modern continental philosophy, absorbed as it is by a rather complex use of jargon and obscure language. For instance Kristeva and Irigaray convey fascinating messages with much relevance to modern feminism, but both can be extraordinarily difficult to read, and even the compressed versions presented here are necessarily some of the more difficult sections of this book. Some of the jargon used in this section can be seen as pretentious, but often the writers are just assuming an academic knowledge of other philosophical, linguistic, and psychoanalytic texts and their writing is difficult to read without that detailed knowledge.

While the first section of this book presented a chronological journey in which there is a relatively clear narrative of how ideas developed and progressed over time, this section is more of a pot-pourri, dipping into some extremely different kinds of thought. Obviously writers within this tradition have influenced one another in many ways, and it would be wrong to pretend that there was no communication between the continent and elsewhere. But rather than attempt to cover all these interactions and influences, we have tended to select representatives of a variety of "isms" to try to convey an idea of broadly varying types of writing and thought.

## *The Prison Notebooks*, 1929–1935

### Antonio Gramsci

*"One of the most important characteristics of any group that is developing towards dominance, is its struggle to assimilate and to conquer 'ideologically' the traditional intellectuals. But this assimilation and conquest is made quicker and more efficacious the more the group in question succeeds in simultaneously elaborating its own organic intellectuals."*

Antonio Gramsci was an Italian writer, politician and political theorist. He founded and at one time led the Communist Party of Italy. Mussolini imprisoned him in 1926 during the fascist regime. Gramsci's writings are heavily concerned with the analysis of culture and political leadership. Academically, he is notable as a highly original thinker within the Marxist tradition. He opposed a "philosophy of praxis" to materialist dialectics and is renowned for his concept of cultural hegemony, a means of maintaining the state in a capitalist society.

He wrote more than thirty notebooks and 3,000 pages on history and analysis during his imprisonment. These writings, known as the *Prison Notebooks*, contain his ideas of Italian history and nationalism, Marxist theory, critical theory and educational theory. Central to these are two major ideas; the notion of *hegemony*, seen by Gramsci as a means of maintaining the capitalist state, and the "organic intellectual" who would create an educated working class.

Hegemony was a concept previously used by Marxists such as Lenin to indicate the political leadership of the working class in a democratic revolution. Gramsci developed this idea to explain why the "inevitable" socialist revolution predicted by orthodox Marxism, had not occurred by the early twentieth century. Gramsci suggested that capitalism maintained control not just through violence and political and economic coercion, but also ideologically, through a hegemonic culture in which the values of the bourgeoisie became the "common sense" values of all. Thus a consensus culture developed, in which the working class identified their own good with the good of the bourgeoisie, and helped to maintain the status quo rather than turning against the ruling class, their oppressors.

According to Gramsci, the working class needed to develop its own culture. This would overthrow the notion that bourgeois values represented "natural" or "normal" values for society. It would also attract the oppressed and intellectual classes to the cause of the proletariat. For Gramsci, culture was fundamental to the attainment of power. In his view, any class that wishes to dominate in modern conditions has to move beyond its own narrow "economic-corporate" interests, to exert intellectual and moral leadership, and also make alliances and compromises with a variety of forces. Gramsci calls this union of social forces a "historic bloc," taking a term from Georges Sorel. This bloc forms the basis of consent to a certain social order, which produces and re-produces the hegemony of the dominant class through a nexus of institutions, social relations, and ideas. Gramsci thought that, in the West, bourgeois cultural values were essentially linked to Christianity, and therefore much of his polemic against hegemonic culture is aimed at religious norms and values.

This theory of hegemony is tied to Gramsci's understanding of the capitalist state, which he claims rules through force plus consent. The state is not to be understood in the narrow sense of the government; instead, Gramsci divides the notion between "political society," which is the arena of political institutions and legal constitutional control, and "civil society," which is commonly seen as the "private" or "non-state" sphere, including the economy. The former is the realm of force and the latter of consent. He stresses, however, that the division is purely conceptual and that the two, in reality, often overlap. It is important that society feels that a government rules by the collective consent of the populace.

Gramsci claimed that in modern capitalism, the ruling class can maintain its economic control by allowing certain demands made by trade unions and mass political parties within civil society to be met by the political sphere. This, in turn, makes the working class feel they have some control over their situation. They continue to vote for members of the ruling class to govern them. In this way, the bourgeoisie engages in "passive revolution" by going beyond its immediate economic interests and allowing the forms of its hegemony to change.

As well as his ideas on hegemony, Gramsci questioned the role of intellectuals in society. It was in these writings that he developed the idea of the "organic" intellectual. One of his most famous statements is that all men are intellectuals, in that all have intellectual and rational faculties, but not all men have the social function of intellectuals. For Gramsci, modern intellectuals were not simply talkers, but directors and organizers who helped build society and produce hegemony by means of ideological apparatuses such as education and the media.

Furthermore, Gramsci made a distinction between a "traditional" intelligentsia which sees itself (wrongly) as a class apart from society, and the thinking groups which every class produces from its own ranks "organically." Such "organic" intellectuals would articulate, through the language of culture, the feelings and experiences which the masses could not express for themselves. The need to create a working-class culture relates to Gramsci's call for a kind of education that could develop working-class intellectuals, who would not simply introduce Marxist ideology from outside of the proletariat, but instead renovate and make the already existing intellectual activity of the masses more critical of the status quo. In other words they would operate from within the working class using the values of working class culture to raise the consciousness of the proletariat.

According to Gramsci, it was necessary to effectively challenge the ideologies of the educated classes, and to do so Marxists must present their philosophy in a more sophisticated guise, and attempt to genuinely understand their opponents' views. He thought the best way of doing this was by taking on board and furthering elements of socialist thought within the working class culture, through education. His ideas about an education system for this purpose correspond with the notion of critical pedagogy and popular education as theorized and practised in later decades by Paulo Freire in Brazil. Many purveyors of adult and popular education consider Gramsci an important voice to this day.

The work of Gramsci is not without its critics. They have charged him with fostering a notion of power struggle through ideas that is reflected in recent academic controversies such as political correctness. Many people find the Gramscian approach to ideas, reflected in these controversies, to be in conflict with open-ended, liberal inquiry grounded in the classics of Western culture.

*The Prison Notebooks*

## The Speed Read

Fancy yourself as a bit of a revolutionary? Become an "organic" intellectual. You need to engage with the working class and unemployed, challenging any ideas they have adopted from the bourgeoisie. Take part in their cultural activities and emphasize their importance in the political views of the proletariat. By doing so you will create a "hegemony" a consensus to rule that appeals to real working class values.

## *Mythologies*, 1957

Roland Barthes

*"Other countries drink to get drunk, and this is accepted by everyone; in France, drunkenness is a consequence, never an intention . . . wine is not only philtre, it is also the leisurely act of drinking."*

Roland Barthes was born in 1915 in Normandy. He studied at the Sorbonne, and developed an academic career in France, Romania, and Egypt. He also contributed to the leftist Parisian paper *Combat*, out of which grew his first full-length work *Writing Degree Zero* (1953). Barthes' earliest work was very much a reaction to the trend of existentialist philosophy that was prominent during the 1940s, specifically the figurehead of existentialism Jean-Paul Sartre.

In his work *What Is Literature?* (1947) Sartre expresses disenchantment with both established forms of writing, and more experimental avant-garde forms, which in his opinion alienate readers. Barthes' response was to try to find what can be considered unique and original in writing. In *Writing Degree Zero* he asserts that language and style are both matters that appeal to conventions, and are thus not purely creative. Instead *form*, or what Barthes calls "writing," the specific way an individual chooses to manipulate conventions of style for a desired effect, is the unique and creative act (a term he sometimes uses for this is "writerly"). One's form is vulnerable to becoming a convention once it has been made available to the public.

This means that being creative is an ongoing process of continual change and reaction. In this sense, Barthes believed that literature and art should be critical and interrogate the world rather than seek to explain it. He saw Albert Camus' *The Stranger* as an ideal example of this notion, for its sincere lack of any embellishment or flair. Barthes felt that avant-garde writing should be praised for maintaining a distance between its audience and its work. By maintaining an obvious artificiality rather than making claims to great subjective truths, avant-garde writers ensure that their audiences maintain an objective perspective when reading their work. This method of examining texts through form and structure rather than meaning and function became generally known as structuralism.

In 1952 Barthes studied lexicology and sociology at the Centre National de la Recherche Scientifique. During his seven-year period there he began writing bimonthly instalments to *Les Lettres Nouvelles*, a popular series of essays that dismantled myths of popular culture and which were eventually gathered together in *Mythologies*. The essays contained in *Mythologies* often interrogate pieces of cultural material to show how bourgeois society used them to impose its values upon others.

In one example, the portrayal of wine in French society as a robust and healthy habit would be a bourgeois ideal perception contradicted by certain realities, in this case that wine can be unhealthy and inebriating. He found semiology, the study of signs, useful in his interrogations. Barthes explained that these bourgeois cultural myths were second-order signs, or significations. His use of the terms "sign," "signifier" and "signified" can be hard to understand. For Barthes, a "sign" is a symbol, an image or a word, which can become signifier or signified. If we stay with the wine example, a picture of a full, dark bottle is a signifier relating to a signified: in this case a fermented, alcoholic beverage – wine. However, according to Barthes, the bourgeois take this signified (the wine) and apply their own emphasis to it, making "wine" a new signifier (instead of a picture of a full bottle), this time relating to a new signified: the idea of healthy, robust, relaxing wine. Motivations for such manipulations vary from a desire to sell products to a simple desire to maintain the status quo. They also sometimes blur the boundaries between signifier and signified.

In his essay, *The Fashion System*, Barthes showed how this adulteration of signs could easily be translated into words. He demonstrated how in the fashion world any word could be loaded with idealistic bourgeois emphasis. Thus, if popular fashion says that a "blouse" is ideal for a certain situation or ensemble, this idea is immediately naturalized and accepted as truth, even though the actual sign could just as easily be interchangeable with "skirt," "vest" or any number of combinations. A picture of a frilly garment worn on the upper torso of a woman's body is the "signifier" of a "blouse," however, a "blouse" through fashion text may become a "signifier" of one's place in the fashionable hierarchy.

Ironically, in the end, Barthes' *Mythologies* was itself absorbed into bourgeois culture. Barthes found many third parties asking him to comment on a certain cultural phenomenon as if he was suddenly an expert in these matters. This turn of events made him question the point of demystifying culture for the masses, thinking it might be a fruitless attempt, and drove him deeper in his search for individualistic meaning in art.

While Barthes found structuralism to be a useful tool and believed that discourse of literature could be formalized, he didn't believe it could become a strict scientific endeavour. Literary theory was beginning to change in the late 1960s. Writers such as Jacques Derrida were aiming to test the bounds of structuralist thinking. Derrida identified the flaw of structuralism as its reliance on a transcendental signified; a symbol of constant, universal meaning would be essential as an orienting point in such a closed off system. This would have to be a metaphysical point of stable meaning. So without some regular standard of measurement, a system of criticism that references nothing outside of the actual work itself could never work. This is because symbols of constant and universal significance don't exist, the entire premise of structuralism as a means of evaluating writing (or anything) is eventually hollow if one accepts this viewpoint.

Eventually, the new thinking taking over the world of literary criticism led Barthes to consider the limitations of not just signs and symbols, but also Western culture's dependency on beliefs of constancy and ultimate standards. He thus reflected on the ability of signs in Japan to exist for their own merit, retaining only the significance naturally imbued by their signifiers (for instance in his book *Empire of Signs*).

Such a society contrasts greatly with the one he dissected in *Mythologies*, which was a study of a society revealed to be always asserting a greater, more complex significance on top of the natural one.

In this period Barthes also wrote the essay *The Death of the Author*, in which he continued to point to the shifting nature of signifiers. He saw the notion of the author (or authorial authority) in the criticism of literary text as the forced projection of an ultimate meaning of the text. By imagining an "ultimate" intended meaning of a piece of literature, that is, looking for what the author "meant" the book to be about, one could infer an ultimate explanation for it. But Barthes points out that the great proliferation of meaning in language and the unknowable state of the author's mind makes any such ultimate realization impossible. *The Death of the Author* is sometimes considered a post-structuralist work, since it moves past the conventions of trying to quantify literature, but others see it as a transitional phase for Barthes in his continuing effort to find significance in culture outside of the bourgeois norms. Indeed the notion of the author being irrelevant was already a factor of structuralist thinking.

In the academic world today, the influence of Barthes' works can still be felt in fields that concern themselves with the representation of information such as photography, music, and literature and art history. However, one consequence of the sheer diversity of his works is that he never spawned a group of thinkers dedicated to his theories. The very fact of his insistence that his work be ever adapting, always refuting notions of stability and constancy means there is no theory to be modelled after.

Barthes was always opposed to the notion of adopting, without criticism, inferred ideologies regardless of their source. He preferred individualist thought and adaptability rather than conformity. However his work remains a valuable source of insight and tools for the analysis of meaning in any given man-made representation.

---

### *Mythologies*

## The Speed Read

"Meaning" is a very precarious ground to walk upon. A sign (something used to represent any object via visual or textual means) can become a "signifier" or "signified." A picture of a bottle of wine becomes a "signifier" for wine. In this case "wine" is what is signified. However, the word "wine" could become a signifier for "alcoholic drink" (that which is signified by "wine"), the picture of the bottle of wine could be a "signifier" for alcoholic, alcoholic being "signified" by a picture of a bottle of wine. Go have a drink and think about it, the bottle, the glass, the drink . . .

---

## *Écrits: A Selection*, 1966

### Jacques Lacan

*"This jubilant assumption of his specular image by the child at the infans stage, still sunk in his motor incapacity and nursling dependence, would seem to exhibit in an exemplary situation the symbolic matrix in which the I is precipitated in a primordial form, before it is objectified in the dialectic of identification with the other, and before language restores to it, in the universal, its function as subject."*

Jacques-Marie-Émile Lacan was a French psychoanalyst, psychiatrist, and doctor. He considered his work to be an authentic "return to Freud". This entailed a renewed concentration upon the Freudian concepts of the unconscious, the castration complex, the ego conceptualized as a mosaic of identifications, and the centrality of language to any psychoanalytic work. His work has a strong interdisciplinary focus, drawing particularly on linguistics, philosophy, and mathematics, and he has become an important figure in many fields beyond psychoanalysis, particularly within critical theory. His only major body of writing, *Écrits*, is notoriously difficult to read. The quote above gives a fairly good idea of how dense his writing is. In *Seminar XX* he remarks that his *Écrits* were not to be understood, but would produce a "meaning effect" in the reader similar to some mystical texts. Part of the reason for this, it should be emphasized, are the repeated Hegelian allusions and similar unheralded theoretical divergences. There are however some critics who accuse Lacan of simply writing deliberately obscure prose for the sake of effect and this should be remembered when reading this summary of some dense, difficult theory.

Following Freud's death, psychoanalytic practice had split into differing schools of thought. Lacan accused some of his contemporary psychoanalysts of a superficial understanding of Freud, claiming they had adhered so cautiously to his ideas that they had served to block rather than encourage scientific investigation of the mental process. Lacan wanted to return to Freud's thought, and expand it in the light of its own tensions and currents. In fact, near the end of his life he remarked to a conference, "It is up to you to be Lacanians if you wish; I am Freudian." It should be emphasized that Lacan insisted that his work was not, for him, an interpretation but a *translation* of Freud into structural-linguistic terms. Lacan insisted that Freud's ideas of "slips of the tongue" jokes emphasized the agency of language in subjective constitution.

The "return to Freud" is therefore primarily the realization that the pervading agency of the unconscious is intimately tied to the functions and dynamics of language, where the signifier is irremediably divorced from the signified in a chronic but generative tension of "lack". (The signifier relates to the signified but even as it relates to it, it is also separate from it, hence Lacan's use of the term "lack.")

It is here that Lacan began his attempt to "correct" Freud from within. The "return to Freud" begins with his paper *The Instance of the Letter in the Unconscious, or Reason Since Freud* in *Écrits*. Lacan's principal challenge to Freudian theory is the privilege that it accords the ego in self-determination. For Freud, the unconscious was ruled by the ego. The central pillar of Jacques Lacan's psychoanalytic theory is that "the unconscious is structured like a language," in the same way that the conscious mind is.

The unconscious, he argued, was not a more primitive or archetypal part of the mind separate from the conscious, linguistic ego, but, rather, a formation every bit as complex and structurally sophisticated as consciousness itself. If the unconscious is structured like a language, Lacan argued, then the self is denied any point of reference to which to be "restored" following trauma or "identity crisis." In this way, Lacan's thesis is also a challenge to the ego psychology that Freud himself opposed.

Lacan described "The Mirror Stage" in the essay, "The Mirror Stage as formative in the function of the I as revealed in psychoanalytic experience," which remains one of his most important papers. Lacan distinguishes between the Imaginary and the Symbolic in the development of the idea of identity. In the Imaginary phase, the recognition of the "self" in the mirror is in a sense a "misrecognition" (*méconnaissance*) – although this is how a child comes to feel it has a coherent self. Lacan describes this as a primordial form which is never really returned to but which is phantasmic since the desire to do so structures the identity of the subject in the Symbolic realm (after the introduction of language, of "difference" into the world of the subject).

Lacan's emphasis here is on the process of *identification* with an outside image or entity. The recognition of one's self and other occurs through the acquisition of language. All that the subject can be certain of is the image that he catches sight of in his mirror. The subject becomes at each stage what he was before and announces himself as what he will have been. The ambiguity of a failure to recognize is essential to knowing one's self. What is seen in the mirror is in part a misrecognition, not a fully coherent self.

It is significant that this process of identification is the first step towards the manufacture of the subject, because all that follows it, the transition from what Lacan calls the "Imaginary" and the "Symbolic" order, is based on this misrecognition. This is the start of a lifelong process of identifying the self in terms of the "Other."

The concept of "Other" is another important term in Lacan's work. In contrast to the dominant Anglo-American tradition of his time, Lacan considered the self as something constituted in the "Other," that is, the conception of the external. This belief is rooted in Lacan's reading of Ferdinand de Saussure and structuralism, and more specifically his belief that Freud's concept of the unconscious prefigured structuralist linguistics. Lacan picks up on Saussure's observation that a signifier is identified through its difference from other signifiers. (For example, "love" is understandable, in part, only through its opposition to "hate," which is in turn understandable only in relationship to "love.") As a result, language is never completely contained – it always contains things beyond what is intended, and these things form an endless chain of signifiers. This signifying chain, and more broadly the structures of language in general constitute the Other. The existence of the Other forces an unavoidable disconnect between the ego and its desire, which is the source of psychoanalytic symptoms. Lacan does not believe in the possibility of a "cure" in the sense of removing all symptoms, since the structure of language cannot be avoided, and so the Other will always be present. Instead, one can hope at best to alter one's symptoms.

Lacan then connects these ideas to the Real – the world as it exists before the mediation of language. The Real can never truly be grasped or engaged with – it is continually mediated through the Imaginary and the Symbolic. Lacan's notion of the Real is a very difficult concept which he, in his later years, worked to present in a structured, set-theory fashion, as "mathemes". (These are mathematical style diagrams, which mainly serve to make Lacan's writing even more impenetrable.)

Some critics of Lacan have accused him of maintaining the sexist tradition in psychoanalysis. Lacan certainly enjoys an awkward relationship with feminism and post-feminism in that, while he is much criticized for adopting (or inheriting from Freud) a phallocentric stance within his psychoanalytic theories, he seems also to provide an accurate portrayal of the gender biases within society. In either case, traditional feminism has profited from Lacan's attempts to show that society has an inherent sexual bias that reduces womanhood to a degrading status of deficiency.

Other critics, including Jacques Derrida, have accused him of simply taking a structuralist approach to psychoanalysis. In particular, Derrida criticizes Lacanian theory for an inherited Freudian phallocentrism, exemplified primarily in his conception of the *phallus* as the "primary signifier" that determines the social order of signifiers. Much of Derrida's critique of Lacan comes from Lacan's relationship with Freud. For example, Derrida deconstructs the Freudian conception of "penis envy," upon which female subjectivity is determined *as an absence*, to show that the primacy of the male phallus entails a hierarchy between phallic presence and absence that ultimately collapses.

A less theoretically detailed, but more pithy attack on Lacan came from Noam Chomsky, who simply described Lacan as "an amusing and perfectly self-conscious charlatan."

*Écrits: A Selection*

## The Speed Read

The analyst Jacques Lacan
Had a very complicated plan.
While Freud blamed his mother,
Jacques' self was the Other,
But his mirror showed only a man.

## *The Accursed Share*, 1967

### Georges Bataille

*"The beings that we are are not given once and for all; they appear designed for an increase of their energy resources. They generally make this increase, beyond mere subsistence, their goal and their reason for being."*

Georges Bataille is probably best known for his semi-pornographic surrealist novels (such as *Story of The Eye*), but he also wrote many books and articles on philosophy and had a particular interest in the works of Marx and Hegel.

Bataille was the founder of several journals and writing groups, becoming the author of a diverse body of work, including novels, poems and essays on innumerable subjects (including poetry, the mysticism of economy, philosophy, the arts and eroticism). A keen fan of Nietzsche, he sometimes published under pseudonyms, and some of his publications were banned. As a philosopher or theorist he was mostly ignored in his lifetime and scorned by contemporaries such as Jean-Paul Sartre as an advocate of mysticism. However, after his death, his work had a considerable influence on authors such as Michel Foucault, Philippe Sollers and Jacques Derrida, all of whom were affiliated with the *Tel Quel* journal. His influence is also felt in the work of Jean Baudrillard, as well as in the psychoanalytic theories of Jacques Lacan.

The controversial work *The Accursed Share* contains three volumes, and sets out a theory of what Bataille sees as the paradox of utility. For Bataille, if being useful means serving a further end, then the ultimate end of utility can only be uselessness. He often took onboard Marxist ideas and in his exploration of them turned them on their heads. Only the first volume of *The Accursed Share* was published before his death. It treated this paradox of utility in economic terms, showing that "it is not necessity but its contrary, luxury, that presents living matter and mankind with their fundamental problems."

Moving beyond Marx, Georges Bataille's theory of consumption sees the "accursed share" as that excessive and non-recoupable part of any economy, which is destined to one of two modes of economic and social expenditure. Either it is spent luxuriously and knowingly without gain in the arts, non-procreative sexuality, spectacles and sumptuous monuments, or it is obliviously destined to an outrageous and catastrophic outpouring in war.

This notion of "excess" energy is central to Bataille's thinking. Unlike the rational writers of classical economy who see the economy as motivated by scarcity (a theory that is at the heart of Karl Marx's work), in Bataille's theory there is normally an "excess" of energy available to it. This extra energy can be used productively for growth or it can be lavishly expended. Bataille insists that society's growth or expansion always runs up against limits and eventually becomes impossible. The wasting of this energy is "luxury." The form and role luxury assumes in a society are characteristic of that society. The result is that the desire for luxury is what motivates the individual, not the fear of scarcity.

The phrase "The Accursed Share" refers to this excess opulence and indulgence eventually destined for waste, creating the ultimate "throwaway" culture. Bataille outlines this concept and provides historical examples of its function: the monastic institutions of Tibetan Lamaism, human sacrifice in Aztec society, and the Marshall Plan along with many others. Bataille's idea of "expenditure" risks being misunderstood if it is construed as a theory that should explain why certain phenomena (such as war, sacrifice, and potlatch) exist, a theory that assigns them an anthropological function. This means ignoring the temptation to see these phenomena as the preservation of the social order, which would result in turning "expenditure" into a useful, conserving, and rational enterprise, which is precisely what expenditure cannot be, according to Bataille. True expenditure must be wasteful, non-rational and useless. Therefore, Bataille's notion of expenditure is paradoxical, because it assigns a use value to certain phenomena (preservation of a society through elimination of energy that cannot be assimilated) even while it identifies the same phenomena as inherently useless and impossible to rationalize. Due to this paradox, it is helpful to consider Bataille's notion of expenditure as an impossibility, a horizon that can never be reached.

He goes further in his paradoxical reading of power, the result being some strange political theories, including that of "authentic" and "non-authentic" pleasure. In later volumes of *The Accursed Share*, Bataille decides that the workers, in their nothing-to-lose Saturday night debauches, are more sovereign than the well-heeled bourgeoisie, despite the latter's obviously greater pleasures and luxury in their lives. According to Bataille, this is because the bourgeoisie always have an eye on their social and economic position. Therefore, they have to hold themselves back from the necessary careless expenditure of energy that *authentic* ecstasy demands (the earn-your-money-and-spend-it-on-Friday-and-Saturday-night lives of the workers).

To achieve this view of the bourgeoisie as uptight killjoys, Bataille has to overestimate the extent to which the bourgeoisie are a slave to their projects and their desire for survival. After all, despite the bourgeoisie's need to keep the show on the road, they most often delegate tasks to and rely on the worker. A member of the bourgeoisie probably fears ruin more than the worker, who is perpetually close to ruin in any case. The worker with no time to call his own and no wealth to burn is more sovereign (the true ruler of the economy) than the bourgeois man who has free time when he wants it and access to all manner of luxury goods. Bourgeois man, with time and money for pleasure, ends up the true slave. Bataille's work in these later volumes of *The Accursed Share* is often dismissed, perhaps fairly, as simply upside-down thinking. Bataille creates an even greater paradox when he finally goes on to declare that only an aristocrat (in the case given in his example, the Marquis de Sade) can enjoy true sovereignty in his effortless swan dive from the heights of bourgeois luxury to the world of the depraved.

### The Accursed Share

## The Speed Read

Blessed are the unemployed working-class, for they rule the world and scare our arch-enemy the bourgeoisie. Take your meagre income or welfare cheque down the pub and drink it in one night and you are hastening the revolution. You will never stop wanting. Your desire for those designer shoes, fur coat and diamonds is simply a desire, a primal need, for more and more. It is a desire that will never be sated however many of these luxury objects you manage to procure. They will go to waste as you continue to crave for something else. The waste will eventually drown society in its depraved wallowing. The real way forward is sacrifice not acquisition.

## *Essays on Ideology,* 1971

### Louis Althusser

*"In order to advance the theory of the State it is indispensable to take into account . . . the distinction between State power and State apparatus . . ."*

Louis Pierre Althusser was born in Algeria and studied at the École Normale Supérieure in Paris, where he eventually became Professor of Philosophy. He was also a leading academic proponent of the French Communist Party. He is generally regarded as one of the leading writers in the field of *structuralist* thought. His work contains an interesting approach to the idea of personal identity.

Althusser considers that, because of Marx's belief in the close relation between the individual and society, it is

pointless to try to build a social theory on a prior conception
of the individual. The subject of observation is not individual human elements, but "structure." For Althusser, Marx
did not explain society by appealing to one factor (individuals), but broke it up into related units called "practices."
He uses this analysis to defend Marx's historical materialism
against the charge that it crudely posits a base and superstructure and then attempts to explain all aspects of the
superstructure by appealing to features of the base, in other
words, that society as a whole could only be understood
through its economic base. Althusser criticizes the idea that
a social theory can be founded on an historical conception
of human needs, he also dismisses the idea that an independently defined notion of economic practice can be used
to explain other aspects of society.

Althusser sees society as an interconnected collection
of "wholes" – economic practice, ideological practice
and politico-legal practice – which together make up one
complex whole. He believes that all practices are dependent
on each other. For example, among the relations of
production are the buying and selling of labour power by
capitalists and workers. These relations are part of economic
practice, but can only exist within the context of a legal
system that establishes individual agents as buyers and
sellers; furthermore, the arrangement must be maintained by
political and ideological means. From this it can be seen that
aspects of economic practice depend on the superstructure
and vice versa.

However, Althusser does not mean to say that the events
that determine social changes all have the same causal status.
While a part of a complex whole, economic practice is, in his
view, a structure in dominance: it plays a major part in deter-
mining the relations between other spheres, and has more
effect on them than they have on it. The most prominent
aspect of society (the religious one in feudal formations and

the economic one in capitalist ones) is called the "dominant instance," and is in turn determined "in the last instance" by the economy. For Althusser, the economic practice of a society determines which other aspect of it dominates the society as a whole.

The most influential essay in *Essays on Ideology* is *Ideology and Ideological State Apparatus*. Althusser held that it was necessary to understand how society constructs the individual in its own image. He felt that within capitalist society, the human individual is generally regarded as a subject endowed with the property of being a self-conscious agent. For Althusser, however, people's capacity for perceiving themselves in this way is not innate. Rather, it is acquired within the structure of established social practices, which impose on individuals the role (*forme*) of a subject. Social practices both determine the characteristics of the individual and give him/her an idea of the range of properties they can have, and of the limits of each social practice. Althusser argues that many of our roles and activities are given to us by social practice: for example, the production of car makers is a part of economic practice, while the production of lawyers is part of politico-legal practice. However, other characteristics of individuals, such as their beliefs about the good life or their metaphysical reflections on the nature of the self, do not easily fit into these categories.

In Althusser's view, our values, desires and preferences are inculcated in us by ideological practice, the sphere which has the defining property of constituting individuals as subjects. Ideological practice consists of an assortment of institutions called Ideological State Apparatuses (ISAs), which include the family, the media, religious organizations and, most importantly, the education system, as well as the received ideas they propagate. There is, however, no single ISA that produces in us the belief that we are self-conscious agents. Instead, we learn this belief in the course of learning what it is to be a daughter, a schoolchild, a steelworker, a councillor, and so forth. For Althusser, our sense of self is a social practice.

Despite its many institutional forms, the function and structure of ideology is unchanging and present throughout history; as Althusser's first thesis on ideology states, "ideology has no history." All ideologies constitute a subject, even though he or she may differ according to each particular ideology. Althusser illustrates this by using the concept of "interpellation". He uses the example of an individual walking in a street: upon hearing a police whistle, or any other form of hailing, the individual turns round and, in this simple movement of his or her body, they are transformed into a subject. Althusser discusses the process by which the person being hailed recognizes himself or herself as the subject of the hail, and knows to respond. Even though there was nothing suspicious about them walking in the street, they recognize that it is indeed themselves being hailed. This recognition is a mis-recognition (*méconnaissance*) in that it is working retroactively: a material individual is *always-already* an ideological subject. According to Althusser, the "transformation" of an individual into a subject has always-already happened. In stating this, Althusser acknowledges a debt toward Spinoza's theory of immanence. That is to say, our idea of who we are is delivered by ideology.

The second of Althusser's theses is that "ideology has a material existence." It maintains that, as such, ideas have disappeared (insofar as they are endowed with an ideal or spiritual existence), to the extent that their existence is inscribed in the actions of practices governed by rituals, defined in the last instance by an ideological apparatus. Therefore, it appears that the subject acts insofar as he is acted by the following system: "ideology existing in a material ideological apparatus, describing material practices governed by a material ritual, which practices exist in the material actions of a subject acting in all consciousness according to his belief." The subject believes that he is acting independently, but for Althusser, we acquire our identities by seeing ourselves and our social roles mirrored in material ideologies.

(A biographical note ... on 16 November, 1980, Althusser strangled his wife to death. This had been preceded by a period of intense mental instability. The exact circumstances are debated. Some claim it was deliberate – others accidental. Althusser himself claimed not to have a clear memory of the event. He was alone with his wife when she died, so it is hard to come to firm conclusions. Since Althusser was diagnosed as suffering from diminished responsibility, he was not tried, but instead committed to the Sainte-Anne psychiatric hospital. He remained in hospital until 1983. After his release, he moved to Northern Paris and lived reclusively, seeing few people and no longer working, except for producing his autobiography. He died of a heart attack on 22 October, 1990 at the age of seventy-two.)

## *Essays on Ideology*

# The Speed Read

Economic base and ideological "superstrucures" form a complex whole of society. Within the ideological super-structure are many practices that mirror the subject back to themselves in material ideologies. We recognize ourselves through society.

# *Of Grammatology,* 1974

Jacques Derrida

*". . . they are angry at what I write. They are angry at my texts more than anything else, and I think it is because of the way I write — not the content, or the thesis. They say that I do not obey the usual rules of rhetoric, grammar, demonstration, and argumentation; but, of course, if they were simply not interested, they would not be angry."*

Jacques Derrida's voluminous body of work had a great effect on contemporary continental philosophy and on literary theory. His work is often associated with post-structuralism and post-modernism although Derrida despised the latter term and repeatedly dissociated himself from it. Even critics of Derrida acknowledge that his philosophical project, whether adequately represented by the term *deconstruction* or not, involved extremely close reading of texts and tremendous erudition. It is this attention to the minutiae "effects" of a text that gives Derrida his reputation of being intensely opaque, if not impossible, to read.

In 1967 Derrida published the three collections of work with which he became internationally recognized. His most significant and least-understood concept, *deconstruction,* began in these books. *Of Grammatology, Writing and Difference* and *Speech and Phenomena* contained essay-studies of philosophers such as Rousseau, Husserl, Levinas, Heidegger, Hegel, Foucault, Bataille and Descartes, as well as anthropologist Claude Lévi-Strauss, psychoanalyst Sigmund Freud, linguist Ferdinand de Saussure, and writers such as Edmond Jabès and Antonin Artaud. It is in this trinity of early works that the "principles" of deconstruction were set out, although significantly not through theoretical explication but by demonstration. He aimed to show that the arguments promulgated by their subjects exceeded and contradicted the oppositional parameters in which they were situated.

This is the kind of approach that gives Derrida a reputation of difficulty. Much of the mystique and confusion surrounding deconstruction stems from Derrida's insistence on not allowing the concept to be immune to critique. That is, Derrida took pains to make his deconstruction as impossible to "theorize" as deconstruction made everything else.

Central to the theory, (if it can be said to have a centre – philosophically there is no "core" in deconstruction), deconstruction is an attempt to open a text (literary, philosophical, or otherwise) to several meanings and interpretations. Deconstruction often takes binary oppositions within a text – inside and outside, subject and object or male and female – which Derrida argues are culturally and historically defined, even reliant upon one another, and shows that they are not as clear-cut or as stable as it would at first seem. The two opposed concepts are exposed as fluid, then this ambiguity is used to show that the text's meaning is fluid as well.

This idea of fluidity stands against a legacy of traditional metaphysics founded on oppositions that seek to establish a stability of meaning through conceptual absolutes where one term, for example "good," is elevated to a status that designates its opposite, in this case "evil," as its perversion, absence or inferior. Drawing from the work of Nietzsche, who had carried out similarly intense interrogations of the meanings of words, these "violent hierarchies," as Derrida termed them, are structurally unstable within the texts themselves, where the meaning strictly depends on this contradiction. This is why Derrida insisted that deconstruction was never performed or executed but "took place" through "memory work": in this way, the task of the "deconstructor" was to show where this opposition or dialectical stability was ultimately subverted by the text's internal logic. You cannot "practice" deconstruction – instead you experience it.

Reading this way, no "meaning" is stable. The only thing that keeps the sense of unity within a text is what Derrida called the "metaphysics of presence," where presence was granted the privilege of truth. *Of Grammatology* is perhaps the clearest study of Derrida's deconstruction of the speech/writing opposition. In this book, Derrida's critique of oppositions is largely inspired by Nietzsche's genealogical reconsideration of "good" and "evil" (especially in *Beyond Good and Evil* and *On the Genealogy of Morals*).

Derrida claims that deconstruction is an "event" within a text, not a method of reading it. Despite this, within literary studies, deconstruction is often treated as a particular method of reading. Although its influence on literary theory is probably the most well-known and most-studied effect of deconstruction, many maintain that its roots are more philosophical than literary. It is also tied to academic disciplines such as linguistics, women's studies, and anthropology (called the "human sciences" in France). Derrida's examination of the latter's philosophical foundations, both conceptual and historical, and their continued reliance on philosophical argument (whether consciously or not), is an important aspect of his thought.

Another of his foremost influences is Martin Heidegger. As Derrida claims in his "Letter to a Japanese Friend" the word *déconstruction* was his attempt both to translate and re-appropriate for his own ends Heidegger's terms *Destruktion* and *Abbau* via a word from the French language, the varied senses of which seemed consistent with his requirements. This relationship with the Heidegger term was chosen over Nietzsche's term "demolition," as Derrida shared with Heidegger an interest in renovating philosophy to allow it to treat increasingly fundamental matters.

Derrida has many critics who view his work as unreadable at best and just plain daft at worst. Linguist Noam Chomsky has expressed the view that Derrida's work is essentially pointless because his writings are deliberately "obscured" with "pretentious rhetoric" to hide the simplicity of the ideas within. Chomsky has frequently grouped Derrida within a broader category of the Parisian intellectual community that he has criticized for, according to him, acting as an elite power structure for the well educated through "difficult writing."

For the most part, Derrida has been criticized for writing about difficult and obscure authors and expecting an elaborate knowledge of Western philosophy from his readers. Derrida has responded to this critique of "difficult writing" by emphasizing that his writing has the potential to change, depending on the context of that which he addresses. By extension, it would be much more accessible in, for example, the case of newspaper articles, and necessarily retaining the utmost deconstructive rigor in properly philosophical texts.

Derrida also pointed out that the popular demand that philosophers write for a wide audience is ideological and does not match, for example, the demands put upon mathematicians or physicists, the specificity of whose argument cannot usually be explained to a general public. Derrida felt deconstruction was an enlivening method and that it held a precipitating effect upon traditionally established institutions – it never "undermines" norms but rather places them within contexts that reveal their developmental and effective features (for instance his treatment of opposed binaries is revealing in this way). In this way Derrida saw himself as stress-testing conventional notions of knowledge and meaning.

*Of Grammatology*

# The Speed Read

*Am I writing this – or are you reading it?*

Reading/writing is an experience of textual effect and must be taken in its contexts of personal and relative meaning, historical and subjective understanding, reader and author and therein revealing meaning or meaning(s) previously overlooked.

## *This Sex Which Is Not One,* 1977

Luce Irigaray

*"It is useless then to trap women in the exact definition of what they mean, to make them repeat (themselves) so that it will be clear; they are already elsewhere in that discursive machinery where you expected to surprise them. They have returned within themselves."*

Luce Irigaray is an interdisciplinary thinker who works between the fields of philosophy, psychoanalysis, and linguistics. Her contributions to feminist theory and continental philosophy are wide and varied and her work mainly challenges traditional conceptions of gender, self, and body. Irigaray was initially a student of the psychoanalyst Jacques Lacan. However, her departure from Lacan in *Speculum of the Other Woman*, where she criticizes the exclusion of women from both philosophy and psychoanalytic theory, earned her recognition as a leading feminist theorist and continental philosopher.

Her writings have raised questions as to how to define femininity and sexual difference, whether *strategic essentialism* should be employed, and assessing the risk involved in engaging categories historically used to oppress women. She is also often criticized, along with other French feminists such as Julia Kristeva, for the opacity of her writing style.

Irigaray's main argument in *This Sex Which is Not One,* is that women have traditionally been associated with matter and nature to the expense of a female subject position. For Irigaray, women can only become subjects in this society if they assimilate to male subjectivity. She argues that a separate subject position for women does not exist. Irigaray's goal, therefore, is to uncover the absence of a female subject position, the relegation of all things feminine to nature/matter, and, ultimately, the absence of true sexual difference in Western culture. Irigaray's analysis of women's exclusion from culture and her use of strategic essentialism have been enormously influential in contemporary feminist theory.

Irigaray believes that all women have historically been associated with the role of "mother" so that, whether or not a woman is a mother, her identity is always defined according to that role. Her point is that, since ancient times, mothers have been associated with nature and unthinking matter. Irigaray contrasts this association with that of men who are associated with culture and subjectivity. Because of the mother association, even while excluded from culture and subjectivity, women serve as their unacknowledged support. Irigaray argues that although women are not considered full subjects, society itself could not function without their contributions. She ultimately states that Western culture itself is founded upon a primary sacrifice of the mother, and all women through her.

Her argument becomes complicated when, based on this analysis, Irigaray insists that sexual difference does not exist. For Irigaray, true sexual difference would require that men and women are equally able to achieve subjectivity. As it is, Irigaray believes that men are subjects (by which she means self-conscious, self-same entities) and women are "the other" of these subjects (e.g. the non-subjective, supporting matter). Therefore, only one form of subjectivity exists in Western culture and it is male. Through rigorous analysis of both disciplines, Irigaray seeks to unveil how both psychoanalytic theory and philosophy exclude women from a genuine social existence as autonomous subjects, and relegate women to the realm of inert, lifeless, inessential matter.

She argues that both influential discourses exclude women from a social existence as mature subjects. Her best-known critical tool is the notion of *mimesis*. Mimesis is a process of interrogating stereotypical views of women in order to call the views themselves into question. A new definition for women has to emerge out of a mimetic engagement with the old definitions, and it is a collective process. It should be stressed that for Irigaray, the key to mimesis is that the stereotypical views should not be repeated faithfully but taken onboard critically. Irigaray's example in *This Sex Which is Not One* is that if women are viewed as illogical, women should speak logically about this view. The juxtaposition of illogical and logical would undermine the claim that women are illogical. This type of mimesis is also known as strategic essentialism. Irigaray's essay *This Sex Which Is Not One*, provides several clear examples of this method.

One example is Irigaray's belief that there is a need to alter the mother/daughter relationship. This is a constant theme in Irigaray's work. Although she believes that women's social and political situation has to be addressed on a global level, she also thinks that change begins in individual relationships between women. Thus she stresses the need for mothers to represent themselves differently to their daughters, and to emphasize their daughter's subjectivity.

To summarize, through mimesis, Irigaray attempts to suggest that women could begin to reconfigure their identity such that one sex does not exist at the expense of the other. However, because she is unwilling to definitively state what that new identity should be like, the argument in the book is problematic. Irigaray's given reason for not prescribing a new identity is that she wants women to determine for themselves how they want to be defined. Given that she is a woman herself one might wish for her to at least put forth some suggestions on the issue.

Irigaray has been criticized by materialist feminists on the grounds that she privileges questions of psychological oppression over social and material oppression. Their argument is that the psychoanalytic discourse that Irigaray relies upon – even though she is critical of it – universalizes and abstracts away from material conditions that are of central concern to feminism. Materialist feminists do not believe that definitive changes in the structure of politics can result from the changes Irigaray proposes in psychoanalytic theories of subject formation.

Irigaray's response to her critics is that, whilst it is important to find ways to challenge the social and economic position in which women find themselves, focusing exclusively on women's material or economic situation as the key to change will only grant women access to a male social role. It will not change the definition of women. Irigaray's theory argues that to first change material conditions would leave the question of a non-patriarchal view of female identity untouched. Due to the force of the oppression of women, it is the definitions that have to be changed before women, as distinct from men, will attain a social existence.

### This Sex Which Is Not One

## The Speed Read

Women do not exist as subjects in contemporary culture since they are defined by a patriarchal, phallocentric ideology. Women need to learn to relate to each other differently to try and create a new discourse in which woman as subject could exist. All women's self-identity is subjugated to male identity. There is no sexual difference. Everything is male.

# *The Postmodern Condition*, 1979

## Jean-François Lyotard

*"This is a period of slackening – I refer to the colour of the times. From every direction we are being urged to put an end to experimentation, in the arts and elsewhere . . .'*

Jean-François Lyotard was a member of *Socialisme ou Barbarie*, a French political organization formed in 1948 around the inadequacy of Trotskyist theory in explaining the new forms of domination in the Soviet Union. *Socialisme ou Barbarie* became increasingly anti-Marxist and Lyotard was prominent in the *Pouvoir Ouvrier*, a group that rejected the position and split in 1963. He is best known for his ideas developed in the late seventies, beginning with a philosophy of paganism that developed, by the 1980s, into his unique version of postmodernism. Lyotard is primarily concerned with the problems of justice that arise between competing interpretations of events.

*The Postmodern Condition* is largely a study of the status of knowledge in computerized societies. Lyotard pinpoints the Second World War as the start of postmodernity. He believes that the technical and technological advancements that have taken place since then are still having a radical effect on the status of knowledge in the world's most advanced countries. Lyotard chooses computerization as a defining element with which to characterize these technical and technological advancements. He sees the problem with which he is dealing, the variable in the status of knowledge, as one of legitimation.

For Lyotard, this is a question of both knowledge and power. He describes knowledge and power as two sides of the same question. That is to say, who decides what knowledge is, and who knows what needs to be decided? For

Lyotard, in the computer age, the question of knowledge is now more than ever a question of government. With vast amounts of knowledge stored digitally in databases, who decides what knowledge is worth storing (what is legitimate knowledge) and who has access to these databases? Lyotard decides that problem lies with multinational corporations. He uses IBM as an example to suggest a hypothetical world in which the corporation owns a certain belt in the Earth's orbital field in which to circulate satellites for communication and/or for storing data banks. Paranoid though this seems, Lyotard's questions are, "Who will have access to them? Who will determine which channels or data are forbidden? The State? Or will the State simply be one user among others?"

Lyotard's work is characterized by a persistent opposition to universals, meta-narratives, and generality. He is fiercely critical of many of the "universalist" claims of the Enlightenment, and several of his works serve to undermine the fundamental principles that generate these broad claims. Most famously, in *The Postmodern Condition: A Report on Knowledge*, he argued that our age (with its postmodern condition – and computer-generated information) is marked by an "incredulity towards meta-narratives." Lyotard sees these meta-narratives as grand, large-scale theories and philosophies of the world, such as the progress of history, the position in which the scientific "knowability" of everything pervades, and the possibility of absolute freedom that is so often sought for. Lyotard argues that we have ceased to believe that narratives of this kind are adequate to represent and contain us all. The world has become alert to difference, diversity, the incompatibility of our aspirations, beliefs and desires, and for that reason postmodernity is characterized by an abundance of micro-narratives (small, relative theories). To illustrate this concept, Lyotard draws on and re-interprets the notion of "language-games" found in the work of Wittgenstein.

For Lyotard, the term "language games" (which he also sometimes called "phrase regimens") denotes the multiplicity of communities of meaning, the innumerable and incommensurable separate systems in which meanings are produced and within which rules for their circulation are created. Lyotard continues from this to try to develop a postmodern theory of justice.

Some have made the criticism that the atomization of human beings implied by the notion of the micro-narrative and the language games suggests a collapse of ethics. This is because it has often been thought that universality is a condition for something to be a properly ethical statement: "thou shalt not steal" is an ethical statement in a way that "thou shalt not steal from Toby" is not. The latter is too particular to be an ethical statement, after all, what's so special about Toby? The statement is only interpreted as ethical if it rests on a universal statement ("thou shalt not steal from *anyone*").

However, Lyotard argues that universals aren't tenable in a world that has lost faith in meta-narratives, and so it would seem that ethics is impossible. Justice and injustice can only be terms within language games, and the universality of ethics is out of the window. Despite this, Lyotard infers that notions of justice and injustice do in fact remain in postmodernism. The new definition of injustice is indeed to use the language rules from one "phrase regimen" and apply them to another. Ethical behaviour is about remaining alert precisely to the threat of this injustice, of paying attention to things in their particularity and not enclosing them within abstract conceptuality. Lyotard is fascinated by the fact that the mind cannot always organize the world rationally. For him, some objects are simply incapable of being brought neatly under concepts. He believes that generalities such as "concepts" fail to pay proper attention to the particularity of things.

Some argue that Lyotard's theories are self-contradictory because *The Postmodern Condition* seems to offer its own grand narrative in the story of the decline of the meta-narrative. Against this, supporters argue that Lyotard's narrative in *The Postmodern Condition* declares the decline of only a few defunct "narratives of legitimation" and not of narrative knowledge itself. It is not contradictory to say that a statement about narratives is itself a narrative, just as when Lyotard states that "every utterance [in his usage of the "language games"] should be thought of as a 'move' in a game" his statement is itself a "move" in a language game.

*The Postmodern Condition*

## The Speed Read

We exist in a state of crisis where we realize the inadequacy of the imagination and reason to each other. We are witnessing the straining of the mind at the edges of itself and at the edges of its conceptuality. Our knowledge is broken down into tiny fragments of belief. We have become both cynical as to the value of this knowledge and yet alarmed at its proliferation and control. We're shattered.

## *The History of Sexuality*, 1976

### Michel Foucault

*"It was essential that the state know what was happening with its citizens' sex, and the use they made of it, but also that each individual be capable of the use made of it. Between the state and the individual, sex became an issue and a public issue no less . . ."*

Michel Foucault is best known for his critical studies of various social institutions, most notably psychiatry, medicine, parameters of educational timeframes, and the prison system, and also for his work on the history of sexuality. Much of his work concerns power and the relation between power and knowledge. His ideas concerning "discourse" in relation to the history of Western thought, have been widely discussed. Foucault's work is frequently referred to in disciplines as diverse as art, history, anthropology, archaeology, communication studies and cultural studies.

In the late 1970s, political activism in France had tailed off and many left wing militants became disillusioned. A number of young Maoists abandoned their beliefs to become the so-called New Philosophers, often citing Foucault as their major influence, a role about which Foucault had mixed feelings. It was during this period that Foucault embarked on his six-volume project *The History of Sexuality*, although he died before completing it. Its first volume, *The Will to Knowledge*, was published in 1976. The second and third volumes did not appear for another eight years, and they surprised readers by their relatively traditional style, subject matter (classical Greek and Latin texts) and approach, particularly Foucault's focus on the subject of knowledge and power, a concept he had previously neglected.

The first volume, *The Will to Knowledge* focused primarily on the last two centuries, and the functioning of sexuality as an analytic tool to look at power, which Foucault related to the emergence of a science of sexuality (*scientia sexualis*). In this volume he attacks the "repressive hypothesis," the widespread belief that we have, particularly since the nineteenth century, "repressed" our natural sexual drives. He shows that what we think of as "repression" of sexuality actually constituted sexuality as a core feature of our identities, and produced a proliferation of discourse on the subject. These discourses ranged from psychiatry and psychoanalysis to philosophy, anthropology, history, literature, and medicine. It is in this volume that he began to examine works with his theory that "knowledge is power." For Foucault much of our identity is related to sexuality and for centuries people have used "confession" as a tool by which we open ourselves up to repressed desires. He shows how over the eighteenth and nineteenth centuries the "confessional" moved from the priest to the psychoanalyst.

Foucault tends to direct his analysis toward the "statement," something that he sees as the basic unit of discourse that has been ignored up to this point. "Statement" is the English translation from French *énoncé* (that which is enunciated or expressed), which has a particular meaning for Foucault. In his writing, *Énoncé* means that certain something that makes propositions, utterances, or speech acts meaningful.

In this understanding, statements themselves are not propositions, utterances, or speech acts. Rather, statements create a network of rules establishing what is meaningful, and it is these rules that are the preconditions for propositions, utterances, or speech acts to have meaning. Statements are also "events." Depending on whether or not they comply with the rules of meaning, a grammatically correct sentence may still lack meaning and inversely, an incorrect sentence may still be meaningful. Statements depend on the conditions in which they emerge and exist within a field of discourse. It is huge collections of statements, called discursive formations, toward which Foucault aims his analysis.

It is important to note that Foucault reiterates that the analysis he is outlining is only one possible tactic, and that he is not seeking to displace other ways of analyzing discourse or render them as invalid. Foucault not only invalidates issues of truth; he also invalidates issues of meaning. Rather than looking for a deeper meaning underneath discourse or looking for the source of meaning in some transcendental subject, Foucault concentrates on analyzing the discursive and practical conditions of the existence for truth and meaning. This does not mean that Foucault denounces truth and meaning, but just that truth and meaning depend on the historical discursive and practical means of truth and meaning production. This stance allows Foucault to move away from an anthropological standpoint, denouncing a priori concepts of the nature of the human subject, and to focus on the role of discursive practices in constituting subjectivity. In order to show the principles of meaning and truth production in various discursive formations he details how truth claims emerge during various epochs on the basis of what was actually said and written during these periods of time. In *The History of Sexuality*, he describes the Renaissance, the Age of Enlightenment, and the twentieth century in particular.

The second two volumes, *The Use of Pleasure* and *The Care of the Self* dealt with the role of sex in Greek and Roman antiquity. Both were published in 1984, the year of Foucault's death. In his lecture series from 1979 to 1980 Foucault extended his analysis of government to its "wider sense of techniques and procedures designed to direct the behaviour of men," which involved a new consideration of the "examination of conscience" and confession in early Christian literature. These themes of early Christian literature seemed to dominate Foucault's work in these books, alongside his study of Greek and Roman literature. His interest in these subjects lasted until the end of his life. However, Foucault's death from AIDS in 1984 left the work incomplete, and the planned fourth volume of his *History of Sexuality* on Christianity was never published.

Foucault always maintained that he believed strongly in human freedom and that his philosophy was a fundamentally optimistic one, as he believed that something positive could always be done no matter how bleak the situation. One might also add that his work is actually aimed at refuting the position that Reason (or "rationality") is the sole means of guaranteeing truth and the validity of ethical systems. Thus, to criticize Reason is not to reject all notions of truth and ethics as some of his critics have claimed.

*The History of Sexuality*

## The Speed Read

Knowledge is power. All methods of "the confessional" from priests, religious orders, education, psychoanalysis and psychotherapy are methods of maintaining a culture of the repressed. Educational policies and the state further compound these and act on our self-identity.

## *Powers of Horror:*
## *An Essay on Abjection,* 1982

Julia Kristeva

*"What we designate as 'feminine', far from being a primeval essence, will be seen as an 'other' without a name, which subjective experience confronts when it does not stop at the appearance of its identity."*

Julia Kristeva is a Bulgarian-French philosopher, literary critic, psychoanalyst, feminist, and, most recently, novelist. She has lived in France since the mid-1960s. She became influential in critical analysis and cultural theory after publishing her first book *Semeiotikè* in 1969. Her works are considered to have an important place in post-structuralist thought. Kristeva joined the "Tel Quel group" in 1965 where she focused on the politics of language and became an active member. Kristeva undertook training in psychoanalysis, under the tutelage of Jacques Lacan, which she completed in 1979. In some ways, her work can be seen as trying to adapt a psychoanalytic approach to the post-structuralist critiques.

Her innumerable books, essays and publications, although seen as academically important, can be difficult to understand with their notions of *intertextuality, the semiotic*, and *abjection*. To explain briefly, Kristeva uses the term intertextuality to designate the transposition of one (or more) system of signs on to another which is accompanied by a new enunciative and denotative position. To put that more simply, it is a fluid interpretation of meaning where one meaning becomes linked to another, which perhaps changes or even negates the previous meaning.

Kristeva's use of the term *semiotic* here should not be confused with the discipline of semiotics (study of linguistics) suggested by Ferdinand de Saussure. For Kristeva, "the semiotic" is closely related to the infantile (pre-mirror) state in the work of both Jacques Lacan and Sigmund Freud (in Freud the pre-Oedipal stage). It is a pre-language state, an emotional force, tied to our instincts, which exists in the fissures and prosody (speech rhythms) of language rather than in the direct meanings of words. In this sense, the semiotic is opposed to the symbolic, which refers to a more direct mathematical correspondence of words to meaning.

In *Powers of Horror,* Kristeva focuses on two areas of discussion: the "body," and "abjection." Feminists link the body historically with the feminine, the female, or woman, and describe it as being denigrated as weak, immoral, unclean, or decaying. In all of her writings, Kristeva has theorized the connection between mind and body, culture and nature, psyche and soma, matter and representation, by insisting both that bodily drives are discharged in representation, and that the logic of signification is already operating in the material body. Kristeva maintains that all signification is composed of the distinction between the "semiotic" and the "symbolic." The "semiotic" element is the bodily drive as it is discharged in signification (the process of meaning).

The "semiotic" is associated with the rhythms, tones, and movement of signifying practices. As the discharge of drives, it is also associated with the maternal body, the first source of rhythms, tones, and movements for every human being since we all have resided in that body (inside our mothers). The "symbolic" element is associated with the grammar and structure of signification (language and meaning). The symbolic element is what makes reference possible. For example, words have referential meaning because of the symbolic structure of language. Without the "symbolic," all signification would be babble or noise. But, without the semiotic, all signification would be empty and have no importance for our lives. This means that for Kristeva, there is no signification without a combination of both the "semiotic" and the "symbolic."

In *Powers of Horror* Kristeva argues that just as bodily drives are discharged into signification, the logic of signification is already operating within the material existence of the body. Kristeva suggests that the operations of identification and differentiation necessary for signification are prefigured in the body's expulsions of food in particular. The maternal body regulates these bodily "identifications" and "differentiations" before birth and the mother carries on this regulation during infancy. Kristeva proposes that there is a maternal regulation or law, which prefigures the paternal law, which Freudian psychoanalysts have maintained is necessary for signification.

So beneath all the rather confusing jargon, Kristeva is basically arguing (partly against Lacan and Freud) that there is a phase before language in which meaning is female rather than male.

For Freud, part of the "oedipal stage" is the point at which the infant recognizes its self and is considered necessary for the child's acquisition of language. (Similarly the Lacanian theory of the "mirror phase" is that once the child recognizes itself in the mirror it recognizes that it is different to other objects around it and it is only after this occurs that the child enters the world of language.) In both theories the child must turn away from the mother and recognize itself as different in order to gain self-recognition. For Kristeva then, the regulation or grammar and laws of language are already operating on the level of matter before this stage.

Kristeva tries to counteract stereotypes that reduce maternity to nature by insisting that the maternal body operates between nature and culture. The mother never ceases to be primarily a speaking subject. Kristeva uses the maternal body with its two-in-one, or "other" within, as a model for all subjective relations. Like the maternal body, we are all what Kristeva calls a subject-in-process. As subjects-in-process we are always negotiating the "other" within, that is to say, the return of the repressed. Like the maternal body, we are never completely the subjects of our own experience.

In *Powers of Horror*, Kristeva develops her idea of "abjection" which she sees as useful in diagnosing the dynamics of women's oppression. She describes abjection as an operation of the psyche through which subjective and group identity are constituted by excluding anything that threatens one's own (or one's group's) borders (in other words, anything that threatens one's sense of self). According to Kristeva, the main threat to the young, developing subject is his or her dependence upon the maternal body. From this idea, Kristeva concludes that abjection is fundamentally related to the maternal function. In order to become subjects (within a patriarchal culture) we must abject (or turn away from) the maternal body. This creates a paradox, since women cannot abject the maternal body with which they also identify as women. They therefore develop what Kristeva calls a depressive sexuality.

Kristeva argues that misplaced abjection is one cause of women's oppression because women have been reduced to the maternal function in patriarchal cultures. Kristeva concludes that, if it is necessary to abject the maternal function to become a subject, and women, maternity, and femininity all have been reduced to the maternal function, then within patriarchy, women, maternity, and femininity are all "abject" along with the maternal function. For Kristeva, the connection between the social and the subject isn't that they represent each other, but rather that they follow the same logic: the survival of the group and subject. Towards the end of *Powers of Horror*, she compares anthropology and psychology and claims that the way in which an individual excludes the abject mother as a means of forming an identity, is the same way in which societies are constructed. On a broader scale, cultures exclude the maternal and the feminine, and by doing this come into being.

### *Powers of Horror: An Essay on Abjection*
# The Speed Read

If you are a woman, you are "cast out" of historical culture. Yet, you understand more than men because you have experience of being both "self" and "other" – you have been an "other" within (inside the womb) and without (at birth and in society) while becoming "self" and have the capacity to create an "other" (separate being) inside you. Since the creation of sperm banks the maternal realm will rule.

## *Symbolic Exchange and Death,* 1983

### Jean Baudrillard

*"The end of history is, alas, also the end of the dustbins of history. There are no longer any dustbins for disposing of old ideologies, old regimes, old values . . . History itself has become a dustbin. It has become its own dustbin, just as the planet itself is becoming its own dustbin."*

Jean Baudrillard is a social theorist best known for his analyses of modes of mediation and technological communication, although the scope of his writing spreads across more diverse subjects. These range from consumerism, gender relations, and the social understanding of history through to more journalistic commentaries on AIDS, cloning, the Rushdie affair, the (first) Gulf War (not "the continuation of politics by other means," but "the continuation of the absence of politics by other means") and the attacks on the World Trade Center (the "absolute event"). He has many critics and his ideas can be seen as a little outlandish.

Baudrillard has affinities with post-structuralism in that his arguments consistently draw on the notion that systems of signification and meaning are only understandable in terms of their interrelation. However, in contrast to Foucault who he is sharply critical of, Baudrillard has developed theories based, not on power and knowledge, but around the notions of seduction, simulation, and "hyperreality", the term with which he is most associated. These notions all share the common principle that signification, and therefore meaning, is self-referential (construed, following structuralist semiotics, in terms of absence, so "dog" means "dog" not because of what the word says but because it does not say: "cat," "goat," "tree" etc.). Baudrillard uses this principle to argue that in our present "global" society, technological communication has created an excessive proliferation of meaning. Because of this, meaning's self-referentiality has prompted, not a "global village," but a world where meaning has been obliterated and society has been reduced to an opaque mass, where the "real" has been reduced to the self-referential signs of its existence. It has become "hyperreal."

Influenced by the work of Georges Bataille, especially *Visions of Excess*, Baudrillard writes of the erosion of meaning via its excess. In the post-modern computer-driven society, for Baudrillard, there is an excess of references leading eventually back to themselves. He has sought to understand the world, not in terms of the subject's desire to coherently know the world, or in terms of the interpolation of power within subjectivity (in the manner of Foucault). Instead Baudrillard sees it in terms of the object and its power to seduce or simulate. As a result Baudrillard has, particularly in his later work, "withdrawn" himself from his own writing, by employing a poetic and ironic dynamic in his books.

In terms of Baudrillard's political standpoint, he increasingly opposes semiotic logic, (that of meaning, sign, signification, and commodity exchange), with that of the symbolic realm. For Baudrillard, this becomes a logic of gift exchange, potlatch (the practice of sumptuous destruction), and through this he analyses the principle of Evil (and what it means to invoke the principle of Evil). Latterly, in his work, this has prompted him to characterize the world in terms of a binary opposition of symbolic cultures (based upon gift exchange) and the ever-expanding "globalized" world, based on sign and commodity exchange, a world which has no answer to symbolic logic.

Throughout the 1980s, Baudrillard moved away from economically based theories to considerations of mediation and mass communication. The best known of these works is *Symbolic Exchange and Death*. Here Baudrillard moved beyond both Saussure's and Roland Barthes' formal semiology to consider the implications of a historically understood, and thus *form-less*, version of structural semiology. Most famously he argued, that Western societies have undergone a "precession (a slow spinning) of simulacra" (the simulacrum being that "truth which hides the fact there is none").

Baudrillard's use of the term "simulacrum" is roughly comparable to the word "idol." This precession, according to Baudrillard, took the form of "orders of simulacra" from the era of the original, to the counterfeit, to the produced, mechanical copy, and through to the simulated "third order of simulacra" whereby the copy has come to replace the original. Baudrillard argued that for present day society, as the simulated copy has superseded the original, so the map has come to precede the territory. Using this line of reasoning, Baudrillard came to characterize the present age as one of "hyperreality" where the real has come to be effaced or superseded by the "signs" of its existence. Baudrillard has drawn heaviest criticism for this typical "fatal strategy" of attempting to push his theories of society beyond themselves, so to speak. In this book Baudrillard's philosophical challenge to himself was not "why is there something rather than nothing," but "why is there nothing rather than something."

Baudrillard also maintained that the "end of history," in terms of a teleological goal, had always been an illusion brought about by modernity's will towards progress, civilization and rational unification. And this was an illusion that to all intents and purposes vanished toward the end of the twentieth century, brought about by the "speed" at which society moved, effectively "destabilizing" the linear progression of history. History was, so to speak, outpaced by its own spectacular realization. This approach to history demonstrates Baudrillard's affinities with the postmodern philosophy of Jean-Francois Lyotard, as he expresses the idea that society – and Western society in particular – has "dropped out" of the grand narratives (or for Lyotard the meta-narratives) of History. Baudrillard has supplemented this argument by claiming that, while this "dropping out" may have taken place, the global world is, in accordance with its spectacular understanding of itself, condemned to "play out" this illusory ending in an extreme way. The global world is acting out the end of the end of the end, *ad infinitum*. Thus, Baudrillard argues that Western society is subject to the political restriction of means that are justified by ends that do not exist.

Baudrillard's writing, and his uncompromising – even arrogant – stance, have led to fierce criticism which in contemporary social scholarship can only be compared to the criticism received by Jacques Lacan. Christopher Norris's *Uncritical Theory: Postmodernism, Intellectuals and the Gulf War* seeks to reject his media theory and position on "the real" out of hand. Others have argued that Baudrillard's position on semiotic analysis of meaning makes his own position on symbolic exchange untenable. These criticisms allude to the common criticism of post-structuralist work (a criticism that can similarly be applied to Baudrillard, Foucault or Gilles Deleuze) that emphasizing interrelation as the basis for subjectivity denies the human agency from which social structures necessarily arise. The most severe of his critics accuse him of being a purveyor of a form of reality-denying irrationalism.

*Symbolic Exchange and Death*

# The Speed Read

The spectacle of the end of the world is a continuously rotating and replaying illusion. Nothing can be declared "a means to an end." Non-existent ends justify the restriction of means. There is nothing. All is simulacra and this can be seen as the "truth which hides the fact there is none." So no truth either then. Nor meaning, nor means nor ends. Nor any point really when you come to think of it. Not even any dustbins to put "nothing" in.

# Index